"As someone who spent an inordinate amount of time watching the Huntsville Stars—go ahead, bet me that I can't name their 1985 championship-winning starting lineup—and can recite Joe Charbonneau's Chattanooga Lookouts stat line by heart, I thought I knew all I needed to about the Southern League. I was wrong. Few history lessons are as entertaining as Never a Bad Game, and few writers are as entertaining as Mark McCarter. This book is proof that the best stories are often found far away from the glare of the big-league spotlight."
—Mark Bechtel, Senior Editor, *Sports Illustrated*

"Mark McCarter has never simply 'followed' Southern League baseball, he's lived it—and he's loved every minute. He didn't need to write a book to prove that. Thankfully, he did anyway. *Never a Bad Game* is a fascinating reminder that even baseball's greatest heroes once rode buses through Alabama, and that some of the most compelling history happened during five-game sets in Southern League ballparks. Mark's passion for pursuing and telling these stories should appeal to everyone who's ever eaten a hot dog in the bleachers."
—John Turner, Deputy Editor, *The Sporting News*

"Having covered minor-league baseball for six years before moving on to cover the Brewers, I can vouch for the minors being a treasure trove of great stories. This is where the game is played without the distractions of labor disputes, megabucks contracts and other off-field maneuverings. Mark McCarter gives you the inside stories of the Southern League that never see the light of day in big-league newspapers. You'll feel like you were right there in Joe Davis Stadium with Mark when you're reading these well-written and entertaining stories of life off baseball's beaten track."
—Tom Haudricourt, *Milwaukee Journal-Sentinel*

Never a Bad Game

NEVER A BAD GAME

Mark McCarter

 **August Publications**

Middleton, Wisconsin

CONTENTS

The Moments

The Life

Never a Bad Game: Fifty Years of the Southern League, 1964-2014

Lineup Books / August Publications
3543 John Muir Dr.
Middleton, WI 53562
608.836.3730
augustpublications.com

Print ISBN: 978-1-938532-16-0
eBook ISBN: 978-1-938532-24-5

9 8 7 6 5 4 3 2

Designer (cover): Jim Tocco.

In memory of my Southern League "Mount Rushmore"

Billy Hitchcock,
who treated a kid sportswriter as if he were a grown-up

Jimmy Bragan,
who gave my daughter her first baby gift

and

Don Mincher,
quite simply my best friend in baseball

INTRODUCTION

A friend of my father ran the scoreboard, punching buttons that illuminated the red, green, and white lights on the distant board so big, so far, so magical that it seemed like one of the Seven Wonders of the World to a kid.

It loomed over the left-field wall, 360-plus-feet from home plate, with a subtle round top, like icing on a cupcake. It bore a gargantuan advertising logo of Krystal, a local institution whose little square, onion-grilled hamburgers sold for a dime apiece (though the customer was always encouraged to "take home a sack-full.") Someone worked from inside the scoreboard, manually dropping in the white digits on big black rectangles to fill out the line scores from cities that sounded so exotic, their team nicknames so indigenous. To read the scoreboard was to take a geography lesson.

From the old Southern Association days, there were the Nashville Vols. Mobile Bears. New Orleans Pelicans. Arkansas Travelers. Shreveport Sports. Atlanta Crackers. When the current incarnation of the Southern League began in 1964, you could add the Lynchburg White Sox. Macon Peaches. Asheville Tourists. The major-league scores were posted there, too, but expansion brought a quandary. There was only room for eight games, four in each league.

I'd catch myself, from our usual seats deep in the first-base grandstand, looking toward my father's friend in the press box. It was a long, backlit rectangle perched atop the stadium roof. I could see the heads and shoulders of men at work in the best seats in the house, smack dab above home plate. My father's friend sat at the far right, the sportswriters in the other seats. Probably Joe Engel was up there, too. He owned the team and the ballpark was named for him. The so-called "Barnum of Baseball" was a cantankerous soul. In the small restroom in the back of the press box, Engel had ordered a picture of himself to be placed as a target in the urinal. He'd growl to the old-time sportswriters like E.T. Bales and Allan Morris and Wirt Gammon that "You pee on me in print, you might as well pee on me in the press box."

Gus Chamberlain was up there somewhere, in a booth off to the side. He was the "Voice of the Chattanooga Lookouts," as grand a celebrity as there was in the city. It was not unusual for Chattanoogans to visit the WAPO radio studio in the Read House, an historic hotel across from the Union Depot train station at Broad and Ninth. Babe Ruth and the Yankees stayed there en route from spring training. Al Capone stayed there en route from Chicago to Florida. Winston Churchill stayed there. Chamberlain would sit behind a plate-glass window and, from information fed to him by a narrow ribbon of ticker-tape, recreate what was happening in the Lookouts' road games for his radio audience, and for those awestruck among us outside.

It would be grossly inaccurate revisionist history for me to say I gazed wistfully at that Engel Stadium press box and imagined myself working there. I do know I looked up there more often than most fans and thinking, in the simple language of a nine-year-old, that it'd be really, really neat to be up there.

And... you know what? It was.

It still is.

In 1976, as a 21-year-old sportswriter for the *Chattanooga News-Free Press*, I was handed the day-to-day beat assignment for the Chattanooga Lookouts, who were bringing pro baseball back to the city after a 10-year absence. I would spend 700 or more evenings in that box atop Engel Stadium, laughing and learning, keeping notes in a tiny scorebook that, upon recent retrieval from the bottom of a filing cabinet, now appear to have been written in hieroglyphics.

I'm still hanging around press boxes, the last 16 seasons while at the *Huntsville Times*. The visits to Joe Davis Stadium aren't quite as frequent as I'd like, but not a night in the Huntsville press box goes by without thoughts of Don Mincher, one of the three men in whose memory this book is dedicated. A Don Mincher-model first baseman's mitt, which he inscribed to me, sits at my desk as these words are typed. Don spent many nights in that press box, sharing stories and wisdom and laughs. He knew the game intimately and respected it immensely.

My first "official" Southern League press box was actually at Crockett Park, an old wooden structure with red-clay floors in the visiting manager's office, tucked away in a leafy neighborhood in

Charlotte. Residents would sit on their front porches and wave as the visiting team buses came through, as regular as Swiss trains, each afternoon. How many future superstars, I wonder, did they greet? I rode the Lookouts' bus to Charlotte that trip, which marked the first games of Chattanooga's return to pro baseball in 1976; the Orioles were back after being out of the Southern League three years. I piled on board with a suitcase, typewriter, briefcase, and Telecopier, a primitive version of the fax machine that could zip a typewritten page back into its mate in our office in a rapid six minutes' time.

The first words the Telecopier spat out the next morning were:

> CHARLOTTE, N.C.—This was a night to remember, a red-letter date for Charlotte as well as Chattanooga. But the most unlikely of heroes found his way into the history books.
>
> Rafael Liranzo sounds as if he should be riding the favored horse at the Kentucky Derby. Instead, he supplied both the charge out of the starting gate and the burst down the home stretch as Charlotte edged Chattanooga 4-3 here Tuesday night.

Hardly Pulitzer-worthy, but sentiment has that page of double-spaced pica type still tucked away in a box in my house. All those sappy notions about first love, and I guess in some ways it applied to my summer of 1976. It was my first great newspaper assignment. I was the age of the players. I was as much friend as journalist, hitching a ride for 40 of the 70 road games. The Lookouts were celebrities that season and I danced on the edge of their spotlight, even as I helped create some of that light.

The manager was Rene Lachemann, whose tobacco-filled cheeks appeared with almost alarming foreshadowing and regularity every time I had unwrapped a pack of Topps bubble gum cards a decade earlier. He did it all in those days, when the only staff was a manager and trainer. He threw batting practice, drove the tractor to manicure the field, and tolerated the constant presence of a callow writer.

As for the players, I can almost name the entire roster off the top of my head. Rightly or wrongly, they became friends more than sources. Denny Walling, who nearly killed me in a Savannah parking lot in an ill-advised 1 a.m. shopping-cart race. Dwayne Murphy and Steve McCatty and Bob Mollenhauer and Matty Keough. Derek Bryant rode with me to the Southern League All-Star Game that year and played on my CB radio. (I did say it was 1976.) Rick Lysander, the trivia whiz. There was Ron Beaurivage; I was a groomsman in his wedding when his New Hampshire running buddies couldn't make the trip south. There was Keith Lieppman, who helped jumpstart my new job in Huntsville in his role as Oakland's farm director.

I still get regular emails from Bruce Robinson and Brian Kingman; they had used to traditionally call me on the eve of spring training. One day in Montgomery, we finagled our way into the office of Alabama Gov. George Wallace. It's not one of the top 50 stories in the history of the Southern League; forgive my indulgence, though, for including the saga in the following collection.

A lifetime of journalism since that 1976 season, I still plop into up a comfortable, swivel office chair in the Joe Davis Stadium press box in Huntsville and watch baseball through a Plexiglas window scuffed and smudged with age, through eyes themselves a bit smudged with age. Much like many cities in the Southern League, I've had my own hiatus or two from baseball, with other jobs in other cities. But I keep coming back, feeling an almost inexorable tie to the league I watched as a kid 50 years ago, going then to those games armed with my trusty Rawlings glove and hopeful of a foul ball, now going with a laptop and hopeful of a good story.

Let me tell you a few of them.

Mark McCarter
Owens Cross Roads, Alabama
April 2014

FOREWORD

I can't really remember how old I was, but growing up in Huntsville, when they were an Oakland A's team, the crowds used to be pretty good and you could get tickets wherever you went in the city. We took advantage of that and went to some games. My parents, Mike and Sandy, knew how much my brothers Matt and Alan and I loved baseball, so we had the opportunity to go watch professionals play at the Double-A level right here in Huntsville. That was cool.

My parents said I told them once when we were at Joe Davis Stadium that "when I grow up, I'm going to play here." I don't remember that specifically. When you're younger, you don't really remember the all things you say and do. But that's what parents are for, to remind you of what you said and did!

I know we went to July 4th fireworks nights, and one of the games I do remember distinctly was when Michael Jordan came to town. That was probably the biggest crowd they ever had. But because we were playing ball so much, every night and every weekend it seemed like, I didn't get out there that much.

You can name all the big Stars that everybody knew—Mark McGwire, Jose Canseco, Tim Hudson. There's been a lot of big league guys step foot and play in that ballpark. When I was with "Huddy" with the Braves, I always told him he was too old for me to remember when he played for the Stars in 1998. I said, "I was probably in diapers when you played here in Double-A."

The Southern League has been around a long time and Double-A baseball is big in our state. When I was growing up in Alabama, that's all we had at the professional level. You have it in Mobile and Montgomery and Birmingham and Huntsville and you don't always have the opportunity to drive all the way to Atlanta to see a game. So you have Double-A baseball, and I know how much it's meant here in Alabama.

I heard some of the stories about the Southern League that are in the book, like Chips Swanson, who threw a perfect game. Not many people heard of him because he never made it to the big leagues, but he went to work on "Cheers." And everybody knows what "Cheers" is.

Having a chance to go back and play in Huntsville in 2009 when I got called up to Mississippi was pretty cool. Especially since that was the first road trip after I was moved up. That was great because we played five-game sets and to come home that long was pretty nice. We played four games—our last game got rained out—and I pitched in two of the four games. I know I walked the first guy I faced, but I got a double-play ball, then struck out the last guy.

I played for Phillip Wellman at Mississippi, and I know there's a story about him here, too. It was after that famous big blow-up against the umpires that was on video. It was definitely one of those things where somebody shows it to you and it was "Guess who you're going to play for. Watch this!"

He was kind of intimidating—Fu Manchu mustache, bald head, a big guy. But when you got to know Phillip you knew he was a good manager, a good guy. I enjoyed playing for him. That moment had nothing to do with what kind of guy he was or manager he was. It was just one of those things that if he was going to do, he was going to do it to the fullest. I got to know his son Brett that year. He was our bullpen catcher.

Then he and my brother Matt wound up playing together at Shelton State Community College.

When I pitched for Mississippi, that wasn't the first time I played at Joe Davis Stadium. Butch Weaver, my coach at Lee High School, always scheduled a doubleheader every year where we'd play one game at there and then go back and play another on campus. I got to pitch there in my sophomore year in high school and I thought that was pretty cool.

They always did an all-star showcase there, too. That's where I met Randy Putman, who was the coach at Wallace State-Hanceville, and I eventually ended up going to school down there. It was the first time he ever saw me pitch. So, really, my career got started because of a game at Joe Davis Stadium.

Craig Kimbrel
Huntsville, Alabama
January 2014

THE HISTORY

Historic Rickwood Field.

FOREBEARS
AND FAILURES

1885-1964

Mythological creatures roamed the earth in those days. Harmon Killebrew jacked homers over the 471-foot sign, past the giant metal Coca-Cola bottle on the distant corner of the Engel Stadium wall. Walt Dropo pounded one a million miles at Birmingham's Rickwood Field that's still marked with an X on the wall. "Country" Brown stole every base in sight.

It was a land of giants, or so it sounded to the generation that grew up at the knee of those who populated the old ballparks of the post-Depression South, back when Minor League Baseball was the sort of religion devoted now to Southeastern Conference football. Major League Baseball was but a 16-team entity. The closest most Southerners got to the majors was the staticky, fickle signal from KMOX out of St. Louis, to hear the Cardinals' games, and the box scores in the next afternoon's newspapers. Television was still a new-fangled thing after World War II. The first Game of the Week telecast came on in 1953, but fewer than half the households in America even had a TV set.

Diversions were few, so you went to the ballpark. You may have been among the 24,600 in attendance the night Joe Engel gave away a house, or one of the 20,074 when Ray Caldwell outdueled Dizzy Dean in the 1931 Dixie Series game in Birmingham. Recalled long-time fan Harold Justice, "My Dad saw the pitching duel between Caldwell and Dizzy Dean. I bet I heard that story dozens of times, probably each time we listened to the Saturday game with Dizzy as the color announcer."

Those days, a fan could watch a player year after year after year.

They were property of the minor-league teams, then sold to teams at higher levels and to the majors. Branch Rickey, the masterful innovator, had established a farm system with his St. Louis Cardinals by the 1920s, but other teams were reluctant to follow the pattern.

The advent of the farm system eased some of the financial burden on the owners. While it was better economically, it also cost them some drawing cards. The Ray Caldwells of the world, who pitched five seasons in Birmingham while in his 40s, and the gentlemanly Roy Hawes, who spent the last of his six years with the Lookouts as a 33-year-old in 1960, were soon as extinct as pterodactyls.

Those mythological players might even come down from Mount Olympus in the offseason. They might open a bar or restaurant or work in a neighboring building. They might find themselves some pretty little local girl and get themselves hitched and become a permanent member of the community. Even decades after their career ended, they'd be introduced as "This is so-and-so. You remember he used to play for the Crackers?" Or Vols. Or Lookouts. Or Bears. Or Barons.

The baseball land in which these giants ruled the earth in the late 1950s and early 1960s had its origins in a league that began in 1885. Professional baseball actually began a decade earlier before various civic leaders formed the Southern League, with teams in Atlanta, Augusta, Birmingham, Chattanooga, Columbus, Macon, Memphis, and Nashville. Birmingham and Columbus dropped out for 1886, replaced by Charleston (South Carolina) and Savannah. New Orleans soon joined the league, dominating play, but economics led to a temporary suspension of play in 1890 and 1891, and again in 1897. Finally, after 1899, the league closed its doors for good.

The Southern Association, featuring some of the same owners and franchises, was unveiled in 1901, with charter members Birmingham, Chattanooga, Little Rock, Memphis, Nashville, New Orleans, Selma (Alabama), and Shreveport. After a few seasons, it would enjoy a remarkable constancy in its membership, with bell cow franchises like Atlanta, Birmingham, Chattanooga, Little Rock, Memphis, Nashville, and New Orleans. It was classified an A1 league in 1936, Double-A in 1946.

In the 1950s, things grew stagnant. American life changed. Instead of being one of 25,000 at one game, maybe you were one of the 25,000 who attended games over the course of a full season in Jacksonville in 1962, the sort of attendance blight that had become pandemic in the early 1960s. By that time, air conditioners stuck out from window sills like a pouty lip in every home. Organized youth baseball was blossoming. Families were at the ballparks regularly, but watching the offspring, not the pros. Obituaries for minor-league franchises were written across the country.

The Southern Association, the predecessor to the current-day Southern League, was not in the best of health, either. After the 1961 season, losing teams and fans, it folded.

Overlapping geographically for decades was the Class A South Atlantic ("SALLY," also written as "Sally") League, though its cities were typically closer to the eastern seaboard, while Southern League teams were further west. With the dismantling of the Southern League, pro baseball was left with a dearth of Class AA teams, featuring just 12 franchises in the Texas and Mexican Leagues to supply 20 major-league clubs.

Sam Smith, the SALLY League president, asked to be reclassified as Double-A, which took place in 1963. But there was a branding issue. The SALLY League was synonymous with Class A ball. The Southern Association was associated with failure. So before the 1964 season, the league owners went back to the future, back to 1899 and the Southern League.

SEGREGATION
AND
STANDOUTS

1964-1970

Sam Smith was like a man who just purchased a creaky old fixer-upper. No sooner than the Swiss-cheese roof gets patched, the plumbing holds a mutiny. That gets fixed, suddenly here come the termites.

The Southern League, in the infancy of the current incarnation, was a handful for the league president, who ran the operation out of his home in northeast Knoxville, in the Holston Hills area on the bank of the Holston River. His wife Louise worked as the league secretary.

From 1964 through 1970, the league remained in a state of flux. It operated in 13 different cities, with Charlotte the only constant. During three seasons, 1967-69, the league operated as a six-team entity.

It was a struggle to do minor-league baseball business anywhere. It seemed on the verge of life-support across the country, a victim of television and a changing mobile economy.

Before becoming Southern League president, Smith was president of the Class A South Atlantic League starting in 1959, succeeding Sam Wolfson of Jacksonville, whose stadium bore his name. The SALLY League was hardly the bastion of stability, either. Between 1957 and 1962, the SALLY League was in 15 different cities. One franchise, Savannah, uprooted and moved in 1962 because of pickets outside Grayson Stadium by the NAACP, protesting the segregation in the stands.

Things were even worse in the Southern Association, which folded after the 1961 season, with franchises in such medium-sized markets as Atlanta, Chattanooga, Nashville, Little Rock, and Mobile. That meant only 12 of the 20 major-league clubs had Class AA affiliates, so Smith led the move to raise the SALLY League to the Double-A level in 1963, bringing Chattanooga and Nashville into the fold along with Macon, Asheville, Lynchburg, Augusta, Knoxville, and Charlotte.

Smith and league owners rebranded their organization as the Southern League in 1964, with Asheville, Birmingham, Charlotte, Chattanooga, Columbus, Knoxville, Lynchburg, and Macon as the charter members.

The most significant change in 1964 was another dramatic step for racial equality in Southern baseball. From a retrospective in the league's 1994 media guide:

As minor-league baseball in the Old South stepped to the forefront of social change three decades ago, something got in the way.

Integration was already a part of baseball. Jackie Robinson had taken care of that in 1947 with the old Brooklyn Dodgers. And as years passed, other outstanding black and Latin baseball players took their place beside white players in lineups from Class A to the Majors. The old Southern Association, one of baseball's premier Class AA leagues since the turn of the century, was ready to make the change in the early 1960s. But that's when politics stepped in. Some cities refused to allow blacks to play and the Southern Association died in 1961.

It was probably the darkest moment in minor-league baseball history in the south. But just as some of the nation's outstanding cities have grown from the ashes of racial strife in the Sun Belt, over the last three decades the ashes of the old Southern Association have produced the Southern League.

One of the factors in the Southern Association's demise were laws in Birmingham and New Orleans that prohibited black and white players on the same team, which defied a Major League Baseball edict in 1961 that teams would be integrated. But when the Birmingham Barons opened for business in '64, the blacks-only bleachers in right field had been removed. The Barons became the first integrated pro team in the state, 10 months after Gov. George Wallace's stand at the schoolhouse door when black students tried to integrate the University of Alabama—but 17 years after Jackie Robinson broke the color barrier in the majors.

Glynn West, the Barons' general manager, would later recall, "Things were tense that first night. But I got a chuckle when the crowd started coming in. The first black fans asked if they could sit behind home plate and when we told them they could, they looked surprised. After sitting out in the bleachers all those years, all they wanted was a better view of the game."

Despite sharing the field, the players often weren't able to share the same hotels and restaurants. Long Island native Fran Kalafatis, the wife of the late George Kalafatis, a slugging Montgomery first baseman from 1967-69, recalled, "We started out in spring training in Florida and people were literally hugging and kissing you and saying goodbye. And I said, 'Well, aren't you going to Montgomery?' Oh, yeah, but you'll see when we get there. We will not be with each other. I didn't understand. They lived in a different part of town whereas in Florida we all lived together. At the games, the black wives sat in the bleachers and we sat in box seats behind home plate. I remember walking down there and sitting with them and remember them saying, I know you think you're helping us, but you're putting us at risk. I felt horrible. These were friends. Our children played together. … We had housing where they put us where we had to sign a lease you would not have people of color come over."

Rene Lachemann was a 19-year-old kid from California who joined the Barons briefly late in '64 and was in Mobile in 1965 (he'd return to the league in '76 as the Chattanooga manager). He remembered a road trip to Montgomery when he saw Dr. Martin Luther King leading a march.

"It was in the middle of racial struggle. I grew up in Los Angeles baseball with a group of black players, guys like Bob Tolan and Bob Watson and Paul Blair. It was a culture shock for me when I saw the towns that were so segregated," Lachemann said, relaxing in the clubhouse of the Colorado Rockies, for whom he was a coach in 2013. "It was an entirely different thing. The black players couldn't stay in the same hotel as us."

Larry Colton, who played in the league in 1966, authored a book, *Southern League*, centered on the 1964 Barons. Wrote Colton, "It didn't matter that the Civil Rights Act had been passed ... most hotels and restaurants in Alabama still didn't serve blacks, and hooded members of the Ku Klux Klan were as common as grits."

For the league's growing pains, instability, and the racial situation, the first seven seasons of the fledgling Southern League brought some sensational personal and team achievements.

Knoxville's Doug Gallagher, a 24-year-old lefty from Freemont, Ohio, threw the first no-hitter in league history, blanking Asheville 3-0 in the first game of a May 3 doubleheader. Three days later, Asheville was shelled by Columbus 22-4. Perhaps more than coincidental to that, Asheville was part of a peculiar swap, with manager Ray Hathaway being sent to Class A Gastonia in midseason and replaced by Bob Clear.

While Gallagher had the no-hitter, the league's dominant pitcher was Manley "Shot" Johnston, who won 20 games and grabbed headlines with three homers in a May 16 contest against Charlotte, including two in the same inning. Johnston was named the league MVP, leading Lynchburg to the title when Birmingham sprung a leak late in the season. Nonetheless, the Barons led the league in attendance at 95,703 and the eight teams combined for 491,444.

The 1966 Southern League media guide would refer to Roy White as "Another Hank Aaron?" Certainly numbers merited the hype for the 21-year-old African-American from Compton, Calif., who played with a Rebel flag on the sleeve of his Columbus Confederate Yankees uniform, an awkward way for Columbus to tout its ties to the New York Yankees while keeping Southern. White, who'd enjoy a solid 15-year career in the majors, batted .300 with 19 homers and 56 RBI. Columbus, playing two fewer games, won the pennant over Asheville by one percentage point.

Mobile made a cameo appearance in the league in 1966 and pitcher Jim Nash, a 6-5 right-hander from the Atlanta suburbs, was sensational. On June 5, Nash struck out 16 Knoxville Smokies. "He was straight, 'Here it comes, brother,'" said Lachemann, who caught that game. "He was over the top and it overpowered you." It also overpowered big leaguers. Nash was promoted to the majors in July and won his first seven decisions for Kansas City, finishing 12-1.

Birmingham returned to the circuit in 1967, with a new general manager in Paul Bryant, Jr., son of Alabama's legendary football coach. The Barons won the league behind players like Reggie Jackson, Rollie Fingers, Joe Rudi, and Dave Duncan; George Lauzerique posted 13 victories, including a seven-inning perfect game.

Asheville and Savannah entered the league in 1968 as Macon and Knoxville dropped out; the latter agonized Smith, by then entrenched in Knoxville with his family. He'd not live to see a minor-league team back in the city.

Asheville, a Reds' affiliate managed by Sparky Anderson, won the '68 pennant despite a 16-game win streak by runner-up Montgomery. Asheville took advantage of the short right-field fence at quaint McCormick Field to lead the league in home runs.

Charlotte went 81-59 in 1969 to win the pennant by three games over 78-62 Birmingham. They were the only teams above .500. After that season, Phil Howser, who worked for the Charlotte club for 32 seasons, retired.

Jacksonville and Mobile rejoined the league in 1970, making it again an eight-team league, and Columbus won the pennant by a mere .001 percentage points over Montgomery. It would be the last pennant Sam Smith would present as league president.

Smith was a native of Troy, Ala., who played football at Auburn as a freshman under Ralph "Shug" Jordan. After four years in the Navy during World War II, Smith graduated from Troy State, then got into coaching. In 1947, he was hired as the assistant to the president of the Alabama State League, then worked with the Dothan team, and in 1954 became president of the Alabama-Florida League.

He was a bold leader, "a real champion of minor-league baseball," Birmingham's Glynn West would say. Smith was prescient and proactive. As early as November 1964, after his first season as Southern League president, there were rumors beginning to circulate about more big-league expansion and he approached Major League Baseball to request a timetable, so that minor leagues could deal with the rumors. He predicted then that Dallas-Fort Worth, Seattle, Oakland and Atlanta would be expansion targets.

"He was always known as a battler," Texas League president Bobby Bragan said of him. "He was always one willing to stand up and be counted—even in the minor leagues' battles with the majors."

"I'm just a country boy and I make plenty of mistakes but I've never been accused of being dishonest," he said in an interview.

Smith was diagnosed with cancer in 1970 and despite the illness helped navigate the Southern League through its agreement with the Texas League to form the Dixie Association for 1971. A week into the season, on April 19, 1971, Smith succumbed to the cancer. He was 50. He was, wrote Marvin West in the *Knoxville News-Sentinel*, "a baseball optimist who never saw a bad game."

ONE YEAR ONLY

The Dixie Association of 1971

On the morning of December 2, 1970, representatives of seven Texas League teams gathered with league president Bobby Bragan in room 2217 at the Biltmore Hotel in downtown Los Angeles. The 11-story hotel, with its ornate carvings and opulent design, had hosted the Academy Awards for several years. John F. Kennedy stayed there during the 1960 Democratic Convention and The Beatles stayed there four years later.

There was some history being made in that meeting room. The Texas League was in a quandary. Its El Paso team was moving to Shreveport, where previous owners had closed operation. It would be left with seven teams—maybe six, if Memphis followed through on its desire to move to the Southern League, which team president Will Carruthers broached during the 1970 season.

The meeting ended with a motion passed unanimously, encouraging Bragan to meet with Southern League president Sam Smith. A marriage proposal of sorts was in the air. "A marriage of necessity," as current Texas League president Tom Kayser called it. The Southern League would be operating in 1971 with only seven teams as well, with Mobile dropping out.

Some six weeks later, it was another hotel, another meeting room. This time, it was the 20-story Birmingham landmark, the Thomas Jefferson Hotel on the west side of the city's downtown. It was known for a quirky accessory: Atop the roof was a mooring mast for airships. Long-since closed, the tower hovers in the skyline not far away from Birmingham's modern Regions Field, the Barons' current home.

Joining Bragan, Smith, and National Association president Phil Piton in the Green Room at 9 a.m. on Jan. 19, 1971, were 17 others, representing the seven franchises each from the Southern and Texas Leagues. Carruthers reiterated his desire to move to the Southern League, but the Texas League would not let him do so without financial penalty. Piton reported that should one of the leagues end up with six teams, Major League Baseball would reimburse it $18,000. With no small amount of harrumphing, the directors adjourned to separate league meetings.

Smith, battling cancer that would take his life three months later, conducted the Southern League meeting in which there was a unanimous vote against a 14-team league. The Southern League tendered invitations to Memphis and Little Rock, but they were not accepted. It was back to a stalemate. A committee that included Art Parrack of Jacksonville, Glynn West of Birmingham, Tom Fleming of Asheville, Ray Johnston of Shreveport, Gene Lawing of San Antonio, and Charlie Blaney of Albuquerque was appointed to solve the problem, but they had no solutions.

With everyone back in the Green Room, it came down to the gist of most meetings: Money. The idea arose to take the $18,000 major-league money and divide it among teams to help with travel expenses. Suddenly, the Southern League unanimous vote dissolved.

"With this settled, both the Southern and Texas League agreed to playing in a combined league called the Dixie Association. This Association will consist of 7 Southern League cites and 7 Texas League cities divided into 3 playing divisions with interlocking schedules," the league minutes report.

At 6 p.m., the meeting adjourned. But the adventure was just beginning.

A league that stretched more than 1,600 miles from Charlotte to Albuquerque would be a challenge. The schedule was quirky. The West division—Albuquerque, Amarillo, Dallas-Fort Worth, and San Antonio—would play a lot of intramural games against the teams from the Central—Shreveport, Little Rock, Memphis, and Birmingham. The East—Asheville, Charlotte, Columbus, Jacksonville, Montgomery, and Savannah—would operate fairly independently, but also play Central teams. Birmingham would find itself on marathon road trips, flying into Texas, then making a nearly three-week bus tour of the state.

By June, the Dixie Association's future was doomed. Bragan

acknowledged that both leagues wanted a return to the old format, saying, "The Dixie was set up for just one year anyway."

The Dixie Association was no great boon for attendance. The seven Southern League teams drew 333,906 and the Texas League drew 733,859. By comparison, the stable Eastern League drew 559,198.

"I remember from a fan's point of view it was confusing," said Jim Baker, then a teenager but who would later cover the league for the *Asheville Citizen-Times*. "You'd go to the ballpark and the Arkansas Travelers would be there and you'd go, 'What are they doing here?'"

The aptly named Travelers, a St. Louis farm club, won the Central as Jorge Roque hit 16 homers and drove in 73 runs. Amarillo, a San Francisco affiliate, won the West, with 20-year-old Gary Matthews, a future big-league standout, supplying 15 homers and 86 RBI while three starting pitchers collected double-digit wins.

It was the Southern League nucleus, the Eastern Division, which provided the greatest drama. Charlotte, a Minnesota Twins' franchise, edged Asheville by 1.5 games. The venerable Minnie Mendoza, 37 years old and in his seventh of eight years in a Charlotte uniform, batted .316 and led the league with 163 hits. Charlotte beat Asheville 2-1 in the first round of the playoffs, and then swept Arkansas 3-0 in the Dixie Series.

This one-year experiment may have been best defined in what amounted to an obituary. Billy Hitchcock, elected as Southern League president that summer, mailed this memo to the league board of directors, dated Oct. 15, 1971:

> It was my honor to be elected President of the Southern League, effective August 1, 1971, and to serve the last two months of the year 1971. During the first two weeks of August, the League office was moved from Knoxville, Tennessee to Opelika, Alabama. At the present time, all League affairs are being administered from Opelika.
>
> The 1971 season was a rather difficult one in many respects for the Southern League clubs. The league was a division of the Dixie Association and played an interlocking schedule with the Texas League clubs. Travel increased; consequently, transportation costs were higher. Texas League clubs playing in

Southern League cities did not stimulate real fan interest. Rainy weather, causing many postponements, and racial disturbances in some of our cities had a decided effect on attendance. In spite of these deterrents, attendance increased appreciably with some clubs, notably Asheville, Charlotte and Savannah. The average paid attendance per opening increased from 659 in 1970 to 769 in 1971. The Charlotte Club is to be congratulated for leading the League in attendance with 69,132 paid....

The Southern League will operate in 1972 as an eight-club league, completely divorced from the Texas League. At this time I am encouraged over the prospects for our eighth club. Macon and Knoxville, both of whom have fine facilities, have expressed interest in returning to the league. Baltimore, Milwaukee and Cleveland have indicated an interest in operating in our League. It is my hope that in the very near future, our League will be set, and we will have a strong, compact, eight-city league, one that will have a continuous operation in the cities involved—all with strong Major League agreements.

We have the greatest product in the world to sell, so let's sell!

MOVING
FORWARD

1972-present

The Southern League that opened for business in 1972 is now just an old yearbook picture, all paisley and bellbottomed and sideburned. It bears little resemblance to the graying, distinguished organization celebrating its golden anniversary.

"Minor-league baseball back then was light years from where it is now," said Dave Fendrick, the Savannah general manager in 1976 and now president of the Round Rock Express.

The league's adolescence after its experimentation with the Dixie Association and adulthood has been a constant evolution. New cities. New stadiums. More importantly, a new way of doing business.

"They're operated so much more professionally," Fendrick said. "In Savannah, it was two full-time people on staff. The concessionaire was a high-school teacher who came in at four o'clock. The city supplied the grounds crew."

Nowadays, a franchise like Birmingham or Jacksonville might have two-dozen full-time employees plus an armada of part-timers and interns. Walk into the Pensacola office and you're greeted by a receptionist and comfortable seats to await an appointment. Walk into a Southern League front office in 1972, you were greeted by a fog of cigar smoke, a No-Pest strip dangling from the ceiling, and an air-conditioning unit that sounded like a bronchitis patient.

On the field, it was the same scarcity in personnel. "You didn't have a hitting coach," said Rene Lachemann, a player in the league in the 1960s and the manager of the year in 1976 at Chattanooga. "You were the hitting coach, the pitching coach, everything."

"The biggest change has been the facilities," said Wayne Martin, formerly of the *Birmingham News*, who covered the league in the 1970s. "They had that old board stadium at Charlotte that burned down. They had some stadiums that were so bad the teams dressed at the motel."

"The ballparks today are miniature major-league stadiums," Fendrick echoed. "Back then, they weren't of that quality. Playing fields, locker rooms, clubhouses, offices, stands, concessions, you name it, it's nowhere near where it is today."

Geographically, the 1972 Southern League looked nothing like it'd look on its golden anniversary, though it was a far cry from the nascent league overseen by Sam Smith in 1964, much less the Rand-McNally extravaganza that was the 1971 Dixie Association. Not that geography wouldn't be flexible.

There is tangible evidence of that in the Southern League office in Marietta, Georgia, an Atlanta suburb. A large conference table sits in the middle of a room on the second-floor loft, which then-president Arnie Fielkow extravagantly and optimistically ordered in 1994. Engraved on the table were the names of the league sites—including Puerto Rico. Fielkow, whose tenure was termed "a big mistake" by a long-time team official, indeed had plans to place a team there before the deal fell through.

Even as the league muscled up in economic stability and attendance, the seasons that followed the baby steps of the 1960s remained a constant evolution.

Billy Hitchcock revived the league from its Dixie Association fling and held the presidency for 10 years before handing off to Jimmy Bragan in 1981. By this time, the league had expanded, to eight teams in 1972, then 10 in 1978 with the addition of Memphis and Nashville. The horizons had expanded, too. In the late 1970s and early 1980s, the old guard of owners and general managers was joined by some brash, imaginative youngsters. They were a good mixture, if not always smooth. The old guard shared wisdom. The youngsters shared ideas.

"It was an unbelievably, aggressively outside of the box league," said Bruce Baldwin, then at Greenville and now president in Pensacola. "It had a lot of young guys that went on to have a great deal of success in minor-league baseball or something else. We had the

Crocketts in Charlotte. Frances had a bunch of cats in her office, but I really liked her a lot. She did a lot of stuff I thought, 'What is she doing that for?' Larry [Schmittou, Nashville GM] was over the top in promotions.

"We were so aggressive, so competitive, but we shared like crazy. You go to the winter meetings, get somebody else's idea and you come home and look like the smartest guy in the world. We had our own marketing committee. We didn't sell anything, but we had a hell of a good time."

"There had been no marketing done at all in the 70s," said Wayne Martin, "and I think that's an outgrowth of the late 40s and 50s. They didn't have to market. They played baseball and people came out to watch."

In the early 1980s, Bragan established a goal of two million fans, an almost absurd notion for a league that combined for 333,906 with its seven teams in the Dixie Association year. Of course, the marketing committee never imagined that the greatest idea to promote the Southern League and sell tickets would come when a basketball player in search of a new challenge decided he wanted to give baseball a try.

A timeline of the Southern League's most recent 40-some-odd years:

1972-1975: With the addition of Knoxville, the SL splits into two divisions. Montgomery begins its dominant run of five championships in six years. Mike Reinbach leads Asheville to the 1972 division title by winning the league's Triple Crown (.346, 30 HRs, 109 RBI). With a combined 88 rainouts in 1975, the league attendance takes a nosedive.

1976-1977: Chattanooga replaces Birmingham and Charlotte replaces Asheville in 1976. A 20-year-old Eddie Murray debuts at Charlotte, and Chattanooga draws a league record 135,144, including 8,305 on opening night when team officials have to rope off a portion of the outfield. The Montgomery Rebels continue to hoist the league hardware, beating Chattanooga for the West title, then taking two of three against Orlando for the 1976 pennant under manager Les Moss. A year later, Eddie Brinkman leads the Rebels to a sweep of both halves and 2-1 and 3-2 victories over Jacksonville in the championship.

1978: Memphis and Nashville are admitted, bringing the league to 10 teams for the first time and nearly doubling the previous season's combined attendance total with 1,054,658. Knoxville wins both halves in the West and beats Orlando two out of three. Jim Bouton receives the Best Hustler Award after his comeback at Savannah. Darrell Jackson, a lefty from Arizona State, makes his Southern League debut with nine hitless innings for Orlando on April 14, but is removed without getting the decision as the Twins win in extra innings. Rod Boxberger, fresh from leading Southern California to the NCAA title, pitches a no-hitter for Columbus in his debut on July 12. Two managers also make their debuts: Tony LaRussa in Knoxville, taking over for Joe Jones, and Jimmy Bragan, replacing John Orsino at Chattanooga. Bigger things are in store for both.

1980-1984: Attendance continues to rise as Nashville and Memphis draw exceptionally well and Birmingham replaces Montgomery in 1981. Nashville qualifies for the playoffs all five years, winning the pennant in 1982 on a 12-inning walk-off homer by Bryan Dayett. Charlotte, with a shortstop named Cal Ripken, Jr., takes the 1980 pennant and again in 1984 as Ken Dixon strikes out 211 batters. Orlando wins in 1981 as Tim Laudner hit a league-record 42 homers; Birmingham takes the 1983 title. Bragan takes over from Hitchcock as league president in 1981, moving the league headquarters to Trussville, Ala. Greenville replaces Savannah in 1984.

1985-87: Huntsville joins the league and Jose Canseco wins the MVP despite a mid-season promotion. The Stars draw 300,810. With Canseco already in Triple-A, the Stars still win the title when crowd favorite Rocky Coyle hits a ninth-inning homer in Game Five of the championship series against Charlotte. The Stars reach the playoffs each of the next two years, losing to Columbus in 1986 in the finals and eventual champion Birmingham in the first round in 1987. Bo Jackson, a Heisman Trophy winner at Auburn, opts for pro baseball instead of football and plays for the Memphis Chicks.

1988-1990: Memphis wins the second half in the Western Division under Sal Rende, a long-time Chattanooga Lookouts star, but his old team beats his new one in the playoffs en route to a three-game sweep over Greenville for the '88 pennant, the last one for Chattanooga in the first 50 years of the league. 1989 brings another sweeping disappointment for Greenville in the championship round, falling 9-1, 9-1 and 3-2 to Birmingham. Jeff Cox, who set a league record with 68 stolen bases in 1977 for Chattanooga, manages the Memphis Chicks to the 1990 pennant, with Jeff Conine winning the MVP award. The Chicks win at home after two days of rainouts.

1991: The Carolina Mudcats come into existence, moving to Zebulon, N.C., from Columbus, Ga. The small town outside of Raleigh is chosen as the site to avoid geographical conflicts with other teams in the area. The new franchise helps the Southern League top the two million mark in attendance for the first time, with 2,127,828, fulfilling Jimmy Bragan's goal. Orlando wins three playoff games by one run and earns its first pennant in a decade.

1992-1993: Greenville wins the first half by 11 games and the second by 16½ in a 100-win season, and then Grady Little's club—with SL MVP Javy Lopez—beats Chattanooga in a thrilling five-game series. The league attendance is 2,318,080. Charlotte leaves the league in 1993, with the Nashville Xpress taking its place and sharing space at Greer Stadium with the Triple A Sounds. The Cubs switch their affiliation from Charlotte to Orlando, the Twins going from Orlando to Nashville. Carlos Delgado wins the '93 MVP award and jumps straight to the majors, while Terry Francona is manager of the year.

1994: Everyone's attendance skyrockets. Michael Jordan plays for the Birmingham Barons and the league has its best year ever at the turnstiles, at 2,596,340. Arnie Fielkow assumes the league presidency from Bragan. He had been deputy commissioner of the Continental Basketball Association.

1995-96: Fielkow's plan to place a franchise in Puerto Rico collapses, and so the Port City Roosters, a Mariners' franchise, take roost in Wilmington, N.C., for two years. By coincidence, Wilmington is Michael Jordan's hometown. Carolina sits in first place for 128 of 154 days and outlasts Chattanooga in a five-game championship series for the 1995 championship.

1997: Mobile takes Port City's place in the league and appears to have the Western Division playoffs locked up before Huntsville's Justin Bowles, in his first Double-A at-bat, hits a two-out, game-tying ninth-inning homer. Despite homers in six straight playoff games by the Stars' Ramon Hernandez, Greenville—with nary a player on the All-Star team—wins the championship series. Pete Rose, Jr. plays for Chattanooga and reaches the majors on September 1.

1998: Gabe Kapler leads the minors with 146 RBI and has 28 homers for Jacksonville. But Mobile wins both halves of the West and knocks off the Suns in the finals. West Tenn joins the league, replacing Memphis.

1999: Orlando, in its final season at Tinker Field before moving to Disney World, wins the '99 pennant over the Diamond Jaxx. Bill Russell's Orlando club plays its last eight regular season games on the road, travels from Huntsville to Jacksonville for a tiebreaker game with Jacksonville, and then rides to Knoxville for the Eastern Division playoff opener. As Hurricane Floyd hits Florida, the playoffs shift to West Tenn with Orlando slated as the home team in Game 3. The teams fly back to Florida for Game 4 and the Rays' clincher.

2000-04: New stadiums open in Tennessee, Orlando, and Chattanooga. In 2000, for only the second time, all playoff series go the distance, with West Tenn winning the title on a 10th-inning Jacksonville throwing error. The 2001 championship series is cancelled because of the 9/11 attacks, with Jacksonville and Huntsville declared co-champions. Birmingham sweeps Jacksonville in three games to hoist the 2002 championship, but Wally Backman's club has to go extra innings in two of them, including a 12-inning victory in Game 3 on Danny Sandoval's RBI base hit. Huntsville extends Carolina to five games in the '03 series before falling, a victim of 80 strikeouts in the series. The Suns open a new park in Jacksonville. In 2004, Orlando moves to Montgomery. For the second time in three years, co-champions are declared, with Tennessee and Mobile sharing the title after Hurricane Ivan wreaks havoc.

2005-07: Mississippi replaces Greenville. Jacksonville sweeps Birmingham in the South playoffs, then avenges its 2000 playoff loss to West Tenn in the finals. Montgomery knocks off Huntsville in both the 2006 and 2007 championship, stealing the latter in dramatic fashion when Stars' closer Luis Pena yields a two-out, three-run, opposite-field ninth-inning homer to Sergio Pedroza, just up from A-ball.

2008-13: The M-Braves do their worst-to-first number in the course of one season, starting out 2-15 and winning the 2008 pennant. Jacksonville wins back-to-back in 2009-10, clinching its fifth championship in 15 seasons. Mobile goes back-to-back with the 2011-12 pennants. Hunter Morris, the first Huntsville native to play for the Stars, leads the league in homers and RBI and is named MVP. The BayBears are dethroned in 2013 by Birmingham, celebrating the opening of its beautiful new park.

THE TEAMS

The 1976 Chattanooga Lookouts.

14 DAYS OF TRIUMPH

1968

The Streak was so magical and relentless, it took two days to finally end it. Before it finally succumbed, The Streak included a no-hitter, two doubleheader sweeps, eight wins against Birmingham, three extra-inning victories, a manager excused for a death in the family, a pitcher excused for a wedding, two injuries suffered at home—not home plate—and something of a managerial debut for a baseball icon.

The Montgomery Rebels won 16 games in a two-week period in July 1968. Otherwise, they were a pedestrian 64-57 that season and would still finish four-and-a-half games behind Asheville in the Southern League pennant race.

But from July 13, 1968, through July 26, they were perfect, outscoring the opposition 70-24.

They were even unbeaten at the end of play on July 27—though they were losing. The Rebels trailed by a run when the power conked out at Savannah's Grayson Stadium, forcing a suspended game. So The Streak wasn't officially ended until the completion of the suspended game on July 28.

The Montgomery Rebels were a Detroit Tigers farm club managed by Frank Carswell, a baseball lifer from Texas who lost four formative years of his playing career to World War II. Carswell, who had been a basketball star at Rice, was a Crash Davis sort, with 209 minor-league homers over 14 seasons. The most famous graduate of the '68 Rebels was a catcher who barely hit his weight and would later earn far more renown once his playing career was finished. His name: Jim Leyland.

They played at Paterson Field, a handsome little park at the base of a kudzu-covered embankment. Across the street was the Crampton Bowl, the site for many years of the Blue-Gray all-star football game. Over Paterson Field's left-field wall was Oakwood Cemetery, where Hank Williams was buried in January 1953.

The Rebels had three pitchers with double-digit victories, Jim Brown (14-9), George Korince (13-7), and Ronnie Chandler (12-8); only Korince would reach the majors, and that for a mere 17 innings. The season before, the Topps Company made an egregious error, using a photo of Brown, an African-American, on a Tigers' rookie card for Korince, who was white.

A lean, 6-foot-3 right-hander from the Chicago suburb of Harvey, Jim Brown was 23 years old but had already bounced between Class A and Class AA for five previous seasons. Brown was 55-57 for his career when he took the mound on Sunday afternoon, July 7, in the first game of a doubleheader at Charlotte. He faced only 23 men in flinging a no-hitter. His ledger included two strikeouts and only three baserunners, walking Charlie Manuel and Red Rambo and hitting Rudy Welch with a pitch.

Twice before Brown had been within one out of a no-hitter in pro ball, in 1964 at Knoxville and in 1965 at Rocky Mount, North Carolina. Roger Repoz broke up the first, Frank Coggins the second. Admitted Brown, "That's all I could think of when [the final batter, Jim] Jenkins came up." Jenkins smashed a line drive back at Brown that he speared thigh-high, preserving the no-hitter. The gem U-turned Brown's season. He had won six in a row to start the season before suffering shoulder woes that left him at 7-6 entering the day.

Eighteen days later, Brown would become the only Southern League pitcher to throw two no-hitters in a season. He even hit a home run in that win, over Birmingham, which came on his 24th birthday.

But, wait. We're getting ahead of ourselves now....

On July 11, Asheville nipped Montgomery 2-1, as Don Anderson homered and the Tourists scored an unearned run. The Rebels managed a mere six hits. It was their eighth loss in nine games and ninth loss in 11 games, dropping them to fourth place. The next evening's game against Asheville was rained out.

The Streak would be born on the following day.

Win One, July 13—Montgomery 4, Birmingham 1. Norm McRae—"Cool Mac" to teammates—scattered six hits and Wayne Redmond supplied a pair of hits.

Win Two, July 13—Montgomery 6, Birmingham 5. Larry Rojas homered in the ninth inning of the scheduled seven-inning game for a Rebels' doubleheader sweep. Korince owned a 5-4 lead in the seventh but yielded a homer to Joe Keough that sent the game to extra innings. Pete McKenzie belted a two-run homer in the second for the Rebs; he sat out the first game after having been at National Guard drills all day.

Win Three, July 14—Montgomery 7, Birmingham 3. Art Todtenhausen had lost seven consecutive games and been sent to the bullpen but he entered with nobody out in the second and allowed only two hits in eight innings of relief, striking out six.

Win Four, July 15—Montgomery 1, Birmingham 0. McKenzie, who committed three errors at third base, drove home Paul Pavelko with a single to right in the 11th inning, giving the win to relief ace Bill Butler. Bob Reed had a no-hitter until an eighth-inning single by the Athletics' Freddie Velazquez.

Win Five, July 16—Montgomery 4, Savannah 1. Brown retired the last 12 batters he faced in a complete-game win, his first appearance since his no-hitter, having missed a turn after suffering a nasty cut on his ankle in an accident at home. Redmond lashed a two-run homer.

Win Six, July 17—Montgomery 2, Savannah 1. Pitcher Ron Chandler had a seventh-inning homer for the winning margin and allowed only three hits in eight-plus innings. Shrugged Carswell, "I gave him the home-run sign."

Win Seven, July 18—Montgomery 6, Savannah 0. After Korince started on July 13, he was married and excused for a two-day honeymoon to Panama City, Fla., with bride Gail. He returned to pitch a six-hit shutout against Savannah that was hardly a honeymoon. He was bit on the pitching hand that day by his dog and was hit by a Frank Biitner line drive just above his pitching elbow. Redmond walloped a homer estimated at 450 feet.

Win Eight, July 19—Montgomery 4, Savannah 2. Reed struck out eight in a complete-game six-hitter and Tim Marting had a two-run seventh-inning single. It was the last that Bob Reed would see of The

Streak. He shipped out for two weeks of National Guard duty after the game.

Win Nine, July 20—Montgomery 4, Evansville 2. The Rebels tested The Streak out on the road for the first time, coming back from a 2-0 deficit. Butler saved the day with six strikeouts in three and two-thirds innings of relief.

Win Ten, July 21—Montgomery 9, Evansville 2. After being held hitless through five-and-a-third frames by Fred Rath, the Rebels scored nine runs in the seventh, aided by four Evansville errors, two bases-loaded walks and a run-scoring wild pitch.

Win Eleven, July 22—Montgomery 5, Evansville 3. The Rebels tied the Southern League record of 11 wins in a row in front of a paltry 163 fans at historic Bosse Field. Rojas broke a 3-3 tie with a two-out RBI single in the eighth. Evansville, too, was streaking. It was the E-Sox' eighth loss in a row and 13th in 14 games en route to a 55-84 record in the city's final season in the league.

Win Twelve, July 23—Montgomery 4, Birmingham 1. The Rebels handed Korince a two-run lead after the top of the first, and he made it stand up with a seven-hit, seven-strikeout complete game.

Win Thirteen, July 24—Montgomery 5, Birmingham 0. "Cool Mac" and Butler combined for a four-hit shutout.

Win Fourteen, July 24—Montgomery 3, Birmingham 1. The Rebels completed their second doubleheader sweep of the Barons during The Sweep when Redmond and Barry Morgan delivered back-to-back homers in the top of the 10th.

Win Fifteen, July 25—Montgomery 3, Birmingham 0. Only an eighth-inning walk to Darrell Evans prevented Brown from a perfect game, but he still registered his second no-hitter in a span of three starts. He struck out 12—seven in a row during one stretch—and homered. Carswell missed the game after returning home to Pasadena, Texas, following the death of his mother. Leyland, in a portent of the future, managed the club in Carswell's absence and was also the starting catcher. "The easiest game I've ever caught," he told the *Montgomery Advertiser*. He had some teasing for Carswell. "Frank's always talking about how he wins them by giving Redmond or Morgan the home-run sign. I didn't even fool with that. I just gave Brown the no-hitter sign."

Win Sixteen, July 26—Montgomery 3, Birmingham 2. McKenzie, a former Auburn University player who would go into the ministry following his brief career in the majors, homered off Mike Olivo in the sixth inning, driving home Redmond.

The following night in Savannah, the Senators jumped on Matt Hoar for five runs and were leading 5-4 when the power went out in the sixth inning, an outage that affected much of the city. When the game was resumed the next afternoon, Montgomery took a 7-5 lead in the top of the seventh, keyed by a Marting homer, only to watch Bob Lucas tie the game with a two-run single. On the play, a relay throw to the infield eluded third baseman Rojas. The baseball disappeared into the Montgomery dugout.

It took The Streak with it.

COMING BACK TO CHATTANOOGA

1976

They landed like one big posse, many of them wearing Western hats that were souvenirs from their spring in the Arizona desert. Even now, hanging on the wall of a guest bedroom in La Jolla, California, there is a group photo of several of them, looking straight from a spaghetti Western. Bruce Robinson. Matt Keough. Brian Kingman. Derek Bryant. Denny Haines. Steve McCatty.

Deplaning that Saturday afternoon in April 1976, they had no idea what lay in store. In the terminal of Chattanooga's Lovell Field were more than a couple hundred baseball fans greeting their arrival. "It was like the big leaguers were coming back after winning the World Series," Robinson said. Offered first baseman Ron Beaurivage, "We didn't have that many coming out to our games in Birmingham the year before."

Pro baseball was returning to Chattanooga after a 10-season hiatus (see Chapter 17), and these were the new Lookouts who were bringing it there. They were an Oakland A's farm club, predominantly players from the West Coast, showing a little trickle-down swagger from the A's big-league reign of that era. They were often treated like big leaguers. After games, they'd head to Dino's Supper Club, a place whose similarities to some romantic Rat Pack night club were few. The players would be escorted past the line of customers and ushered in through the kitchen, seated at private VIP tables where their evening was comped. It was the same sort of rock-star treatment they'd get at the Brass Register or Yesterday's, or especially at a seedy garage across the Georgia line that became headquarters to the Bleacher Bums, a band of oft-lubricated fans who'd follow the team on short road trips in a dilapidated bus painted in Lookouts' green and gold.

"It was a remarkable year in so many respects," said Robinson, sitting on a deck at his Idaho home, overlooking the Snake River. "We were so fortunate to be the first team back. It was very heartwarming."

"It was magical for minor-league players and for anybody, really, with all the history in that stadium," Kingman said from Phoenix. "People seemed interested in the game and the players. It seemed like a simpler, better America."

The man behind the return was a small, soft-spoken gentleman named Woodrow Reid. Everyone in town knew his company. Reid House Salads were in every grocery's dairy case, and commercials peppered the airwaves. They were not to be confused with the stately landmark hotel called the Read House; in those less-litigious times, Reid's company could get away with the similarity, which was likely propitious. However, few people knew Woodrow Reid. He was certainly a stranger to *Chattanooga News-Free Press* sports editor Allan Morris, who got the call that Reid and Southern League president Billy Hitchcock had some news for him, that a plan to return baseball to the city was in the works.

The club would play at Engel Stadium, once a sparkling gem in the glory days of the colorful Joe Engel, but since the end of a dismal 1965 season, it had been left to the University of Tennessee at Chattanooga baseball team, the Orchard Knob Junior High football team, and hundreds of pigeons. There was a modest clean-up project by friends and family when UTC's baseball team called it home, but it was like trying to scour a sewer with a toothbrush. Wrote Morris, "Paint is peeling off the walls and seats, the floors are filthy, the roof is falling down, and it looks like a tornado hit the place." It was not the best of signs when Oakland farm director Syd Thrift and Hitchcock had to jimmy open a window and crawl through for their first tour of the stadium.

But Reid was able to land a working agreement with the Oakland A's. The city came through with some assistance. Reid invested a considerable amount of money himself. A few splashes of paint, some repair work, a lot of scouring, and the ballpark was ready for the season.

It was a shoestring operation. Reid's son, Mark, was the team president. His wife, Sarah, had a box seat behind the dugout, assuming a maternal role toward the players that met with mixed results. The general manager was Jerry Lambert. The only other full-time office staff member was Brenda, an assistant who became part of a running joke. When things weren't just quite right, the mantra was, "Brenda will get around to it by the next home stand." There were some part-time employees, like Jimmy Rowe, who dated back to the Joe Engel Era, and the organist, Charlie Timmons, who was once ejected from the ballpark by umpire Joe West for playing, "Three Blind Mice." In the umpire's defense, the tune serenaded a two-man crew, West working with fellow future big-league ump John Shulock.

Rene Lachemann was the manager, and players fed off his leadership. "The best thing about Lach, he was a players' manager," Beaurivage said from his home in Manchester, N.H. "His philosophy was, you don't like something, then come to the office and shut the door. Then we'll deal with it. Then the door will open and we'll both walk out. No reports. No carrying it over."

Lachemann was a catcher in the Kansas City Athletics system, playing at Birmingham and Mobile in the Southern League in the early 1960s, hoping for a call-up to the majors. He'd still belt out a refrain or two from "Goin' to Kansas City" around his players. Lachemann, a Dodgers' bat boy as a kid along with best pal Jim Lefebvre, was called up to KC in 1965, but by '66 Phil Roof was ensconced as the A's catcher. Lach was sent back to the minors. By the time he was 23, he had played his final big-league game. He was a mere 30 years old when he began as Chattanooga's manager, a rung on a ladder that would see him ultimately manage in the majors at Seattle, Milwaukee and Florida.

Chattanooga's Keough, Kingman, and McCatty—who'd make the cover of Sports Illustrated as Oakland's "Five Aces" in April 1981, before manager Billy Martin treated their arms like swizzle sticks—along with outfielders Dwayne Murphy and Denny Walling all went on to have extended major-league careers.

But it was the team's character—and characters—that appealed to the populace and built the sort of clubhouse chemistry that saw the Lookouts win the first-half division title. (Alas, they lost to Dave Rozema and the dynastic Montgomery Rebels—"they were flippin' loaded," Robinson said—in a one-game playoff for the league championship in August.) There was the volatile infielder who prompted Lachemann to buy a sandbag on which the player could take out his anger, saving water coolers, light bulbs, and sanity. There was another infielder who chose to spend much of his hotel time in the nude and almost missed a bus departure, with only time to wrap a motel towel around his waist and sprint to the bus. There was the almost daily contest to launch a fungo over the 35-foot-tall scoreboard/billboard in left field, more than 360 feet from home plate.

The Lookouts opened their season on the road, starting 1-4 before Beaurivage produced an inspirational poem about perseverance before a Sunday afternoon game at Savannah, and Chattanooga salvaged that one. They returned for the home opener, on April 20, against Charlotte. Mark Budaska hit a grand slam in the fifth, Kingman scattered eight hits in seven innings, and Rick Tronerud closed the door in relief. The crowd was announced at 8,305. Reid, Lambert & Co. had to rope off sections of the outfield to enable fans to sit there. "The greatest crowd I've ever seen," Tronerud said afterward. "I got chill bumps when I came in."

"I'm just sorry we missed 10 years," Reid said. It was not a night without some hiccups. But Brenda had 'em fixed by the next home stand.

CHIPPER AND GRADY'S JUGGERNAUT

1992

Chipper Jones, dressy casual in a gray suit and open-collared shirt, a cross necklace at his throat, sat on a tall barstool on stage at the Chattanooga Convention Center, just a few miles and 21 years removed from a night he came into that city and walked away with a Southern League pennant. While he was there to offer some inspiration to an audience of young athletes, he also served up some nostalgia about the winningest team in Southern League history.

"I won a Double-A championship in this town in 1992 when I was with Greenville," Jones said. "I remember it was a mighty big poke to center field (at Engel Stadium).

"But what I remember most"—he begins to chuckle—"was almost starting a brawl during one of the playoff games. I questioned the ancestry of this dude's mother after I thought he was trying to hit me with a pitch. It was pretty intense. But we ended up winning and got our pictures made with a five-foot trophy, which was probably the biggest thing I'd ever seen."

He neglected to mention that he had to take a brief leave during the championship series, and for good reason. While still a Single-A infielder at Durham, he had scheduled his wedding that week and it couldn't be moved.

Anything but a gargantuan trophy would have been inappropriate for the '92 Braves. They were the only team in league history to win 100 games in a season. They were 30 games better than Eastern

Division runner-up Charlotte, 10 games better than Western Division champ Chattanooga, which had the most wins in franchise history (Southern League era) and still didn't win a pennant. Greenville saw to that by winning the best-of-five series, three games to two, including a 10-3 thrashing in the finale at Engel Stadium.

The Braves had eight more wins than the previous record of 92, set by Charlotte in the 1971 Dixie Association season, and 11 more than any team since (manager Trent Jewett's Carolina team, with 89 in 1995.)

Quite simply, "It was loaded," said G-Braves radio broadcaster Mark Hauser.

It's never easy to get a manager or coach into the business of comparison, but Grady Little, the G-Braves' skipper, acknowledged it was the best minor-league team he managed.

Check some of the names.

Javy Lopez, the league's MVP, notched a .321 average and 60 RBI in 115 games. Eddie Perez, his backup, amassed 41 RBI. Tony Tarasco, who went on to become a Baltimore Orioles outfielder (and is still waiting to catch that Derek Jeter fly ball intercepted by Jeffrey Maier in the 1996 ALCS), hit .286 with 54 RBI. The team's blue-chip prospect, Golden Spikes Award winner Mike Kelly from Arizona State, batted .229 but still socked a team-high 25 homers and drove in 71. Mike Bell drove home 63 runs. Melvin Nieves, the youngest G-Braves starter, hit .283 with 18 homers and 76 RBI.

And, of course, Chipper Jones himself, with a .346 average, 42 RBI and nine homers in 67 second-half games. Said Little, "He was a player with so much ability, we did everything we could not to mess him up."

"That was a borderline big-league team," said Brad Rippelmeyer, catching then for the Braves' Class A team in Durham, North Carolina, and wondering exactly what a guy is supposed to do when Javy Lopez and Eddie Perez are ahead of you on the depth chart. "The Braves were stacked. Not just catching-wise but at every position. That's what helped them go on a run for about 15 years there."

"It was a well-rounded team, a great mix of veterans," Hauser said. "They knew they were going to win when they took the field."

Revisionists might want to believe this was an obvious powerhouse even in spring training, but at least one baseball expert looked at things very conservatively early on—Debi Little, the manager's wife.

"My wife would always ask, 'Who is your closer?' because she knew that was going to determine a lot of success," Little said. In this case, it would be Don Strange, who had saved 19 games and displayed impeccable control as Little's closer in Durham in '91. Still, this was a difficult leap to the Southern League for the six-foot right-hander from Springfield, Mass.

As it turned out, Strange had 18 saves for the championship team. The thing is, the explosive G-Braves simply didn't leave the bullpen with any tense, game-closing situations. "Their numbers were cartoonish," said Curt Bloom, the Birmingham Barons' broadcaster. He recalled poring over game notes and statistics to prep for games when the Barons met the Braves, "and every single stat they kept, whether was against righties or lefties, day games, extra innings, whatever—it was enormous. You can't beat them."

"We played American League-style of baseball," said Little, who would ultimately manage in the American League with Boston (2002-03) before later moving to the National League's Los Angeles Dodgers (2006-07). "We just outslugged a lot of people that year. We had some good pitching on that team, not very many of them who pitched much in the majors. They were always pitching with a lot of run support." Indeed, Greg McMichael, with 160 starts, and journeyman reliever Pedro Borbon were the only G-Braves pitchers to spend significant time in the big leagues.

As loaded as Greenville was offensively and with top prospects, Little knew it was the other pieces that made the difference. "Usually you win those pennants with your supporting cast of players. They've got to be better than everybody else in the league," Little said. Indeed, players like Mike Mordecai, the starting shortstop before Jones' promotion; third baseman Ed Giovanola; outfielder Pat Kelly; Jose Olmeda and Perez gracefully handling his backup role were "big parts of that team."

You could make the case the most valuable player in all this—in fact, for 20 years of Atlanta Braves history—was a righthanded pitcher who had gone 6-13 for Huntsville the year before, walking 90 of the 607 batters he faced.

Todd Van Poppel was a whiz-bang phenom out of Martin High

School in Arlington, Texas, with the misfortune of labels like "the next Nolan Ryan." He was on everybody's draft list. But he told the Braves not to put him on theirs. They had the first pick in the 1990 draft after another of their abysmal years of the 1980s, and even though Bobby Cox went on a mission trip to Texas to plead otherwise, Van Poppel told him not to waste the pick. He was going to play college ball for the Texas Longhorns. (Oakland took a chance, chose him with the 14th overall selection, and agent Scott Boras worked out an instant-millionaire deal, the Longhorns on the hook.)

The Braves' consolation prize was Larry Wayne Jones, an infielder from The Bolles School in Jacksonville. He'd merely become an NL MVP, an eight-time All-Star, and enjoyed a career that put him on a definite path to Cooperstown. "It's kinda summed up by saying I was never surprised by anything he accomplished," said Little. "You could see the handwriting on the wall when he was a youngster."

Chipper Jones batted only .229 in 44 games of rookie ball as an 18-year-old, but hit .326 with 15 homers and 98 RBI at Macon in 1991, and then .277 in the first half at Durham in 1992. Ozzie Smith, he was not. Jones committed 56 errors at Macon and had 14 at Durham.

Hauser remembered sitting down with Little on the eve of Chipper's Greenville debut and saying, "Is this going to help us?"

Responded Little, "We're going to be the best team in baseball with this kid coming up."

As it turned out, Greenville was the best team in Southern League history.

CUE-BALL'S
SUPER STARS

1997

When D.T. Cromer belted a two-run homer with two out in the first inning, it wasn't especially notable. That's how a lot of Huntsville Stars games seemed to get jump-started in that summer, with somebody going deep.

But on July 18, 1997, Cromer's homer was a mere appetizer. Before the Stars got through pummeling the Chattanooga Lookouts 22-3, they had homered seven times, tying a league record. They piled up 23 hits, totaling 47 total bases. Outfielder Ryan Christenson, in only his seventh game since a promotion from Class A, had a grand slam, went 4-for-6 and drove in six runs.

"What do I remember about that year?" Christenson said. "Kicking everybody's butt."

"Batting practice was fun," recalled pitcher Steve Connelly. "There wasn't a lot of shagging. Just watching balls go over the fence."

The Stars were one of the most productive offensive teams in the first half-century of the Southern League, able to put a slowpitch softball team to shame. Huntsville scored a league record 942 runs, crushed 164 homers, and compiled a team batting average of .268 and slugging percentage of .461. Said Steve Koryna, the team's broadcaster, "It was just obscene."

Mike Quade, the Stars' manager, a future skipper for the Chicago Cubs, said that "never in all my years have I had a club hit like this one. It's the best I've had and one of the best I've seen." In 139 games, Huntsville was never once shut out. By the same token, the team only posted a lone shutout victory.

"From what I remember, as a pitching staff we needed that many runs," Connelly laughed, sitting in the conference room at his downtown Huntsville office, only a few miles from Joe Davis Stadium.

Indeed, the team ERA was 5.16. Said Kornya, "The pitching staff looked worse than it did because the hitting was so awesome." And the hitting wrecked everyone else's ERA. Fat as 5.16 seems, the league average was 4.78.

Huntsville outfielder Ben Grieve was the league's MVP that season, batting .328 with 24 homers and 108 RBI in 100 games. "He was a natural," Kornya said. "The game looked so easy for him." Mike Neill set a league record with 129 runs scored, batting .340. Third baseman Mike Coolbaugh, who would be killed by a line drive while coaching for Tulsa in 2007, led the league with 30 homers and 132 RBI. Miguel Tejada had 22 homers and 97 RBI, Cromer 15 homers and 121 RBI.

The nucleus of the team grew up together in the Oakland system. Ties were even deeper for Cromer and Rob DeBoer, teammates at South Carolina, where DeBoer was also a running back on the football team. Nineteen of the 42 players would eventually make it to the major leagues. Quade, an affable bald guy appropriately nicknamed "Cue-ball" by his players, had the perfect touch for the team: patience with the pitcher, the proper distance from hitters to not mess up their groove, and a wicked sense of humor. After a newbie outfielder joined the team and misjudged a fly ball, letting it plunk him in the chest, Quade ordered him to wear a chest protector the next day during batting practice. He could deal with fragile psyches, like Tejada, who left the clubhouse after a two-error, 0-for-4 performance in the first game of a doubleheader and began walking back to his apartment.

(An aside: One of the players' girlfriends had a connection to a Huntsville businessman who owned an apartment complex. As the team opened the season with a week on the road, the wives began to move in, only to be more than a little unsettled by a shooting that took place directly across the street. One day, Steve Connelly left his apartment to discover eight total strangers piled into his convertible Mustang, taking pictures of each other behind the wheel. Suffice it to say, leases were broken as resoundingly as batting records.)

The only team that could stop these Huntsville Stars was the parent club, the Oakland Athletics. By mid-August, the organization ravaged Huntsville by calling up Grieve, Christenson, and Tejada. Those moves played an instrumental role in the Stars' decision a year later not to continue the working agreement with Oakland.

Quade's Stars still won the second half of the Southern League West Division, setting up a playoff series against Mobile. There was no shortage of familiarity. A quirk in the schedule had Huntsville ending the regular season in Mobile, so they settled in for a nine-day visit.

The Stars won the opener, but blew a four-run lead in the second game and lost on an 11th-inning Wiki Gonzalez home run. They lost 8-3 when the series moved to Huntsville, but kept alive in a Game 4 that remains locked in Stars' lore.

Justin Bowles, a former LSU outfielder, was in Class A all season and flew home to Houston, where he received orders from Oakland farm director Keith Lieppman to join the Stars in Mobile. He headed back to the airport, where he got stuck in traffic at a railroad crossing and missed his flight. No matter. He didn't get off the bench until Game 4, when Quade called upon him to pinch hit for shortstop Jose Castro with two on and two out in the bottom of the ninth, Huntsville trailing 5-2.

Bowles fell behind in the count 3-2. In the press box, Huntsville general manager Don Mincher said, "If he gets hold of one, he'll never forget it the rest of his life." Bowles fouled off a pitch, then drove the next one out of the park over the right-field fence to send the game into extra innings, where a Neill homer won things in the 10th. When the Stars scored seven in the first inning of Game 5, capped by a Ramon Hernandez grand slam, they were on their way to the championship series against Greenville, which was no less eventful.

Hernandez, a native of Venezuela who'd still be catching in the majors at age 37, belted another grand slam in the first game against Greenville, giving Billy King the win. As he walked to the plate, Hernandez recalled, "I was like, 'Wow, what if I hit another one right here?' I was thinking, 'Nobody would believe it.' "

He finished with homers in seven of eight postseason games, including six games in a row.

Hernandez had an RBI single and Neill a two-run homer to hand a 3-0 lead in Game 2 to Blake Stein, a 6-foot-7 right-hander the A's acquired from St. Louis on July 31 as part of the Mark McGwire trade. Then came "the monsoon, one of the hardest rains I ever saw," Connelly said. The grounds crew hustled out and players even helped pull the tarp, but the field was already soaked. The game was washed out after three innings and a new league rule mandated play-off games could not be suspended, they had to start from scratch.

In the makeup, Marc Lewis, a Braves' outfielder from Decatur, Alabama, a 30-minute drive west of Joe Davis Stadium, cracked a three-run homer to enable Greenville to tie the series 1-1. The '97 slugging Stars reappeared in Game 3, with five homers in a 15-3 romp for a 2-1 series lead. Then, it was Lewis again—this time with a three-run double in the first off Stein in Game 4, helping Greenville force a pivotal Game 5.

The Southern League Championship Series finale was not close. Greenville mugged King for five runs in the first and, with Cromer sidelined with a finger injury, Hernandez finally cooled, and Grieve, Tejada, and Christenson on the other side of the country, Mike Quade's explosive Stars were suddenly mortal.

Mike Neill, who'd have a brief stint in Oakland the following year and then star for the 2000 gold medal-winning U.S. Olympic baseball team in Australia, sat in a cramped, stunned Stars' locker room after the championship series defeat.

"I think it makes it harder," Neill told the *Huntsville Times*. "Because I realize there may not be another chance. I think if we'd won this thing, we'd have gone down as one of the best teams in league history, but now we're just another team."

History would argue otherwise.

MISSISSIPPI'S MIRACLE BRAVES

2008

They not only won the Southern League championship in a stupendous and surprising fashion, they went and got themselves a proclamation from the state of Mississippi. Featuring more than a few therefores and whereases, the Mississippi Braves were honored in HR 35, a resolution from the Mississippi State House of Representatives.

HR 35 celebrated how "the Mississippi Braves AA Baseball Team, led by Manager of the Year Phillip Wellman, completed the greatest turnaround in team history by winning the Southern League Championship on Saturday, September 13, 2008, when the M-Braves defeated the Carolina Mudcats 3-2 in 10 innings to claim their first championship."

It noted how "the Braves went on top early in the championship game with Carolina, only to see the Mudcats twice tie the score, before, in the bottom of the 10th, J.C. Holt scored the game-winning run from second base to give the Braves the win and their first Southern League Championship."

It praised the first winning season in a decade and various individual award and accomplishments.

"Be it resolved," it read, "that we do hereby commend and congratulate the Mississippi Braves AA Baseball Team, Manager of the Year Phillip Wellman and General Manager Steve DeSalvo for an incredible 2008 season."

If anything could transcend partisanship in government, it was the agreement that something magical had taken place that summer at the spiffy ballpark nine miles southeast of the state capitol in Jackson, Miss.

The M-Braves that began the season were, in a word, "terrible." That, from Wellman. They started off 2-15, finishing April at 6-20. It was a lean year in the cyclical nature of abundant prospects, and that was showing. Only three of the '08 players would be on the Atlanta roster a half-dozen years later.

The M-Braves that continued the season were, in a word, "resilient." That, too, from Wellman.

"We didn't have a whole lot of what the organization considered prospects on the team. But they didn't like losing and they enjoyed working hard and they just kept at it and kept at it and kept at it and we started winning a few games."

Whereas, they won the pennant.

The M-Braves may have ended the first half 30-40, but as the second half opened they were absolutely untouchable. They won 10 of 12 to start the second.

"I started to sense for the first time all season they truly believed they could win," Wellman said. "To have started out like that, it would have been very easy for them to fold their tents. It proved the high character of the people they were by continuing to come to work and put in a blue-collar work and get better." By the time they swept Chattanooga in late July, with three shutouts in five games, they were finally above .500 and sprinting away from everyone.

Team effort though it may have been, the season was marked by a pair of individual accomplishments.

Matt Young was a 5-foot-8 outfielder, an undrafted free agent out of the University of New Mexico. He good-naturedly accepted constant ribbing about his height, like the night in Class A ball when teammates noticed a midget wrestling bout would be held outside the stadium at Charleston, S.C., and they asked, "Aren't you supposed to work after the game?"

Young began 0-for-3 on July 24, and then, in the sixth inning of a game the Braves would uncharacteristically lose 11-6, he singled to center against Birmingham's Ryan O'Malley. It was a whimper of a beginning of a Southern League record. Over the course of 11 official at-bats, Young had a hit.

The following game he went 4-for-4, then stretched his streak to seven by going 2-for-2 the next night before being hit by a pitch and walking on his next two trips. Facing Chattanooga on a hot Sunday, July 27, in front of 2,412, Young smacked a single in the first off Travis Wood, added a two-run single to left in a five-run second, led off the fourth with a triple, and greeted reliever Lee Tabor with a single to open the sixth. However, Tabor coaxed Young to ground out to second in the eighth, putting the scissors to the streak.

On the opposite end of the spectrum was 6-foot-6 pitcher Tommy Hanson, on a path to becoming the top-rated pitcher in the Atlanta system. Tom and Cindy Hanson traveled from their California home and settled into the stands on June 25 as their son went to the mound against Birmingham. Nothing in the first inning indicated history would be made. He walked the leadoff man, threw a wild pitch, hit a batter, and walked another before escaping with a pop-up to the catcher. Hanson hit the leadoff man in the second before a screeching U-turn. He proceeded to retire the next 20 he faced, 11 on strikeouts. But in doing so, his pitch count was adding up.

"[Pitching coach] Derek Botelho and I were sitting there in the eighth inning and I distinctly remember Hanson going to the opposite end of the dugout when he left the field. He didn't come in at my end," Wellman said. "I told Bo he doesn't want any part of us thinking he's done. But he had like nine pitches left on his pitch count."

Hanson spent those nine getting Javier Colina and Cole Armstrong on flies to centerfielder Jordan Schafer. Wellman didn't budge from the dugout. "Please, Tommy, get this guy out," he remembered saying to himself, adding, "Can you imagine the fan reaction if I'd gone out there with my hand sticking out?"

The last batter, Ricardo Nanita, hit one on the screws, right at Schaefer. Tommy Hanson had his no-hitter.

Hanson's arrival from Class A Myrtle Beach and the move of Kris Medlen from the bullpen solidified the pitching staff. Jairo Asencio, an off-season free agent acquisition, saved 26 games. Jason Parry gave the offense a lift with 13 homers and 41 RBI in 38 games before going to Triple A. "By then," Wellman said, "we had really started to believe we could win on a consistent basis."

Todd Redmond went 13-5 to be named the Southern League Pitcher of the Year, and he threw a five-hit shutout, with nine strikeouts, to beat Birmingham in the playoff opener 1-0. Schafer's 11th-inning sacrifice fly was the difference the next night, then the M-Braves completed the sweep on a Medlen shutout back at Trustmark Park.

The Braves hit the road for Zebulon, N.C., in the opposite corner of the league's geography, as the championship series opened. They split the first two games, then the M-Braves had the luxury of flying back to Jackson while the Mudcats traveled by bus. You'd have never known it. Carolina clobbered 16 hits in rain-delayed Game 3, before J.C. Boscan singled home Schafer in the 13th inning for a Game 4 victory.

Series MVP Kala Ka'aihue delivered a two-out RBI single in the first inning of the decisive Game 5 to give Jonny Venters and the Braves an early lead, but Carolina's Lee Mitchell countered with an RBI double in the second. Holt doubled in the fifth and scored on an infield hit by Young, snapping a prolonged skid; the author of the 11-consecutive-hit stretch in July had been 0 for his last 13. Wellman called upon Redmond in relief in the eighth, and the ace put down the Mudcats 1-2-3. In the ninth, however, Scott Cousins led off with a game-tying homer, and the game moved to extra innings.

Holt and Young cracked one-out singles in the 10th, and the surprise season had one more twist. A wild pitch sent Holt and Young trying to advance and when catcher Brad Davis tried to nail Young at second, the throw bounced up, hit Chris Coghlan in the face and bounced away.

Whereas, Holt scored the clinching run.

Therefore, the Mississippi Braves were champions.

THE PRESIDENTS

Don Mincher.

BILLY HITCHCOCK

Mister Billy / 1971-1980

The amusing irony is that one of the most oft-repeated stories about Billy Hitchcock is the most uncharacteristic.

It was 1948, in an exhibition game in Florida between Hitchcock's Red Sox and the Braves. He was on first base and began taking a generous lead. The Braves pitcher made a few pickoff attempts, but Hitchcock scampered in safely. Finally, the pitcher uncorked a high throw. Diving back to the base, Hitchcock grabbed first baseman Earl Torgeson's leg so he couldn't jump for the ball. Weeks later, they got tangled up in an exhibition in Boston, this time with Torgeson punching Hitchcock in the mouth and triggering a benches-clearing brawl.

Hitchcock was hardly a brawler but he was competitive. That was evident from his days as a football player at Auburn, a player in the majors, then a manager, then ultimately as the Southern League president from 1971-1980. He wasn't shy about taking on owners. One of his first decisions as president changed the fate of the league and perhaps assured the years of growth and financial success it has since enjoyed, determining the Southern League's partnership with the Texas League to form the Dixie Association in 1971 would be dissolved. The Southern League would strike out on its own, thank you very much.

Hitchcock was a kind soul who'd be reverentially referred to as "Mister Billy" for many of his later years. He had a voice rich and thick like syrup, a pipe often clinched in his teeth. You'd have to resurrect Clark Gable to find the perfect actor to play Hitchcock in a movie about his Southern League presidency.

"One of the finest gentlemen I ever knew," said Bob Mayes, who covered the league for *The Huntsville Times* in the 1980s.

He navigated the Southern League through expansion, putting teams in Memphis and Nashville. He helped facilitate moves from crumbling markets into Chattanooga and Charlotte, where baseball flourished—even it meant crawling through a broken window to inspect a shuttered, dilapidated Engel Stadium in Chattanooga.

"Just a joy to work with," said Larry Schmittou, the former owner of the Nashville Sounds. "He had such a great history as a player and manager and executive. He was really concerned about his franchises. He laid a great foundation for presidents to come."

He was far from his Opelika, Alabama, home when the Southern League hired him. League members had contacted Hitchcock to gauge his interest in becoming president, succeeding the late Sam Smith, who had been ill for some time. But when the league met in the fall of 1971 to determine its president, Hitchcock was on a long-planned Scandinavian vacation with his wife, Betty Ann.

It didn't take long for Hitchcock to earn his pay. Clint Courtney, the Savannah manager, and Billy Gardner, at Jacksonville, had a running feud between themselves and their teams that Hitchcock had to tamp down, Once he fined Courtney $25, only to have Courtney pay the fine with 2,500 pennies. In July 1972, Hitchcock was forced to suspend Pablo Torrealbo for the season after the pitcher, angered by a called third strike, struck umpire Fred Spenn across the back with a bat.

Hitchcock served as league president through the 1980 season, when he was succeeded by Jimmy Bragan. There is some symmetry there. In 1966, Hitchcock succeeded Bragan's older brother Bobby as manager of the Atlanta Braves. It was the first year the club was in Atlanta and the Braves were 52-59 when Bragan was fired; Hitchcock was elevated from a coaching position. And when Hitchcock assumed the presidency and the Southern League-Texas League "merger" was ended, it was Bobby Bragan who was the Texas League president.

Billy Hitchcock's first game coincided with a seminal moment in Atlanta baseball history, an event that long-time Braves fans recall with reverence. Denny Lemaster, a Braves lefty who grew up an hour's drive from Dodger Stadium, faced Los Angeles icon Sandy

Koufax in front of 52,270 at Atlanta Stadium. It grew into one of those nights where, if you would believe everyone who said he was there, there would have been closer to 522,700 in the park. Lemaster countered Koufax's four-hitter with a three-hitter of his own, Atlanta winning on an Eddie Matthews walk-off home run—back before the phrase was coined—off Koufax with one out in the ninth.

Hitchcock, who had managed Baltimore in 1962-63, would steer the Braves home with 33 wins in their final 51 games, but he wasn't immune to the axe. Atlanta went 77-85 the next season and Hitchcock was gone. The Southern League was the beneficiary.

Upon his retirement from the Southern League, Hitchcock remained a fan of his beloved Auburn, catching the occasional football and basketball game and owning box seats for Auburn baseball, played in a stadium that would become known as Hitchcock Field at Plainsman Park. The annual Billy Hitchcock Golf Tournament raised funds for the school. Ironically, on the day he died, Auburn won that very tournament. He was an avid supporter of the nearby Camp ASCCA, an undulating piece of property on an Alabama lakeside that provides traditional summer-camp experiences for disabled children.

The Hitchcock Field honor was a shared one. His brother Jimmy was also an Auburn athlete. (James and Sallie Louise Hitchcock had four sons, Billy, Jimmy, Jake, and Walter, widely known as "Bully." They made up the entire infield of a semi-pro team in Union Springs, Ala., in 1933.) Jimmy Hitchcock, who passed away in 1959 at the age of 47, was Auburn's first All-American in football, leading the team to an undefeated season in 1932. He was also an All-American in baseball and signed with the Boston Braves. He played nine years in the minors and was with Boston in 1938. He returned to Auburn and became head baseball coach and an assistant in football before moving onto the school's Board of Trustees.

Billy Hitchcock scored the first bowl-game touchdown in Auburn history, in a 7-7 tie with Villanova in the 1937 Bacardi Bowl in Havana, Cuba. That spring, he led Auburn to its first SEC championship in baseball. He played a year with the Tigers before missing three seasons while serving in the Army, earning a Bronze Star. He wrapped up his playing career, as a journeyman infielder, in 1953.

"It's hard to be in baseball for as long as he was and not have detractors," Auburn baseball coach Hal Baird said upon Hitchcock's death. "He didn't. I never met a man in baseball with more dignity and class. I've never heard a person say a bad word about Billy."

Baird obviously never talked with Earl Torgeson.

JIMMY BRAGAN

The Sunday School teacher / 1981-1994

The last day of the season, a fan made a run to the copy machine. Dozens, maybe hundreds, of simple, 8 x 10 signs were distributed at Engel Stadium, the stately relic of a ballpark by a railroad viaduct in Chattanooga. Pleaded the signs:

COME BACK

BRAGAN

Jimmy Bragan was the interim manager of the Chattanooga Lookouts. He had related to the fans. He lit a fire under an underachieving team that awarded him almost universal respect.

"He liked managing. The fans like him. It was unbelievable. That was a nice tribute," recalled Sarah, his wife of 51 years.

John Orsino, the burly former major-league catcher, began that 1978 season as the Lookouts' manager. Following the engaging Rene Lachemann and the courtly George Farson as the Chattanooga manager in this, the third year of baseball's return, the brusque, intense New Jersey native didn't appeal to the cadre of loyal season-ticket holders who'd miss a family wedding before they'd miss a game. Orsino packed a temper. One postgame, as the beat reporters headed toward his office in the cramped clubhouse toward his office, Orsino could be heard in a booming, profane voice bemoaning a Lookouts' mental miscue. At first, the writers cringed for the poor soul inside, only to realize Orsino was alone. As the writers took one more step toward the threshold of his office, a beer bottle flew across the room in front of them, exploding against a concrete wall. Game stories the next day were published without the benefit of managerial quotes.

Jimmy Bragan was the polar opposite of his predecessor, at least on the surface.

"He was the most Sunday School teacher of all the brothers," said his nephew, Peter Jr. "I loved him. He kept you on the straight and narrow."

"A real committed Christian," Sarah Bragan said.

That didn't mean he couldn't be tough, or even a little salty. John Arnold, a Lookouts pitcher in 1978, remembered Jimmy finally snapping at an obnoxious fan over the visitors' dugout one night, silencing the fan by saying, "Better check on your wife. We've got a player missing."

Bragan would not come back as the Lookouts' manager. Better, bigger, more important things would be in store. In 1981, he succeeded Billy Hitchcock as president of the Southern League, upon Hitchcock's recommendation. It was a considerably less dramatic transition, one gracious Alabama gentleman and baseball lifer passing the baton to the next, than it was to follow Orsino. Here's an odd twist: In 1966, Hitchcock had succeeded Bragan's older brother Bobby as the manager of the Atlanta Braves.

Jimmy and Bobby were two of seven brothers (along with two sisters) in the Bragan household in Birmingham. One of Jimmy's best pals was Alex Grammas. The two wound up at Mississippi State together—at one point, seven Birmingham players were on the Bulldogs' roster—then Bragan signed with the Dodgers' system. He never reached the majors, but established himself as a quintessential "organization man." The Dodgers enlisted him to manage in the low level of the minors, then Cincinnati hired him as a scout, eventually calling him to coach on Dave Bristol's staff from 1967-69. He went on to the Montreal organization, then to Mississippi State as head coach for a year before Grammas was named the Brewers' manager in 1976 and brought Bragan to Milwaukee as coach. Bragan was scouting for the Cleveland Indians, for which Chattanooga was the farm club, when minor-league director Bob Quinn prevailed upon him to take the manager's job.

Jimmy, with Sarah as loyal assistant—"the remarkable balance to Jimmy's life," said Bruce Baldwin, then at Greenville—took over from Hitchcock and opened up the Southern League office in 1981 in the northern Birmingham suburb of Trussville. His 13-year tenure was coincided with great growth and progress. It was a boom time for minor-league franchises, and their worth went from less than six digits into the millions.

"The thing he was most proud of was he brought baseball back to Alabama," Sarah Bragan said. Under Jimmy, Huntsville joined the league, the groundwork was laid for Mobile, and Montgomery moved to Birmingham, although the last was an in-state relocation.

There were parallels to Hitchcock in many ways. Wayne Martin, who covered the league for the *Birmingham News*, said, "The integrity of the game was the single most important thing of the game for them. Like keeping the rules of golf and telling on yourself, it was the integrity of baseball. With Jimmy, it was that way totally." Martin moonlighted alongside Bragan, going to the Trussville office every Monday to put together the league newsletter that, in those primitive days, was mailed to teams and media across the breadth of the league.

A newer breed of owners brought a different challenge for Bragan in the 1980s and he often had to get the hair up on the back of his neck.

"He could be combative," said Nashville owner Larry Schmittou, who for a while had control of a pair of teams in the league.

Some outsized personalities were present in the league meetings and "at times we liked to think Jimmy was the puppet president and we ran the league," said Baldwin, now Pensacola's president. "It was not the case at all."

"There was no gray area with Uncle Jimmy," said Peter Bragan, Jr.

"Sometimes he'd have an umpire or manager or somebody on the phone and he'd close the door, but it didn't make a difference," Martin said. "Sarah would just sit there and cringe."

In May 2001, Bragan was enshrined in the Alabama Sports Hall of Fame in a class that included Charles Barkley and Alabama football great Derrick Thomas. (Hitchcock was inducted in 1975, Don Mincher, the league president in the early 2000s, in 2008.) Weakened by chemotherapy in the battle with the cancer that would take his life on June 2, he gave a stirring talk about his faith and his life. It was one of the few times in his life that Charles Barkley found himself upstaged.

He had been retired from baseball for seven years by then, living on a farm in Westover, 30 miles east of Birmingham, growing hay and a breed of muscadine grapes called scuppernongs, "some as big as Ping-Pong balls," he once boasted.

When it was time to walk away from baseball, no one could pronounce the benediction as well as the old Sunday School teacher. This is what Jimmy Bragan left for posterity in a Southern League media guide:

> I can't remember the first time I stepped onto a baseball field. I'm sure it wasn't much of a field, just a vacant lot somewhere near my home in the Druid Hills neighborhood in Birmingham. I'm sure I followed one or more of my brothers, G.W, Walter, Lionel, Bobby, Peter or Frank. And I'm sure somewhere along the way I ran into Alex or Cameron Grammas or my good buddy Robert Karasek.
>
> The point is, I've been stepping onto baseball fields all my life, first as a player on sandlots, then at Phillips High School and then at Mississippi State University. I was fortunate enough to play professionally and although I never played in the major leagues, I did have eight rewarding years on the major league coaching staff of some outstanding baseball people—Dave Bristol, Cincinnati Reds; Gene Mauch, Montreal Expos; and Alex Grammas, Milwaukee Brewers. There were a couple of years of college coaching and several years of scouting.
>
> I can't imagine doing anything more rewarding, professionally, from slapping a clean single to the outfield or turning double play or to coach and teaching the game to others, to watching a kid like Lee May or Sammy Ellis play on the same sandlots that I played on in Birmingham, signing them and watching them develop and mature into outstanding major league players.
>
> The game is the greatest game on earth and I will never know why God blessed me with the abilities to a part of it on so many different levels. I'm just glad he did.

DON MINCHER

Huntsville's Mr. Baseball / 2000-2011

Pat Mincher stopped to glance at one picture among the dozens on the wall in the second-floor room her husband used as an office at their home on a leafy Huntsville cul de sac. She couldn't help laugh at the memory behind the photo. How fussy Don Mincher was the night that photo was taken.

It was shot at the Baseball Winter Meetings in 2010 in a ballroom at the Walt Disney World Swan and Dolphin Resort. Mincher is wearing a crown and robe and holding a scepter in the photo, with Pat and their children, Mark, Lori, and Donna, next to him. He was crowned "King of Baseball" that night. It was a total surprise to him, but not to his children, who had secretly flown to Orlando. When Don and Pat entered the banquet hall that night, he stubbornly tried to grab a table near the back of the room. But, for convenience's sake, seats near the front of the room had been reserved. Pat wove through the tables, Don reluctantly and slowly in her wake, hounding her to stop. Finally, she turned to him as they reached the appropriate table, "Don, if you don't stop doing that, you're going to make me cry."

Which is why, when a stunned Mincher was called to the stage and presented his honor, he began his speech, "The first thing I need to do is apologize to my wife…"

Don Mincher did many great things in baseball. He hit a home run off Don Drysdale in his first World Series at-bat. He was selected for two All-Star Games. He played 12 years in the big leagues. He got his first major-league hit off Whitey Ford and his last off Nolan Ryan.

More than that, he did many things in baseball in a great way. As he said one afternoon over a platter of chicken fingers, "I'm proud of my career, but I'd like to be recognized not only for what I did as a player, but doing other things in the game."

Mincher helped launch a minor-league team in his hometown, then assured it'd remain afloat. He took over a league that needed a baseball man in charge, and got it on an even keel. He served as Southern League president from the spring of 2000 until October 2011, when he was named president-emeritus. By that point, he was battling poor health that eventually took his life on April 4, 2012.

To his family, he was G-Daddy.

To an entire city, "He was Huntsville's 'Mr. Baseball,' and always will be," said John Pruett, former sports editor of the *Huntsville Times*. "He was the heart and soul of the Huntsville Stars."

To his employees, like former Stars general manager Bryan Dingo, "He was a second father-figure to me."

"A consummate baseball man, a mentor, a role model, the best boss I ever had," said former Huntsville broadcaster Steve Kornya.

"There was probably no more humble guy, especially when you think of the breadth of his career," said Pat O'Conner, president/CEO of Minor League Baseball.

Don Mincher was one of Huntsville's best all-around athletes, more widely referred to in those days as Donnie. He was the only child of George and Lillian and lived in the Lincoln Village area, where the textile industry was still thriving as NASA's influence was beginning to be felt in Huntsville. George Mincher was a welder who worked on the cage in which NASA placed its chimpanzee astronaut, Ham, in 1961.

Tucked away on a bookshelf in Mincher's old office is a framed letter from J.B. "Ears" Whitworth, the former Alabama football coach, offering Mincher a scholarship to play for the Crimson Tide. ("Where my second year I would have gotten Bear Bryant as a coach and he'd have probably run me off the second day," Mincher would often say.) Instead, he decided to sign a contract with the Chicago White Sox in 1956 and headed off to Duluth, Minnesota, with a suitcase packed by his mother, Lillian, a Bible right on top of neatly folded clothes.

After a month, homesickness kicked in. He wanted to come home but George Mincher was firm. "You made a commitment. You have class. You signed with those people and promised to give them one year and that's what you'll do," he said. He hung in there and steadily climbed a long, steep ladder in the minors, eventually being traded to the Senators, for whom he made his major-league debut on April 8, 1960.

Mincher played for the Senators, Twins, Pilots, Angels, Rangers, and A's alongside a half-dozen Hall of Famers, among them Harmon Killebrew, one of his closest friends. Still hanging in the office is the jersey Mincher was wearing during the Twins' pennant clinching celebration that Killebrew grabbed and, not knowing his own strength, tore nearly in two.

On Oct. 6, 1965, Don and Pat met his parents for breakfast near their hotel in Bloomington, Minn. The first pitch of the World Series was only hours away. The entire breakfast, Don "never said one word," Pat said.

In the bottom of the second, Minnesota trailing 1-0 and with two out, Mincher came to bat for the first time in a World Series. He was 160 miles from Duluth—or 160 light years away. Mincher took a sinker down and away for a ball, then Drysdale delivered a fastball on the inside half of the plate, straight as a Baptist deacon. Mincher swung and immediately knew it was a home run. "You get that feeling," he said.

Mincher coolly circled the bases, then reached the Twins dugout and "I started shaking. All of a sudden it hit me what I had done, in front of possibly everybody I knew looking on. ... That one defining three minutes, it's just forever in my mind."

In the postgame interview, a snarky Drysdale said, "My sister could have hit that pitch." Mincher didn't take the bait. "You've still got to hit it when a Hall of Famer throws it."

After the locker rooms emptied, Mincher found his father in a waiting room down in the clammy, dim basement of Met Stadium. They embraced. When the hug ended, the son looked at the father. Tears were rolling down that narrow, weather-beaten, ruddy face. "It was the first time I ever saw my father cry," Mincher said, retelling the story one afternoon at Joe Davis Stadium, his own eyes misting at the memory. He gave out a laugh. "Besides him breathing a sigh of relief for me getting out of high school, that was the proudest moment of our lifetime."

Retiring after his 1972 World Series with Oakland, he opened a trophy shop in Huntsville and resisted the baseball itch pretty well until 1984, when it was announced that Huntsville would have a team in the Southern League. He contacted Larry Schmittou, the team owner, who asked him to become general manager. Then, when Schmittou wanted to sell the club, Mincher galvanized a group of local owners to keep the team in Huntsville; he served as team president. In the late 1990s, the other league directors elected him vice president. It was a purely honorary title, he figured, until Arnie Fielkow resigned and the presidency landed in his lap. He was the fourth of five league presidents, after Sam Smith, Billy Hitchcock, and Jimmy Bragan, to be an Alabama native.

Several years before his children joined him for his coronation as "King of Baseball," Don and Pat took 14 members of the family to Minneapolis for a reunion of the 1965 Twins. "They heard some stories I wish they hadn't heard," Mincher said.

The family took a shopping trip. They went to the Mall of America, the gargantuan, shopping center that rests on the site of the old Metropolitan Stadium, where the Twins originally played.

Shoppers, if they look closely enough, can find an historic marker. The Mincher family made sure to find it. They found a home plate inlaid in the Mall of America tile, at the exact spot where it was for Twins games, the exact spot where the future King created a defining moment in his career.

LORI WEBB

From "Help Wanted" to pioneer / 2012-present

Seneca Falls, N.Y., rests in the webbing between the Finger Lakes of upstate New York, equidistant between Rochester and Syracuse. So blessed with quaint and small-town charm, it proclaims itself as the inspiration for Bedford Falls in Frank Capra's enduring Christmas film, "It's A Wonderful Life."

Seneca Falls is also known as the birthplace of the women's rights movement. It was home to Elizabeth Cady Stanton, a pioneer in the women's movement and organizer of a pivotal 1848 convention in the city during which this resolution, among others, was declared: "Woman is man's equal—was intended to be so by the Creator, and the highest good of the race demands that she should be recognized as such." The city is home to the National Women's Hall of Fame and Stanton is namesake to a local school.

Lori Smith grew up in Seneca Falls, rooting for the Yankees, watching her older brother pitch "more times than I could count," playing in the vacant lot behind the family's home in the warm months, ice-skating on a frozen lake in the winter. She was well aware of the history of the women's movement, as was most everyone in town. It's an intrinsic part of the experience, much the way Southerners grow up accustomed to battlefields and old cannons sprinkled around their towns. "Our little town is historic that way," she said.

But Lori, in her own words, "wasn't a women's libber."

"I got married at a young age. I wanted to be a wife and a mom and [perhaps] I could help my husband out financially. I stayed at home with my kids until they were in school."

Instead, Lori Smith Webb became a pioneer herself. On August 2, 2012, she became the first female president of a Minor League Base-

NEVER A BAD GAME   77

ball circuit, succeeding Don Mincher as the sixth president of the Southern League.

"I'll be 100 percent honest with you, it never occurred to me that there had never been a woman president before," Webb said, sitting at her desk in the league office in the Atlanta suburb of Marietta, the league's current standings on a whiteboard on one wall, a bookcase full of commemorative baseballs and other mementoes along another. On the credenza behind her, the spine of a looseleaf notebook read, "FINES." It was a thick notebook.

"I didn't think about it until [the election] was over and everybody started to make a big deal about it. I just felt like it was a natural move for me."

A year into the job, it has been smooth, but it's been "something different all the time." There are, for instance, the issues that fill that thick looseleaf notebook. On this late-season morning, after some on-field controversy between a pair of teams, Webb fielded a call and nicely snuffed out the fire. A few minutes later, a 42-year-old document was brought to her attention. It was a memo from former president Sam Smith to his umpires, mandating, among other things, that they were not to call him at home with controversies and issues.

Said Webb, laughing, "I want to save that and read it at the next league meeting and see how that goes over."

Funny what can happen when you answer a Help Wanted ad in the *Marietta Daily Journal*.

Jim and Lori Webb had just relocated to Georgia in 1994 with their children, Melanie, Andrew, and PJ; the last of whom would serve as the league's media-relations director. Lori started looking for a job and noticed the ad for "Professional Baseball League seeks executive assistance."

Said Jim, "You're not going to get a job out of the want ads."

Replied Lori, "Well, it can't hurt."

Jim was coaching youth league ball at the time, with Andrew and PJ playing. Lori was a team mom. "I thought this would be perfect for me," she said.

Arnold Fielkow, formerly a lawyer in Chicago and the deputy commissioner of the Continental Basketball Association, was the new league president, taking over for Jimmy Bragan and establishing an office in the square in downtown Roswell, northwest of Atlanta.

Some 20 candidates for the job showed up for an interview session on the same day. Lori Webb was called back for a second interview, along with "this very sharp looking little blonde," Webb remembered. "But Arnie's wife [Sue] was there for the second interview. I was more down to earth. I was a mom. Sue took a liking to me. And I got the job."

On Webb's first day on the job, September 1994, Fielkow picked her up at home at 5 a.m. and they drove to downtown Atlanta, where they caught Amtrak for a four-hour trip to Birmingham. The entire trip—"what seemed like 10 hours," she said—she was taking notes from Fielkow on a steno pad. Bragan was waiting on them in his pickup truck and drove them to 225 Main Street in Trussville, on the northern fringe of Birmingham. Movers were throwing boxes of Southern League property into the back of a rental truck. Bragan and Fielkow sat down to discuss the business of transition, while Webb sat with Sarah Bragan, signing checks to pay bills from the 1994 season and close out the Alabama bank account. Fielkow and Webb then drove the rental truck back to Georgia, where Fielkow proceeded to neglect the fuel gauge. They ran out of gas at 11 p.m. once they reached Marietta. While Fielkow tried to find a station with diesel, Webb went to a fast-food restaurant and found a cell phone to call Jim. Laughing, Webb said, "I don't know why I stayed after that."

She remained as executive assistant to Fielkow, except for a brief hiatus, until his resignation in 2000, then remained on board as Don Mincher assumed the presidency, with Webb promoted to vice president-operations. It was a perfect marriage. Webb maintained the business side of things in Marietta while Mincher could work out of a computer in his Huntsville office—truth be told, he was much more familiar with Goose Gossage than Google—and travel the league. As Mincher grew ill, Webb ran the day-to-day operations, and then Steve DeSalvo stepped in as interim president as Mincher moved into emeritus status.

Eventually, Webb decided to apply for the job herself. Well, it can't hurt, right?

THE LEADERS

Engel Stadium, the house that Joe Engel built.

TOMMIE AARON

More than the Hammer's brother

Some places the Savannah Braves traveled, in those days of low-budget motels scattered across the South, Tommie Aaron would approach the front desk with the team trainer to collect room keys. The South had finally emerged from segregation, when black players often had to stay in rooming houses or different hotels from their white teammates.

When Aaron would request the key to the manager's room, he'd occasionally get a funny look and some hesitation before getting the key.

The manager? A black man?

On Friday, June 15, 1973, Aaron was promoted to become the manager of the Savannah Braves, becoming the first black manager in league history. Clint Courtney had been promoted suddenly to Class AAA Richmond, and Aaron had been a player-coach under Courtney at Savannah. A group of men, including Savannah general manager Miles Wolff, lobbied for Aaron to get the job.

This, in a city that relocated its franchise in 1962 and went without a minor-league team until 1967 because of controversy and protests over segregated seating policies, with black fans forced to sit in the left-field bleachers and separated by a brick wall from white fans.

"I don't care anything about being a pioneer or crusader," Aaron would say at the end of the 1974 season, when he began to be mentioned as a potential major-league manager. Frank Robinson would ultimately become the first black manager in the majors, hired by Cleveland in 1975.

Tommie, the younger brother of Henry "Hammerin' Hank" Aaron, never had the opportunity. Though he was promoted to the

Braves' coaching staff in 1978, he was diagnosed with leukemia in 1982 and died on August 16, 1984, at the age of 45.

"I don't know if he felt [like a pioneer] or not," his wife Carolyn said. "He just did the job he had to do. There were a lot of people that didn't want him to have that job he got. He did it, and he did it well, I thought."

(Older brother Hank was himself something of a pioneer, the first black player in the Class A Sally League, at Jacksonville in 1953. He won the MVP award and, quipped one writer, "led the league in everything but hotel accommodations.")

More than his historic and baseball achievements, what would Carolyn Aaron want you to know about her late husband? "That he was a wonderful person, that he loved baseball, he loved his family. He was a great guy. Everybody that met him liked him. He met no strangers."

Tommie Aaron is part of a trivia question: What brother combo has the most career major-league home runs? That would be the Aarons, with Hank's 755 and Tommie's 13. Said Tommie in a *Sports Illustrated* article in 1973, "You can't compare Henry and me. He's gonna do his thing, and I'm gonna do mine. I found out a long time ago I'm not as good a player as he is, but if I had let it bother me, I wouldn't have stayed around this long. When I first came up with Milwaukee in 1962, everybody expected me to hit 20 to 25 home runs with 100 RBI. But no two men are alike, and nobody understands that more than me."

"They were close," Carolyn said. "They weren't with each other all the time, but when Tommie was in Savannah, Hank was his boss [as the Braves' farm director]. They would have to talk every night."

While Hank hit 190 of his 755 homers in Atlanta-Fulton County Stadium, it was Tommie who made history. In an April 9, 1965, exhibition game at the ballpark after the Braves broke camp and were headed to Milwaukee, Tommie became the first to homer there, victimizing the Tigers' Hank Aguirre. The Braves moved to Atlanta in 1966.

After Tommie reached the majors in 1962, he and Hank were occasional roommates. As Hank wrote in his autobiography, *Aaron, r.f.,* "you know how brothers are. You want to know the other one is around, but you don't want to be too close, unless there's trouble.

Then you can get as close as fur on a cat's back." Hank recalled that on a trip to St. Louis, an air conditioner caused the trouble. There was a sudden loud noise, a puff of smoke "and all of a sudden the room was on fire."

There were those who cruelly suggested Tommie rode his brother's name into the managerial job, but their brother-in-law, the late Bill Lucas, told *Sport* magazine that "if his name was Tommie Jones instead of Tommie Aaron, he would have gotten a better shot."

Tommie Aaron—"T-Bone" to fans and his players—was an instrumental figure in a farm system that created a solid Atlanta team in the late 1970s and early 1980s. He managed such players as Dale Murphy, Glenn Hubbard, Rick Camp, and Rick Mahler. Said Murphy years ago, "Tommie Aaron taught me how to have a good attitude, to be easy going and not get uptight."

Aaron could be superstitious. On a win streak, he'd make sure to park in the same spot every day. He could be contentious with umpires. "He tried to treat everyone with respect," Carolyn said. "I never saw him angry with anybody. Except umpires."

Before she met Tommie, she had never been to a major-league baseball game. She was living in Milwaukee and was friends with Nancy May, then the wife of outfielder Lee May. She went to a game with Nancy and was waiting outside the clubhouse for Lee when Tommie emerged. They went out that night and were soon engaged.

"I didn't know much about baseball," Carolyn said. "I went because Nancy asked me to go, and I got lucky enough to meet Tommie. And he was the love of my life."

They had three children, Efrem, Tommie Jr., and Veleeta, and Carolyn found out more about baseball than she'd ever imagine. When school was out for the summer, she and the kids would join him in Milwaukee or, when the managing days began, in Savannah or Richmond.

"He tried to do a good job because he was the first black manager in the Southern League and in the International League," Carolyn said. "And I believe if he had lived he would have managed in the major leagues. I think he would have been a good manager. Leukemia took him too soon."

BRUCE BALDWIN

Coast to coast

He was wearing the tires off his old Chrysler Cordova. It was a car with "reeeech Coreeenthian leather," he said, employing a TV slogan those of a certain generation will recall. Driving West Coast to East Coast for the first time, in the pre-Mapquest, way-before-GPS days, to a little burg to which his bosses couldn't give him precise directions. Then back to the northwest, then southeast again.

One thing Bruce Baldwin learned—"There's only one radio station in Oklahoma." He leaned back in his desk chair, assuming a poker face. "Well, there may be 100. But they all play the same music."

He was just an old gym-rat in those days, tip-toeing into a new challenge he wasn't sure he wanted, since he thought he had it made already. He was just worrying about having enough air for the basketballs. Who knew he'd go off on this adventure where he'd build new stadiums, launch new teams, conjure up some ideas so silly, why, there was no way they wouldn't work and that he'd be hunkered down at this desk in this tidy office in this handsome ballpark in Pensacola, Fla., that might well have the best setting in all of minor-league baseball?

Baldwin is the president of the Pensacola Blue Wahoos, who sold out 40 games their first season in the league, in 2012, and sold 3,000 season tickets for a park that seats 5,038. He was named winner of the Jimmy Bragan Executive of the Year award, 25 years after he first won it. He's not the longest tenured official in the Southern League, but his history arcs back farther than almost anyone, to his days as general manager of the Savannah Braves in 1984. It gets Baldwin's mind to racing, which is not a difficult thing to make happen.

"This league I thought then, and still think today, was probably the best league, with all due respect to all the leagues out there. An unbelievably aggressively outside-of-the-box league. Jimmy [Bragan] was president. It had a lot of young guys that went on to have a great deal of success in minor-league baseball. Larry Schmittou [in Nashville]. The Crocketts. Frances had a bunch of cats in her office. I really liked Frances a lot. She did a lot of stuff I thought, 'What is she doing that for?' but it made sense. Larry was over the top in promotions. Bill Lee was in Chattanooga. Art Clarkson was in Birmingham. He just called me. He's in Green Bay now, doing indoor football. He said, 'Bruce, how many rainouts have you had? By the way, I've had none.'

"I remember we were in Orlando at a scheduling meeting. It's 10:30 at night. We couldn't decide anything. I propped a chair on the door and locked the door and said, 'If you're going out, you're going through me.' We got it done. We were so aggressive, so competitive, so over the top. But we shared like crazy. We had our own marketing committee. We didn't sell anything, but we had a hell of a good time."

The last sentence is half-wrong when it comes to Bruce Baldwin, half-right. He has sold baseball in Pensacola, where he was enlisted by owner Quint Studer to help this ballpark built on what was once a depressing area of weeds, giant oil-refinery tanks, and a sewage facility. Then he convinced the owner that a Southern League franchise was the way to make it all succeed. "The cost in getting in the club is exorbitant, but the payoff will get to you if you sell it or own it the next 112 years," he told Studer, with a modicum of exaggeration. So even if the owner was starting to feel like a walking ATM, Baldwin went out and made that happen, too. He's had a hell of a good time doing it.

It all started innocently enough. He was coaching at a South Eugene High School in Oregon. He had "the best gig in America." He didn't teach. He didn't have to go to PTA meetings. He could wear shorts to work. "And I got paid for doing this?"

Separated by a small patch of grass and Amazon Parkway sat Civic Stadium, built in 1938 and now sitting as surplus property. It was home to the Eugene Emeralds. Dean Taylor, who'd later become general manager of the Milwaukee Brewers, was the Emeralds' GM and a friend of Baldwin. He convinced Baldwin to work for the club as assistant GM when school was not in session. Turns out, Baldwin had some experience in promotions and marketing. Their first year together, the Emeralds drew 69,000 after only 15,000 the previous season. To which Taylor noted, "How do we top this?" Well ... by drawing 93,000 the next year.

That drew the attention of Bob Freitas, one of the minors' most respected individuals, who nominated Baldwin for a pair of jobs. Bruce declined, wanting to keep the coaching job. Finally, the Atlanta Braves called. Their Pulaski, Virginia, team needed a general manager and Baldwin could work it in between spring and fall semesters. Off he headed in that Chrysler Cordova, driving through some places "where you swear you could hear the banjo music" before arriving in Pulaski, in the southern corner of Virginia that reaches into the Appalachians. Then back in the car in time for football season in Eugene.

But the Braves had another offer. Finish football, then move to Savannah, Ga., in December and take over that club. He drove back across the country, arriving at a lame-duck franchise with two employees and a Vietnamese family that made killer egg rolls for the concession stand. He made $18,000, with a bonus that he could pocket 10 percent of the profits. "They never told me in the 13-year history of the ball club it had lost its (rear end)," Baldwin said.

The next year, it was on to Greenville, opening a new stadium there. He got so good at that, Atlanta had him opening stadiums in Richmond and Gwinnett County (Georgia) before it was all said and done. "I had a great job with the Braves," he said. "I'm still very passionate about the Braves. They offered me a unique opportunity." They even allowed Baldwin, while orchestrating the transition between Richmond and Gwinnett, the opportunity to do consulting work. That led to his meeting with Studer.

That, in turn, led to a freezing night in downtown Pensacola, where thousands of the citizenry annually gathers for "Gallery Night," a festivity that promotes the arts and, more importantly to much of the citizenry, permits free-flowing, public consumption of adult beverages. Baldwin was there, passing out miniature bottles of water that had been branded with the Blue Wahoos logo. A bus was nearby, pulling onto a red carpet. A Native American was chanting and drumming, ostensibly to ward off evil spirits. A woman dressed as Cleopatra tossed rose pedals on the streets. A trumpeter blared his horn and from the bus emerged Kazoo, this ugly-cute Wahoos' mascot. "You didn't know," Baldwin said, "my middle name was Barnum, did you?" The Blue Wahoos sold $4,500 worth of T-shirts that night and inspired no telling how many future season-ticket purchasers.

"We've created this expectation where nobody knows what to expect," Baldwin said. Except maybe a hell of a good time.

PETER BRAGAN, SR.

Ring the bell

In the cluttered world of ballpark trinkets and geegaws, a mere bob-blehead was not sufficient to immortalize Peter Bragan, Sr. Instead, the Jacksonville Suns remembered the team patriarch with a small wobbly-headed figurine sitting atop a black pedestal, a miniature railroad bell next to him. Push a button and you hear Bragan's honey-dipped Southern voice, the sentence punctuated by the excla-mation point of the bell clanging.

How many thousands of times did Bragan ring his CSX railroad bell, signaling a Jacksonville Suns' home run or victory? How many fans left the gorgeous Baseball Grounds of Jacksonville with that joy-ous sound echoing?

Few ballparks have such an iconic symbol as the bell. Even fewer had the sort of character as Peter Bragan, Sr., atop the company masthead.

"He was a one-of-a-kind guy," said his son, Peter Bragan, Jr., bet-ter known as "Pedro" throughout the league. "There was a magic about him."

Bragan, who died on July 7, 2012, four days after his 89th birth-day, bought the Suns in 1984 for $330,000, venturing into the league where his brother Jimmy served as president. He was selling cars in Birmingham when he bought the Suns, and with business inter-ests in Alabama, was often flying back and forth between Jack-sonville and Birmingham. It was on one of those flights he met and befriended Gerald Nichols, a Kentuckian who was the chief oper-ating officer of CSX Railroad, headquartered in Jacksonville. They struck a deal, with the railroad buying signage at the ballpark and holding an annual night for the employees.

On a Wednesday afternoon before the 1996 season, both Peter Sr. and Peter Jr. went to visit Nichols in his massive office to finalize a contract. On a shelf that separated Nichols' workspace from a conference table was a railroad bell. "Man, get me one of those bells," Peter Sr. pleaded. Nichols responded that "these are for senators and governors and people like that." Turns out, they were also for titans of baseball. On May 18 of that season, as CSX held its night at the park, Bragan was beckoned to home plate. There, under a huge purple velvet cloth—"it looked like a giant Crown Royal bag," Pedro said—was a railroad bell.

It was taken to Bragan's permanent seat in the mezzanine and when the Suns rallied back from a 3-0 deficit on a three-run home run, "the old man reached over and rang the bell," Pedro recalled. A tradition was born, arguably the Southern League's most charming ritual. After every home run and win, Bragan would ring the bell. When he was ill in 2005 and missed two months of games, the Suns enlisted a "celebrity du jour" to handle the role. After Bragan's death, Pedro and other relatives handled the duties.

On a day after the bell was never rung, Peter Bragan was in his office at the Baseball Grounds. The Suns went homerless and lost their final game of the 2013 season, missing a shot in the playoffs because of an 11th-inning error. And "he'd have been mad about it," Peter Jr. said of his father.

"He cared about the on-the-field product more than a lot of owners," said Suns broadcaster Roger Hoover, who'd share his daily game notes with Bragan Sr. and often field questions from him about various players or decisions that were being made. It's not surprising, considering the baseball family into which he was raised. Bobby and Jimmy were both in pro ball and George Bragan, Sr.—"Papa Bragan"—was a left-handed catcher on the Birmingham sandlots. Pedro hinted that Peter might have been "the favorite son" because he was the only lefty of the seven brothers.

George Sr. was a sergeant in the U.S. Army during World War II, following Patton's tanks across France and Germany. He was married 69 years to Mary Frances, a constant partner at the ballpark and baseball events. He inherited his father's business acumen, whether it to sell cars or baseball. He liked a good cigar and was a fashionable, sometimes flashy dresser; that's understandable considering the years of wearing his brother's hand-me-downs or Uncle Sam's fatigues.

"He was a man of such strong character. He dominated any room he walked into," Peter Jr. said. "He had a mannerism where he could mix with the millionaires at the country club or he could get out of the car and get down on his haunches and talk to the farmers about the corn or the cotton crop. He had that manner about him that would make anybody comfortable. He was a dynamic personality."

One of Bragan's friends in Jacksonville was Jake Godbold, the city's mayor when Bragan bought the Suns. "Senior was tough to deal with sometimes. He was a growler and a griper. You just had to give it right back to him," he once told *The Florida Times-Union*. "But over the years, you learned to love the guy. There was a mutual respect for each other."

The team operated out of Wolfson Park, with its rich atmosphere of history and tradition becoming tarnished by the years. A new park was needed, and Godbold wanted to make it happen. Bragan was an active supporter in the campaign. However, Godbold lost in an upset to John Delaney, and when Bragan met with the new mayor and broached the subject, he was told, "Why don't you ask Jake to build it for you?"

Instead, in an indirect way, it was the National Football League which built Bragan his new stadium. Wayne Weaver, owner of the NFL's Jacksonville Jaguars, was awarded the Super Bowl for 2005. The Jags' beautiful stadium sat adjacent to aging Wolfson Park and an unattractive, UFO-looking arena. The football stadium needed better set decoration than that. Delaney decided he'd build a baseball park, too.

The Baseball Grounds of Jacksonville boasts 11,000 seats and has a nostalgic feel with its brick construction and ornate rotunda entry way. Palm trees ringing the stadium give you the "I'm in Florida" feel. The grounds incorporate the historic Old St. Andrew's Episcopal Church, just beyond the third-base stands and adjacent to a lush berm area for fans to sit behind the left-field fence.

Up behind home plate, on the mezzanine level, is the seat where Peter Bragan, Sr., sat each night, watching intently. He was the team's greatest ambassador, referring to each fan as "Buddy," and waiting eagerly on the chance to ring the bell. "He made sure people had a great time at the ballpark," said Hoover.

It "was never more evident," Hoover remembered, than an 83-degree, partly cloudy Saturday evening in September 2010, with 4,133 in the ballpark. It was Game Four of the Southern League championship series, with the Suns hosting the Tennessee Smokies. Tennessee won the opener at home 5-0, allowing only four hits. The Suns received a sac fly in the ninth to win Game 2, 7-6. Two days later in Jacksonville, Brad Hand and two relievers stopped the Smokies on three hits. Game 4 was a tense duel between Craig Muschko of Tennessee, in what would be his final professional start, and Jacksonville's Jose Rosario. It was scoreless when Suns catcher Chris Hatcher led off the ninth, lugging in a 0-for-13 performance in the series.

Hatcher socked Luke Sommer's first pitch over the leftfield wall for a walk-off, pennant-winning homer.

Hoover was then the Smokies' broadcaster. As he did his mournful postgame radio show, he kept hearing the incessant ringing of a bell. "Surely Mr. Bragan's not still down there," Hoover thought. As Hoover signed off, packed his equipment and made his way downstairs, the ringing continued. There, in the mezzanine, an endless line of Jacksonville fans stood, waiting for their chance to ring Peter Bragan's bell in celebration.

JOE ENGEL

The Barnum of Baseball

There was the shortstop traded for a turkey. Wait. How about the girl pitcher he hired, who struck out Babe Ruth and Lou Gehrig? Or how about the night he gave away a house, and 26,639 showed up at the ballpark that bore his name? He had to rope off the outfield and let spectators sit and stand there. So ingenious was he, fearing that too many routine outs would become home runs, he put the baseballs in a freezer before the game.

Each Joe Engel story leads to another, an endless game of "can you top this?" courtesy of the fertile mind of the Chattanooga Lookouts' legendary president. A former major-league pitcher, primarily with the Washington Senators during the World War I era, Engel had a discerning eye for baseball talent. So much so, that when a struggling Engel was farmed out to the minors, Senators' owner Clark Griffith told him to determine which new teammate should be ultimately sent to Washington in his place. He often scouted and signed players for the Chattanooga club, selling their contracts to other teams as they improved.

But it was as a promoter that Engel was most famous. "The Baron of Baloney," he was called. "The Barnum of Baseball." Few team presidents were as synonymous with their club as was Engel. He was a pioneer in conjuring up gimmicks and promotions to fill the seats. When his Nashville Sounds were luring in a half-million people a year in the teams' Southern League infancy, team president Larry Schmittou flatly admitted his promotions were "borrowed from things Joe Engel was doing 30 years ago" in Chattanooga.

But the Nashville Sounds never faced Babe Ruth. Or signed Jackie Mitchell to a contract. Jackie was a shy, tomboyish girl of 18 who had grown up as a neighbor to major leaguer Dazzy Vance in Memphis. She learned to pitch from him and was playing on a women's team in Chattanooga when Engel signed her to a Lookouts' contract in the spring of 1931. As it happened, the New York Yankees were barnstorming their way north after spring training and had a stop in Chattanooga. Engel had Mitchell enter the game in relief in the first inning, just in time to face Ruth and Gehrig, as well as Tony Lazzeri, whom she walked. Those were the only batters she faced in men's professional baseball. The next day, Commissioner Kennesaw Mountain Landis voided her contract. Decades later, Jackie Mitchell Gilbert would sit in the den of her suburban Chattanooga home, scrapbook in lap, and vow it was more than some Joe Engel publicity stunt and denying that the Yankees took intentional dives.

Joe Engel was forever creating clever ideas. He was terrific copy for the competing newspapers and a constant source of news. This presented trouble; one enterprising writer found himself on the outs with Engel when he decided to sneak into the president's office and forage through his trash can rather than wait on the promoter's latest revelation.

Engel gave away a house in 1936, then swapped shortstop Johnny Jones to Charlotte for a turkey—"I still think I got the worst end of the deal," Engel groused, cooking the turkey for a feast with local sportswriters—and achieved almost regal status in his adopted hometown.

Drive the narrow roads leading from East Brainerd toward the Georgia line, just before the railroad track bisects the countryside, to Julian Road. There, perched atop posts at the end of a brick wall, were two concrete baseballs, bigger than beach balls. They signified then, and for years later, even as the countryside gave way to progress and saw golf course McMansions sprouting nearby like mushrooms, that it was Joe Engel's place. Passing drivers would slow and rubberneck at the estate where Engel lived and raised racing pigeons and thoroughbred horses. One of his horses, Hallieboy, named for his wife Hallie, ran in the 1950 Kentucky Derby.

Engel's history with the Lookouts dated back to 1929, when he represented his patron saint, Clark Griffith, in a purchase of the Southern League franchise. The deal included a dramatic $180,000 renovation of the existing park, called Andrews Field. It had almost absurd dimensions—more than 450 feet to dead centerfield, where the word LOOKOUTS was spelled out in white concrete blocks—but so much the better when the outfield had to be roped off for an Engel-palooza. The concourse was a baseball history lesson. Engel commissioned an artist to paint murals on the wall of Hall of Fame players.

Alas, Engel's time in the current incarnation of the Southern League was all too brief. The Griffith family sold the stadium to the city in 1961 and the club ownership to the Lookouts Booster Club. The team struggled at the gate, though the '61 club did capture the championship. There was no team in 1962, but Engel landed an agreement with Philadelphia for 1963, a ball club that broke Chattanooga's pro baseball color barrier. The Lookouts joined the Southern League in 1964 and 1965, with Engel's involvement waning. There was a "Save the Lookouts" night promotion that drew only 355 fans. Barely more than 27,000 attended Lookouts' games in 1965, a thousand more than were there in one night, when the Baron of Baloney gave away a house.

Engel died in 1969 at age 76. A couple of sportswriters were in the brace of pallbearers. He was laid to rest at Forest Hills Cemetery, at the foot of Lookout Mountain, where 19 years later a shy, tomboyish lady named Jackie Mitchell Gilbert would be laid to rest.

CHARLIE O. FINLEY

From Birmingham to Oakland

To read the biographers' various attempts to capture the enigmatic life of Charles Oscar Finley is to get a sense of reading a Dickens novel. Finley grew up in Ensley, Ala., on the cusp of Birmingham, in the 1920s. The city was a gray, dirty industrial center, full of flinty Southerners who'd come from the country towns of Jemison and Opp and Cottondale and all over to work in the searing atmosphere of the steel mills.

Charles Finley's grandfather and father, one of 11 children, worked the mills. As a boy, the enterprising young Finley sold newspapers and magazines. He made homemade wine. He started a lawn mowing business but soon had his friends doing the chores while he knocked on doors and pitched the business.

He tried a gimmick—a great idea that failed with some controversy, perhaps a precursor to his professional career—to sell eggs failing what was called a "candling test." Inspectors would examine eggs with bright light to see if the embryo had begun to form or if it was safe to market the eggs. He bought the rejected eggs and sold them for profit, a business that lasted only until customers began cracking open bad eggs.

Finley was also a bat boy for the Birmingham Barons. He made 50 cents a game and often took home a scuffed, unusable baseball. Thus began a lifetime affair. He scuffed up the sport of baseball a little bit, and in many ways he made it better, having gone onto achieve a fortune in the insurance business before returning to his first passion.

Finley, who died February 19, 1996, three days shy of his 78th birthday, grew up to become the owner of the Kansas City Athletics, later moving the team to Oakland. He was an innovator, an icono-clast, an irritant. He could micromanage his operation, but he also made it a winner. The A's won three World Series, from 1972-74, and images of Finley waving an Oakland pennant in joy are as much a memory of those days as the players themselves, with their barber-shop quartet mustaches, vivid yellow jerseys, and ivory britches.

Upon Charlie Finley's death, Jim "Catfish" Hunter—his very nick-name a pure Finley invention—gave a statement, saying Finley "was the type of owner who knew a lot about baseball and knew how to get great players and win; he was 10 to 20 years ahead of his time."

Finley's Oakland tenure would produce three Hall of Famers and a Grammy winner. The former are Hunter, Reggie Jackson, and Rollie Fingers. The latter demonstrated his empathy for bat boys. He hired an 11-year-old kid from the projects named Stanley Burrell, whom Finley discovered selling used baseballs and dancing outside his sta-dium. He gave Stanley a job as batboy and "gopher," though many A's would claim his main job was to spy and give reports to Fin-ley. The players noticed the kid's uncanny resemblance to a young "Hammerin' Hank" Aaron, and began calling him Hammer. Some even provided financial support as the young man later burst onto the scene with great success as rapper MC Hammer.

Finley's purchase of the Athletics in 1960 provided a welcome bonus. It led to a homecoming of sorts, coming back south after his family moved to Gary, Indiana, when his father, Charles Sr., lost his job in the steel mill. Kansas City's Class AA franchise was in Shreveport when Finley bought the club, then moved to Albu-querque and Binghamton before he arranged with the Barons' own-ership to bring them to Birmingham in 1964. That was short lived. The team drew only 28,001 in 1965, finishing 25 games out of first, and ownership moved it to Mobile. Ultimately, Finley took com-mand and yanked the team back to Birmingham in 1967, loading it with the talent that would become the nucleus of Oakland's champi-onship teams, like Jackson, Fingers, and Joe Rudi.

The owner was heavily involved in those days. Finley, who often had barbecue air-freighted from Birmingham's Double-L to his Chicago office, would have the late Birmingham sportswriter Alf Van Hoose call him from the Rickwood Field press box and give him play-by-play updates.

He once brought one of his defending world-championship teams to Birmingham for an exhibition game, only to have monsoons hit the city. Finley ordered up helicopters to swoop in and dry the field, maintaining he'd have his team play barefoot just to get the game in. Catastrophe was avoided when another blast of rain hit, making the field a quagmire. Finley considered putting his Class AAA team in Birmingham, but Wayne Martin of *The Birmingham News* remembered that Finley erupted when he flew to town and none of the city panjandrums were waiting at the airport to greet him. Even as they sold him on the city's progress, Finley growled, "All you've done is build a blankety-blank freeway, and even that ends at (suburban) Fairfield."

Briefly, the team even used the A's moniker, an abrupt move from the traditional Barons' name. The players also used Oakland hand-me-downs. Ever frugal, Finley had his minor-leaguers using uniforms that had been previously worn in the majors. Former Barons first baseman Ron Beaurivage can recall taking the field in Ken Holtzman's old jersey and Sal Bando's old pants.

By that point, baseball's luster had begun to again fade in Birmingham. Finley's appearances became rare. He came in once for a speech, droning about his orange baseballs and other gimmicks. Rickwood Field's neighborhood was growing seedier. Players wouldn't leave the park at night unless they were in groups. The team was losing. The farm system that had built the championship teams grew dry. The team was purchased by a Chattanooga businessman named Woodrow Reid and moved to that city in 1976, leaving Birmingham without a pro baseball team until 1981.

When Finley brought the Barons back for their debut in the "new" Southern League in 1964, it was the stuff of history. The Barons were finally an integrated team, the first pro sports team in Alabama to have black players. John "Blue Moon" Odom was on the pitching staff. Tommie Reynolds, who had been in the majors in '63, was on the club. Rickwood Field, which had consistently segregated black fans in a right-field bleacher area, opened the grandstands to all races. Times could still be tense, though. Odom was once stopped by a Birmingham cop, suspicious to see a young black man driving a fancy new Ford Galaxie.

Charles Oscar Finley, the savvy, hustling urchin from Ensley, came home for the game as Birmingham hosted Asheville.

He worked three innings that night as the Barons' bat boy.

BILLY GARDNER, SR. AND JR.

Managing, the family business

His old man was managing the team, so sure, the clubhouse doors swung wide-open for him. He was respectful, no mistaking that. This was no playground for a spoiled kid. It was his father's workplace. It even became Billy Gardner Jr.'s workplace that summer of 1973, this Connecticut kid transplanted in the heat and humidity, chasing his seventh birthday. He had his own uniform. He got to be the Jacksonville Suns' batboy.

A pretty good Suns team, it was. Al Cowens was there on the way up. Zoilo Versailles, eight years removed from his American League MVP award, was there on his way down. Frank Ortenzio, a 47th-round draft pick who'd sip nine games worth of coffee that year with the Royals, batted .307. The Suns won 76 games. The bat boy's old man was named Southern League Manager of the Year. Jacksonville won the Eastern Division but got beat in the championship series by Montgomery, three games to one.

Fans of symmetry can appreciate this: Billy Jr. grew up to become the manager of Montgomery's team, 34 years later. In 2012, the former bat boy was named Southern League Manager of the Year. The Gardners are the only father-son tandem to win the award, the only father and son, in fact, to manage in the league.

"He's a smart kid," the father bragged. "I think he's going to do well. He's been around and I think eventually he's going to make the big time."

The elder Gardner made the big time as both player and manager. He was a second baseman by trade, with four years in Baltimore from 1956 through 1959. Brooks Robinson was just around the corner at third, and more than a half-century later, Gardner would recall him as the epitome of professionalism. Gardner was the quintessential "scrappy" second baseman of that generation, "a blue-collar player in a blue-collar town," as former *Baltimore Sun* columnist Bob Maisel called him. He once took a ground ball in the mouth during spring training in 1957, knocking out eight teeth and necessitating six stitches, but he was back in the lineup the very next day. He would bat .262 that season, leading the American League in doubles, and he had the best fielding percentage among AL second basemen.

Baltimore traded him down Route 295 in April 1960, swapping him to Washington for Clint Courtney; in 1973, Gardner's Jacksonville club would win the Southern League East by 6 ½ games over the Savannah club managed by Courtney.

Gardner wrapped up his career with first the Yankees, collecting a World Series ring in 1961, and then with the Red Sox. It was appropriate for his geography. Retirement would find him somewhere in Waterford, Conn., located comfortably between the two cities, following either the Yankees or Sox almost nightly on television.

Billy Gardner, Sr., managed the Suns three seasons (going 218-195) before moving to Class AAA Omaha in 1975. He was replaced by the iconoclastic, bombastic Billy Scripture, best known for gnawing the covers off baseball with his bare teeth and standing astride home plate, taking batting practice pitches in the chest just to prove to his players it didn't hurt. Gardner returned to the Southern League in 1979 at Memphis, going 82-62 and reaching the Southern League playoffs for the third time in his four years.

Billy Sr. finally got his shot to manage in the majors in 1981, replacing Johnny Goryl as Minnesota Twins skipper mid-season, and serving through 1985. In 1987, he was working as the Royals' third-base coach when manager Dick Howser was diagnosed with cancer, forcing Gardner to take over at the helm. Billy had the team sitting at 45-35, but the Royals went on a spiral when Bo Jackson left the club to return to pro football. He was fired in September, and the Royals finished two games behind his old Minnesota club. Replacing him as Kansas City manager was John Wathan, his old catcher from the '73 Jacksonville club.

Even in his big league managing days, the old blue-collar guy lived at a Super-8 Motel adjacent to a truck stop at an interstate exit on the fringe of Minneapolis. "The people are nice to me, I get along great with the drivers, and there's a Denny's nearby," he once told a Twin Cities reporter.

"What makes him special is he's very down-to-earth guy," Billy Gardner, Jr., said, sitting behind a neatly arranged desk in a cramped visiting-manager's office. "He never forgot where he came from. He came from nothing. He was very poor growing up. He signed when he was 16 and went on to have a pretty good career in the major leagues and went into coaching, but he never forgot his roots. He was an ordinary guy who'd go down to the local gin mill and play cards with the guys. And he worked every off-season, pumping gas or selling hot dogs for the Norwich Beef Company."

"We never made that much money when I was playing," Billy Sr. shrugged.

It was never a given that the son would follow in the family business. William Frederick Gardner, Jr., was a 50th-round draft pick of Royals in 1987, coming out of Mitchell College. Suffice it to say, the bonus payment from that round didn't send him to any nearby Ferrari dealerships. He spent two seasons in the minors, then enrolled at the University of Hartford to complete his degree. He assisted head coach Dan Gooley with the baseball team and had some odd jobs in the athletic department to make some extra money. Along the way, he ran into Paul Beretta, a Mets scout, who told him the manager's job with the short-season Pittsfield, Massachusetts team was open.

"Next thing you know, I get a call from [Mets' director of minor-league operations] Gerry Hunsicker, who hired me," Billy Jr. said. "And the rest is kind of history. I just fell into it."

He was 24 years old at the time. Before taking the plunge, he talked about it with his father. "He was on board with whatever decision I made. He never forced me into anything, whether it was sports or anything else. He offered his insight into it. He didn't steer me away from it by any means."

That's the business of family, and it's following in the family business.

PHILLIP WELLMAN

The SL's most famous heave-ho, in retrospect

He was the winningest manager in the first 50 years of the Southern League, the only manager with more than 1,000 games in the league, a man held in such high regard he was twice voted the Best Managerial Prospect in the league, though he said, "It's like being named MVP twice. Why aren't you moving on?"

He has captured the league pennant, clinched four half-season championships, won over friends among fans and players and media, and amassed 544 regular-season victories.

Phillip Wellman has spent over 3,000 triumphant, productive hours in Southern League dugouts managing games, yet he knows he'll be remembered for what may be the most famous, widely-viewed three minutes in the first half-century.

"I don't run from it. I don't hide from it. It's out there for the whole world to see," Wellman said.

"It" is a video from a June 1, 2007, game when his Mississippi Braves were playing at Chattanooga. Wellman erupted at the umpiring crew. His ensuing theatrics included yanking both third and second bases from the ground and lobbing, hand grenade-style, the rosin bag at an umpire. It was caught on video by Rick Nyman of WDEF-TV and was quickly sent to ESPN and CNN. Twenty-four hours later, the video had gone viral.

"I had done some stupid stuff," he said. "My wife and kids will tell you they've seen better. It just so happened there were no TV crews there [on those occasions]."

Wellman helmed games with a passion and has a big personality. There's a little showman to him. But he's not the quintessential hothead, a manager destined to be thrown out of a game every two or three weeks.

Wellman managed eight years in the Southern League, going 544-568. Closest to that tenure were Billy Gardner, Jr., who wrapped up his seventh year at Montgomery in 2013, and Harry Warner, with five years at Charlotte and one at Orlando. Wellman was at Chattanooga four seasons (1999, then 2001-2003) in the Reds' farm system, then at Mississippi from 2007-2010. "I loved where I worked," said Wellman, who also spent three years in the league as a hitting coach. "I used to joke with [late league president] Don Mincher, who was one of my favorite people, that I had more time in the Southern League than he did."

Wellman grew up in Marlin, Texas, a town of 6,000 located a half-hour south of Waco. He was the oldest of four boys raised in modest means. "We went without new dining-room furniture, but [our parents made sure] we never went without spikes and never went without gloves." He played at Sam Houston State and Southwestern, then signed with the Braves. He was a minor-league outfielder from 1984-87, showing some power and strong plate discipline. The Braves offered him a coaching opportunity in 1988, at Pulaski, Virginia. The Baltimore organization offered him his first managerial job, at age 30, with their rookie ball team in Bluefield. He managed a couple of co-op teams after that before entering a span of seven years in Cincinnati's employ, including four years at Chattanooga, where he and wife Montee purchased a home after the 2013 season.

So it was familiar territory when the Mississippi Braves went to play the Lookouts, back in a park where he had been a fan favorite. June 1 was the umpiring equivalent to a bad-hair day for the crew of Brent Rice, Jeff Latter, and Rusty Barnett, with a rain delay and several other screwy instances.

Two M-Braves had bickered with Barnett, and Wellman went to their defense. Then Rice made a call on the first pitch of the third with which Wellman disagreed. He burst from the dugout and flung his cap to the ground as he got in Rice's face. Wellman covered home plate with dirt, then drew an outline of a much larger home plate for Rice's benefit. From there, he stalked to third and blasted Barnett. He tugged third base from its moorings and flung it into the outfield. Ditto second base. Between second and pitcher's mound, he dropped to the ground and did a belly crawl. He grabbed the rosin bag and threw it toward Rice, landing just as the ump's feet, an absolutely perfect throw. With the crowd loving it, with Wellman blowing kisses, with his players hiding their faces in their gloves, Wellman headed toward the clubhouse beyond the outfield wall. To get inside, a door had to be opened in the wooden fence. The advertisement on the fence was appropriate for his antagonists: Chattanooga Eye Institute.

Wellman sat at a Frisco, Texas, hotel in midsummer 2013, his own hindsight 20-20, and recalled the incident.

"Somebody brought it up to me the other day. They asked how has that affected your life? It's affected my life in a positive way," Wellman said. "Wherever we go—and it's not in a paranoid sense—it's ingrained in my mind there's probably a camera or a microphone. I had no clue what YouTube was until six years ago. I had a flip phone for 15 years. I never even knew phones had cameras on them. It's made me more aware of things, to try to be more a role model and not do anything stupid that might get caught on camera. Because if it does, I know what YouTube is now."

It was wildly entertaining for both Mincher and Braves general manager John Schuerholz, but also challenging for both. They had to drop the hammer. "You know I love you and I can't quit laughing, and I know you were putting on a show," Schuerholz told Wellman. "Now, let me put my GM's hat on. We have to do something." He served a three-game suspension.

"When we got back to Chattanooga, (team owner) Frank Burke told me attendance was up 50 percent. They wanted to see if I was going to make an ass of myself again. I heard a lot about it. Every close call, people were in the stands, howling, 'Go get him.' It hit me people were spending money to see if I was going to do something stupid. In Carolina, there was this elderly lady in a wheelchair behind our dugout. About the fifth inning, I was coming in and I could see her almost stand up. She yelled at me, 'Wellman, do something!'

"Every time somebody (argues frantically with umps) in the big leagues, it pops up on ESPN. It's not my proudest moment. But I choose to embrace it rather than run from it."

The 2008 season brought moments of true pride for Wellman. After his Mississippi team started dreadfully, the Braves rallied to win the second half, then beat Carolina in five games for the Southern League pennant, only the third one for an Atlanta Double-A franchise in league history.

"They were loaded with prospects," Wellman said of the Mudcats. "After we beat them in the championship, they sent like five guys to the big leagues. We celebrated and sent nobody to the big leagues and went home."

That night, he thought about James Wellman, the man who made sure his four sons had plenty of baseball equipment, even if it meant sacrificing some luxuries. "All the stuff you taught me growing up, all the sayings like you get out of it what you put in it, never giving up is the only way to fix something, Dad, they all came through," he told his father.

Years before, Phillip Wellman made up his mind about something. The first championship ring he ever won, he'd give to his dad. "I just had no idea it'd take 25 years to do it," he said.

He boxed up the ring and shipped it to his father with a note included. Phillip's phone rang after the package arrived. His mother Janie was on the other end of the line. "For the first time in I don't know how long," she said, "I saw your dad cry."

THE PLACES

Regions Field, Birmingham.

BIRMINGHAM, ALABAMA

Storybook season in the Magic City

The sky over Red Mountain was a Crayola concoction of black, orange, and gray clouds on a Friday night in Birmingham, with stormy weather in the area. Vulcan, the enormous statue that stands sentinel above Birmingham as tribute to the city's iron industry, stared down at the Barons-Huntsville Stars game.

If you were hermetically sealed inside the second-tier lounge, sipping a craft beer and eating a designer sandwich, or if you were somewhere in the stands with a draft and a dog, a giveaway Jared Mitchell bobblehead doll tucked under your seat, you were part of a magical memory tour created by the 2013 Birmingham Barons.

"You can't write a more storybook season than what we had," said Barons general manager Jonathan Nelson.

First, a beautiful new ballpark, Regions Field, that opened in downtown on April 10. Then came a first-half division championship, a postseason with enough nervousness to sell a boatload of ulcer medicine, the Southern League pennant and MVP and a pile of awards for off-field excellence.

The magnificent ballpark itself didn't come without some nervous moments, and with a few areas where you assumed you might need a hard hat to enter when the gates first opened. (Full disclosure from the Barons: Not only were gates open that first night, so were enough gaps in the perimeter fencing that pretty much any industrious and shameless fan could have walked in for free.) The concrete was so freshly poured, it was fortunate that footprints weren't left along the way like one big Graumann's Chinese Theater. Construction experienced weather delays and other typical complications. An internet live-cam on a building above the stadium showed the progress, which was being closely monitored in Arizona, where the future Barons were in spring training at the White Sox complex. The Barons weren't able to move into their permanent offices at the stadium until the Monday morning two days before the opener. Said Nelson, "We were feeling our way around in the dark."

The massive undertaking began in November 2010 when visionary owner Don Logan reached an agreement with the city of Birmingham for the new park, estimated then with a $48 million price tag; eventually the cost was reported at $64 million.

It was the third ballpark debut—or re-debut, if you will—in 32 years and signaled baseball's return to Birmingham proper. It also planted the seed, believed the city fathers, to a hub for urban redevelopment in an area that had been left to old warehouses, closed businesses, and empty lots along the path of the railroad tracks that bisect downtown.

Birmingham's first stadium "debut" came at a familiar location. Art Clarkson was the general manager of the Memphis Chicks and doing remarkable business in an old, small park. Jimmy Bragan, the Birmingham native and Southern League president, broached the idea of Clarkson doing the same for Birmingham. With an ownership group molded together by Birmingham sportswriter Alf Van Hoose and University of Alabama broadcaster John Forney, Clarkson brought the Montgomery Rebels into the city in 1981 after baseball had been absent for five seasons, re-opening historic Rickwood Field with a flourish. More than 9,000 fans were at Rickwood on April 14, 1981, when Mike Laga hit a two-out, 11th-inning homer just inside the right-field foul pole to beat Jacksonville.

Even then, gussied up for baseball's return, Rickwood was showing its age. Even more, underneath, her bones were brittle. When Clarkson decided to move the Barons, he didn't write the death sentence for Rickwood. Fact is, it was the best thing for Rickwood's future. The more use, the more abuse. "I was wearing out a 75-year-old ballpark," Clarkson said. "Pipes were cracking. Keeping the power on was a challenge." He learned a new use for a baseball bat in those days: the handle end to pry out a blown fuse, the butt end to pound the new one in.

When Rickwood first reopened, it was functional and comparable to many of its brethren in the league. But sparkling Joe Davis Stadium in Huntsville became Clarkson's great example for a new stadium. At Rickwood, parking was at a premium. Clarkson could stand on the roof 30 minutes before a game and see cars U-turning because the spots were gone. Safety was also a concern in a decaying neighborhood. Clarkson insisted "we never had an incident [during games] during seven years I was there. But we probably had 30 break-ins into my office."

The city of Birmingham wasn't offering any help. Representatives of the communities of Hoover, Homewood, and Trussville met with Clarkson and Hoover Mayor Frank Skinner showed Clarkson a piece of hilly, wooded property just outside Interstate 459 that would test anyone's imagination as being a spot to develop anything more than a Robin Hood movie sequel.

Clarkson has always insisted the construction of the Hoover Met was the "lightning rod" that drew more development in the area, as a high school, residential development, and some businesses bloomed nearby. Indeed, Hoover had fewer than 20,000 citizens in 1980, a figure that would quadruple in 30 years, but Birmingham's waistline was already expanding and this area south of town, just beyond the tony communities of Homewood and Vestavia Hills, was a logical place for growth.

The Barons, with Jack McDowell as their starting pitcher, played their final game at Rickwood Field on September 9, 1987, a 5-4 loss to Charlotte in Game 2 of the Southern League Championship Series. Rondal Rollin, the face of the franchise, struck out to end the game. It was 10:54 p.m. It was the only game the Barons lost in the series; they went on to win the next two in Charlotte to snatch the pennant.

On April 18, 1988, in front of a crowd of more than 10,000—and many more impatient fans stuck in a nightmare traffic jam—the Barons moved into what was originally known as the Hoover Met before various temporary tattoos of corporate sponsors with naming rights were placed on the building.

The Southeastern Conference, whose offices are in downtown Birmingham, set up camp at Hoover for its annual baseball tournament in 1988, six times breaking the six-digit mark in tournament attendance. And, of course, for one memorable season, the ballpark was home to a former Atlantic Coast Conference basketball player named Michael Jordan.

Martin is convinced that the Hoover Met—especially its amenities and security aspects—was a determining factor in Chicago assigning Jordan to the Barons for his fling with baseball in 1994.

Like many cities in recent years, Birmingham began the movement to return its citizens downtown for dinner, entertainment, shopping, and housing. Birmingham opened Railroad Park, a greenway alongside the tracks that trundles Amtrak's Crescent from New Orleans to New England. It's on the cusp of the mushrooming UAB campus. "We saw the positive energy of going downtown," Nelson said. "People saw something downtown, something they were so proud of. It's a mini-big league ballpark. When visiting teams came in, it was as if they came into Yankee Stadium."

It may have felt a little like playing some team from a Yankee dynasty, too. The Barons opened with a 9-5 comeback win over Montgomery in the inaugural game, triggered by a homer from Marcus Semien, the eventual league MVP. They went Usain Bolt on the rest of the field in the first half, winning 44 games to comfortably take the South Division title by nine games over Chattanooga. Despite the inevitable second-half call-ups that often cripple first-half champs, they responded from a 33-37 half with a dramatic playoff run. (Birmingham's other "debut" teams had nowhere near the success. The '81 Barons were 71-70, while the first team at Hoover went 62-82).

Outlasting Tennessee in a five-game South Division playoff series set the Barons up for an I-65 Championship Series against the Mobile BayBears. Birmingham won the first two at Hank Aaron Stadium, but lost their mojo at home. The BayBears, the back-to-back champs in 2010-11, won each of the next two games at Regions Field before a 4-2 Barons victory in Game 5 gave Birmingham the pennant. Playoff MVP Micah Johnson set the tone, leading off the first inning with his first Barons' homer.

"Day 1, I said this was a special team, and it is," manager Julio Vinas.

A special year it was.

"One of those seasons I've never been a part of before, where everything went our way," Nelson said.

The Barons never had a rainout. The enthusiasm for the team never wavered. The team won.

Nelson was one of two members of the 2013 Birmingham front office who was also around for the Michael Jordan season. "I constantly told our staff it was so similar to 1994 because of the attention and the pressure, but the uniqueness and the fun as well," he said. "But unlike '94 when Michael Jordan was a one-hit wonder, this is long-lasting. This is permanent. This is something that is going to positively impact this community for a long time."

The storybook season is trending toward "happily ever after."

JACKSON, TENNESSEE

Of Jaxx and Generals

Charles Farmer served 18 years as the mayor of Jackson, Tennessee, a modest-sized city clinging to Interstate 40 between Memphis and Nashville. "One of my many flaws," Farmer said, laughing, "is undue optimism or extreme recklessness, whichever you might choose."

There were barely 100,000 people in the metro area, even fewer in Jackson proper, when Farmer and other civic leaders optimistically began searching for a possible minor-league team to bring to town. "I don't know why we were crazy enough to think we could get a Double-A baseball team," Farmer said. Still, he added, "I never had any doubt it would work"

After putting out some feelers that went nowhere, Jackson learned that David Hersh was having difficulties in Memphis, some 80 miles to the southwest. He was still doing business with the Class AA Memphis Chicks in Tim McCarver Stadium, named in 1977 for the city's most famous baseball name. It had opened in 1968 on the Fairgrounds, near the Liberty Bowl and the Mid-South Coliseum, by then pretty much relegated to minor-league pro basketball and some major pro wrestling events. Hersh wanted a new stadium, but the city fathers weren't budging. Hersh struck a deal with Jackson.

The city had the land and it had help in building up the infrastructure. It was ahead of the curve in selling naming rights to the stadium, enlisting the manufacturers of locally produced Procter & Gamble potato chips to alliteratively christen it Pringles Park.

The team needed a nickname and fans were urged to submit suggestions. Ron Arnett saw the contest mentioned in the *Jackson Sun* and showed it to his grandmother, Jane Des Ormeaux. The ad had a diamond in the design.

"And there were suggestions we should give credit to our town," Des Ormeaux said. "So I said, 'How about Diamond Jaxx?' "

The grandson sent in the entry and "I was absolutely shocked when they decided on that name," she said. "There were some people who have said it was the worst name they ever heard. I'd say, 'You had the chance to send one in.' "

Des Ormeaux and her son-in-law, Ron Arnett, Sr., were among the first people in the ballpark for opening night. Barely had the 2013 season ended before Des Ormeaux, at 96 years of age, purchased her season ticket for 2014.

It was standing-room only in the 6,000-seat-capacity park on April 17, 1998, when the Diamond Jaxx won on a walk-off hit-by-pitch. They drew a league-best 313,775 that season, three times the population base and almost nearly three times what Hersh drew the previous year in Memphis. Brian McNichol won 12 games and Kyle Farnsworth, then a starter, later to find work in various major-league bullpens, won eight. The next season, Julio Zuleta drove in 97 runs and manager Dave Trembley's club reached the championship series before losing to Orlando.

Manager Dave Bialas took a prospect-filled team back to the 2000 championship series to face Jacksonville. Both the Diamond Jaxx and Suns needed five games to win their division playoffs and this was destined for five games as well, only the second time all three series went the maximum distance since the best-of-five format was adopted in 1980.

West Tenn vaulted to a 1-0 lead in the series behind a pitching gem from Joey Nation. The lean left-hander from Oklahoma was a second-round draft pick of the Braves who became the proverbial "player to be named later" in a deal that sent Cubs reliever Terry Mulholland to Atlanta. Nation made his major-league debut in a six-inning stint against the Cardinals at Wrigley Field once the league playoffs ended—Farnsworth would come on in relief—but the following spring a medical exam would reveal he had an enlarged heart. The diagnosis ended his pro baseball career.

In Game 2, Jayson Bass socked a grand slam and Eric Hinske a solo homer to enable the Jaxx to head home with a 2-0 series lead, sitting pretty with 11-game winner Nate Teut pitching. The 6-foot-7 lefty threw a complete-game one-hitter—but the lone hit was a homer by Jacksonville third baseman Brian Rios, enough for a 1-0 Suns victory. The Suns then romped 12-3 in Game 4, and the series was tied.

Nation started Game 5 against Shane Loux. The game went to the eighth inning, Jacksonville leading 3-2. With two out and one on, Suns manager Gene Roof called on ace reliever Kris Keller, who had pitched in 62 games and notched 26 saves. Keller whiffed Corey Patterson to escape the eighth, but created his own threat in the ninth, walking the first two men before recording two outs. At that point, Peter Bragan, Jr., the Jacksonville general manager, left his seat to find his way to the field for the postgame awards ceremony.

Coming to bat was Mike Amrhein, the Jaxx catcher. His life would take a tragic turn a dozen years later. A 10th-round pick out of Notre Dame, he played six years of pro ball but never reached the majors. He retired to go into coaching and was working at a Chicago-area high school when he committed suicide in 2012, leaving behind a wife and two children.

Amrhein slammed a double off the wall, missing a walk-off winner by two feet. It chased home pinch-runner Dennis Abreu from second, tying the game. Bass, trying to score from first, was tagged out in a Richter-scale collision at home with David Lindstrom.

West Tenn reliever Courtney Duncan sat down the Suns in order in the top of the tenth. In the home half, the Diamond Jaxx' Jaisen Randolph drew a one-out walk, and Franklin Font followed with a routine ground ball to Brian Rios at third. However, as Jaxx broadcaster Matt Park wrote, Rios's "throw to first base went wide and bounced into the offseason." Randolph sped home with the winning run and the title. As David Thomas of the *Jackson Sun* pointed out, the Diamond Jaxx played 28 innings of baseball at home, never led until the error—and still got to fly a pennant at Pringles Park. Joey Nation, whose baseball career would soon be over, was named Championship Series MVP.

Things wouldn't always be so glorious. The iconoclastic Hersh was not inaccurately described in the *St. Petersburg Times* in 2003 as being "known in the league for his dealmaking [and] demanding temperament." His welcome was being worn out in Jackson, too. As Hersh sold the team to the Lozinak family, he was in a court battle with the city over $150,000 in ticket surcharges. The Lozinaks owned the team for nearly six years before selling to a group led by David Freeman, a part-owner of the NHL's Nashville Predators, and Reese Smith III, part of the group that owned the Nashville Sounds.

They began putting their own signature on the team. Jane Des Ormeaux's nickname for the team was scuttled. The franchise was rechristened the Jackson Generals in 2011, a throwback to the Class D Kentucky-Illinois-Tennessee League team in the 1930s through the 50s and a nod to the city's namesake, General Andrew Jackson. There was some consolation; the final night they played as the Diamond Jaxx, Des Ormeaux threw out the first pitch.

Charles Farmer, who retired as mayor in 2007 having navigated the city into pro baseball and through a pair of devastating tornadoes, grew up wanting to be a pitcher for the New York Yankees. The closest he came to playing professional baseball was in a pregame exhibition at Pringles Park when Hall of Fame knuckleballer Phil Niekro appeared and pitched to a raft of local celebrities. "I think I hit a slow dribbler back to the mound," Farmer said.

Farmer did stride to the pitcher's mound on opening night at Pringles Park, light years from Yankee Stadium but no less electric. He was throwing out the ceremonial first pitch.

"I think I more or less insisted on it," Farmer laughed. "There were some who wanted the governor to, but there was a discussion about it. And I think I won."

KNOXVILLE, TENNESSEE

At the steps of the Great Smoky Mountains

Opening Night, April 20, 2000. Cars were backed up for miles on Interstate 40 on the northeast side of Knoxville, waiting to peel off at Exit 407. The ballpark, 13 months in the works just outside the tourist mecca of Sevierville, was state-of-the-art. Local businesses poured out their support.

A helicopter hovered above the diamond; belonging to a local company that flew tourists around through the Smoky Mountain foothills, it was enlisted to shoot aerial photographs of the scene. A Lockheed CJ-130 Super Hercules refueling plane from the Tennessee Air National Guard stationed at nearby Tyson-McGhee Airport was set to fly over as the national anthem was completed.

What could go wrong?

Nothing... except that the Tennessee Smokies staffer who enlisted the helicopter didn't tell the pilot about the CJ-130. And the staffer who convinced the CJ-130 crew to zoom over the ballpark as part of a routine training run didn't know about the helicopter.

"We almost had a mid-air collision over the stadium," Brian Cox, the Smokies' general manager, remembered.

Fortunately, the CJ-130 made a hard right turn, a trail of smoke in its wake. Fans had to figure it was just part of the show.

Moments later, leadoff-hitting Chattanooga Lookouts outfielder Gookie Dawkins was part of the show as well. He had agreed to a request by Smokies manager Rocket Wheeler that he take the first pitch thrown to him by Leo Estrella, so the baseball could be preserved for history. The next pitch was unscripted. Dawkins hammered it down the left-field line for a homer. It was one of seven homers and 27 hits on the night. "We realized then it was not going to be a pitcher's park," Cox said. Jay Gibbons supplied two of the homers for the Smokies, who won 10-7 in front of 7,318.

The Tennessee Smokies were off and running to a 70-69 record in 2000. They were the only team in the Eastern Division to finish above .500, yet because of the split-season schedule they failed to qualify for the playoffs. Considering the track record, that may not be surprising. The Smokies' franchise was a Southern League member for 46 of the first 50 years—during the league's hiatus, the league office (under president Sam Smith) was, ironically, still located in Knoxville's Holston Hills—but the city has claimed only three pennants and 18 playoff appearances. Ten times, it has been the division runner-up.

The Smokies operated out of Bill Meyer Stadium from 1964-1967, and then again from 1972 until after the 1999 season. It was a typical old-time ballpark, with a wooden roof, iron beams, and charming quirks. For instance, there was no lack of a tunnel between the dugouts and the clubhouses, meaning the only way into the clubhouses was through the main concourse. Pity the poor, struggling pitcher who got the hook and had to leave the dugout, exit the field at the end of the grandstand, then trudge up a concrete ramp to the hallway past the same fans who had just been booing him.

Bob Kesling is the radio voice of the University of Tennessee football and basketball. His first job was at Bill Meyer Stadium, convincing then-general manager Bill Reep to hire him between his spring and fall semesters at UT. Kesling was named assistant general manager, "which meant I was the No. 2 man on a two-man staff," he said. Jim Napier managed the Knoxville Sox, a Chicago farm club, to the pennant that season. Kesling still has the championship ring.

Kesling moved up from selling hot dogs and tickets and into the press box a few years later, eventually becoming the team's radio broadcaster. Somewhere along the line, he lost a bet. The press box was inhabited by some old-school sportswriters who learned that the young man had played the cello in high school. Whatever the bet—the details are fuzzy to Kesling—he lost and had to play the national anthem on the cello at home plate one night.

Knoxville dominated the league in 1978, with Tony LaRussa serving as manager in the first half. The Sox swept both halves, then beat Savannah 2-1 in the playoffs. It would be the last pennant the franchise won on the field. (Tennessee shared the 2004 title with Jacksonville when Hurricane Ivan forced the cancellation of the championship series.)

When Toronto partnered with Knoxville in 1980, the club's fortunes sank from first to worst. They finished 57-87. "We used to give out a player of the game award, a free meal at the [since-closed] Regas Restaurant, and we'd go a whole homestand and not be able to give it a Knoxville player," Kesling said.

Bill Meyer Stadium sat just inside a bend in the interstate snaking through Knoxville, at Caswell Park. The original stadium there burned to the ground in 1953, and the new Municipal Stadium was built there for $500,000. It was named in honor of Meyer, a Knoxville player in the 1910s and driving force for the sport for years later, in 1957. The stadium was leveled in 2000, but a baseball park remains at the spot. Ridley-Helton Field is part of a recreation complex at the site, named for Neil Ridley, who owned the team for years, and Knoxville native Todd Helton, the retired Colorado Rockies' first baseman and former Tennessee football and baseball star. Two plaques are at the site, one telling of the field's namesakes, the other listing immortal players who competed at Bill Meyer Stadium.

After Don Beaver bought the franchise from the Blue Jays, who had purchased it from Ridley, the team began looking for a new location. Bill Meyer Stadium simply didn't have enough parking, amenities, or even office space for a growing franchise. Cox, then the assistant GM to Dan Rajkowski, worked in an office in a hallway with a door at either end, the only entrance to the staff restroom in that hall.

Between 1994 and 1998, team officials examined nearly three dozen sites for a new park. They had their hopes set on a plot of ground near the site of the 1982 World's Fair, but that was instead dedicated to a convention center.

Sevierville mayor Bryan Atchley wooed the Smokies to his neck of the woods. Initially, they contemplated a site nearer the population center of the community, but the convenience of the land adjacent to the interstate made most sense. To help convince the rest of the Sevierville poohbahs to buy into the deal, they brought in two secret weapons: Luke Waring and Harrison Chambers, 10-year-old players in the Greater Sevierville Little League. Luke and Harrison appeared at a joint meeting between city and county officials and pleaded for a minor-league team. It might as well have been the first turn of the shovel in construction.

A KOA campground sat on a hill high above the site for the stadium. John Mueller, who owned the grounds, could see deer, foxes, and quail below his home before the dozers and construction equipment moved in. Often the campers' dishes would rattle and homes shake when workers used dynamite.

"We sat and watched them build it," Mueller said. "And we'd walk down there after the contractors left to see what they'd done." The campground received some business because of the Smokies' presence, and hitting coach Hector Torres lived in a camper on-site, his wife working in the KOA's restaurant. Mueller had a unique vantage point on Smokies' games; he could watch from high atop the hill above left field or he could use his season tickets on the first row behind home plate.

John Mueller was there on opening night, though he brought a secret with him: the first game played at Smokies Park was held long before that evening. His grandkids—elementary schoolers Ian, Craig, Samuel John and Heaven Leigh—had long ago played ball on the same carved-out diamond where the Smokies now went to work.

MOBILE, ALABAMA

Something in the water

Climb the short flight of wooden steps, a hollow clomp with each step, and walk onto the porch, which offers a soft creaking sound below your feet. Shake off the damp semi-chill. This happens to be what passes for a wintry day just a few miles from the wide mouth of Mobile Bay, opening into the Gulf of Mexico.

Enter the white, clapboard house that was built in 1942 by an enterprising dockworker named Herbert Aaron on Edwards Avenue in the Toulminville section of Mobile. Aaron purchased a pair of lots, for $53 apiece. The home was originally 700 square feet; a couple of additions later, it grew to 1,200 square feet. It was home to Herbert and his wife Estelle, and their eight children. Now, though, where bedrooms and dining rooms and a kitchen once were, a shrine to the home's most famous resident has been created. The walls are lined with glass display cases, with mementoes, photographs, and other historical artifacts.

The boyhood home of Hank Aaron is now an anachronistic appendix to Hank Aaron Stadium in Mobile, transplanted from across town to the stadium grounds and opened in 2010 as as a museum. It's also the grandest symbol of Mobile's baseball history, a legacy unmatched by any city its size in the United States.

Mobile is birthplace to more Baseball Hall of Fame members per capita than anywhere. The list includes Aaron, Willie McCovey, Satchel Paige, Ozzie Smith, and Billy Williams. Just outside Hank Aaron Stadium, home to the Southern League's Mobile BayBears, each of the five is represented with a plaque in Hall of Fame Circle.

But they only start the lineup of Mobile baseball greats. The list of former and current major leaguers is astounding: Ted "Double-Duty" Radcliffe, the Negro League star so named because he pitched one game of a doubleheader and caught the next; Charlie "Home Run" Duffee, the first Alabamian to reach the majors; the all-Mobile outfield of Cleon Jones, Tommie Agee, and Amos Otis of the 1969 world champion Mets; and more. There were the Bolling brothers, Frank and Milt. Jim Mason. Terry Adams. Juan Pierre. Dave Stapleton, often Bill Buckner's defensive replacement with Boston, but, to the chagrin of Sox fans everywhere, still on the bench when Mookie Wilson came to bat in the bottom of the tenth inning, Game 6, of the 1986 World Series. Jake Peavy, the 2007 National League Cy Young Award winner, is a Mobile native who pitched for his hometown Southern League BayBears both on the field and off the field; he worked in the club's front office one off-season, selling tickets and ads.

The city's standouts aren't limited to one gender. Robin Wallace, Delores "Dolly" Brumfield White, and Marge Holgerson, greats in women's pro baseball, are also Mobile natives.

"I used to tell people there was something in the water, something that made guys play as hard and as well as they did," Billy Williams told Tommy Hicks of the *Mobile Press-Register.* "Every player that played in the majors from Mobile was proud of that [legacy]."

Minor-league baseball has been part of the city's core since early 1887, when they were known as the Swamp Angels. Another incarnation of the team would be called the Mobile Oyster Grabbers. Attendance for minor-league games in those halcyon years was so great, team officials pushed for an exemption to Alabama's strict "blue laws" to enable the team to play on Sundays.

As with many cities, there were good years and lean ones. Ballclubs shifted in and out of Mobile, leagues folded. A new stadium, Hartwell Field, was opened in 1927 at the corner of Ann and Tennessee Streets after bleachers at the team's previous stadium were leveled by a hurricane. A nearby candy store sold candy in the shape of baseballs. A nearby factory was constantly replacing windows shattered by foul balls. In 1947, the Bears enjoyed a championship season behind the popular George "Shotgun" Shuba and future actor Chuck Connors, who'd go on to become both a Brookyn Dodger (for one game, anyway) and TV's "The Rifleman." Cleon Jones proudly recalled years later attending a game at Hartwell Field and catching a foul ball off the bat of Shuba. Frank Bolling and Otis remembered chasing foul balls, to either be used in sandlot games later or to "cash in" as free admission to Bears games.

Hartwell Field remained the home of a Southern Association team through 1961, but it sat empty for three seasons before the Kansas City A's Southern League affiliate was transferred there from Birmingham in 1965. They won the league championship by 9½ games but were back in Birmingham a year later. The White Sox placed their Double-A team in Mobile in 1970, but attendance was miserable and the franchise moved to Asheville, N.C.

An independent league team called the Bay Sharks popped up in 1994, playing at the University of South Alabama. (Hartwell Field had gone the way of the wrecking ball.) The Bay Sharks created enough interest to encourage Mayor Mike Dow and Dr. Eric Margenau, a sports psychologist who would be the BayBears' original owner, to join the Southern League. The BayBears opened the stadium on April 17, 1997—108 years to the day that Charlie Duffee made his major-league debut as the first Alabama player in the big leagues. Affiliated with the expansion Arizona Diamondbacks, the Mobile BayBears led the Southern League in attendance, and then knocked off Huntsville and Jacksonville in the '98 playoffs to bring a championship to the city.

Hank Aaron, naturally, threw out the first pitch in the stadium debut. Aaron maintained strong ties to the city and the franchise; coming back home gave him "goose pimples and things like that." On April 14, 2010, slightly more than 36 years after a home run off Al Downing enabled him to pass Babe Ruth, the Hammer's boyhood home was unveiled as a museum adjacent to the BayBears' stadium—a stadium that bears his name. Willie Mays, Ozzie Smith, Bob Feller, Bruce Sutter, Rickey Henderson, Reggie Jackson, and baseball commissioner Bud Selig were on hand; McCovey, whose relationship with his hometown is not nearly so sentimental, was conspicuously not present.

Before the ceremony, Hank Aaron gave an interview with the *Press-Register's* Hicks, who asked what inspiration the museum might be for youngsters.

"I hope they take away the idea that here's a kid, a black kid, that went all the way to the top and is enshrined in Cooperstown," said Aaron. "That it was not easy, the things that he went through and some of the things that happened to me in my quest for greatness was the fact that I had to overlook a lot of things. I want all kids to understand that the path is not easy sometimes, but they should not turn their back on anything. They should always look forward to being a lot stronger and they should always give everything they've got to reach to the top."

NASHVILLE, TENNESSEE

Like the Taj Mahal

Most summer nights, Farrell Owens still makes his way out to the ballpark. Old habits die hard. When it's 95 degrees in mid-July, he might arrive fashionably late and might not make the first pitch. Indeed, it was more than a little welcome relief to hunker down on a comfy divan upstairs in air-conditioned comfort in the stadium he and his fellow Cohn High School graduate Larry Schmittou built with relentless faith and the assistance of some famous guitar-pickers.

Schmittou was coaching Vanderbilt's baseball team but just had his salary whacked from $20,000 to $14,000 when a new director of athletics took away his duties with the Vandy football team. Owens was coaching at Pearl High School and preparing to go into real estate to help supplement his income.

So it was pretty audacious that they determined, as Owens said, "we were the ideal guys" to bring professional baseball back to Nashville after it vanished in 1963. They weren't exactly rolling in money; Schmittou would later have to mortgage his house to help pay for stadium construction. But, said Owens, "We knew everybody."

It was the fall of 1976, and Schmittou had seen the success Chattanooga enjoyed after ending its 10-year hiatus from pro ball. "I thought if we got a park in Nashville, we could do even better than that," he said. After bumping into Farrell Owens at a high-school football game, Schmittou tracked his friend down the next day where Owens was studying for the real estate exam.

"We just drummed it up right there," said Owens.

Larry Schmittou drew up plans for a park. He convinced the city of Nashville to provide the land, pledging to build the stadium on a hillside not far from the Nashville skyline. Schmittou and Owens flew to Los Angeles for the winter meetings and put handwritten notes in the mail slots of each major-league team, asking to discuss the potential of locating a farm team there. "We were from Nashville," Owens said. "They thought we were stars. We knew Roy Acuff. We didn't really, but they thought we did."

Schmittou did know Jerry Reed, though. And they both knew Snuffy Miller, a long-time sessions drummer who knew Conway Twitty, a huge baseball fan. (Miller would eventually become the Sounds' bus driver.) Twitty jumped in to buy 20 percent of the club. Singer Cal Smith bought a chunk of the team. So did Reed and the songwriter L.E. White. They had a pretty good stake to start building a stadium they estimated at a half-million dollars—except it came up with a $780,000 price tag.

The Sounds hooked up with Cincinnati as the parent club. The Reds had grown weary of the cold weather in Trois-Rivieres, a city in Quebec an hour and half north of Montreal. Schmittou and Owens sealed the deal with Reds farm director Sheldon "Chief" Bender at a vacated Hertz Rental Car booth in the hotel lobby at the winter meetings. But the Nashville winter of 1977-78 was nearly Canadian in its cold, slowing construction. After workers poured concrete, they had to use huge gas heaters to cure the wet mixture. The seats they installed were second-hand, purchased from the Atlanta Braves, who were renovating their own stadium. When the Sounds opened in 1978, there were no offices for the staff, most of the restroom facilities were portable, and the field was not level. The first grass that was planted died. One day Owens went on the radio and announced a "sod party," and dozens of fans showed up to help lay the new turf.

They christened the ballpark Herschel Greer Stadium, the president of the old Nashville Vols.

Early that season, Memphis manager Felipe Alou groused to Schmittou, "Worst field I ever saw. Worst field I ever saw." But the Chicks swept a doubleheader that night, winning both by nearly a dozen runs. "Best field I ever saw," Alou told Schmittou afterward. "Best field I ever saw."

The Nashville Sounds soundly beat Savannah 12-4 on April 26, but they floundered otherwise, finishing eighth. Nonetheless, they drew 380,159 fans.

In those glorious early days of Southern League baseball in Nashville, the Sounds brought out more stars than the Grand Ol' Opry. Players would peer into the stands from both dugouts with "Wow, look who's here tonight" awe. It could be Loretta Lynn or Larry Gatlin, Barbara Mandrell or any of a number of Oak Ridge Boys. Other entertainers bought into the franchise. Schmittou, a promoter at heart, had something off-beat going every night. He was a former Vandy football recruiter, after all, and was inspired by the former University of Tennessee football recruiter and track coach Chuck Rohe, who helped create the "Big Orange Country" theme.

In 1979, the Sounds won the pennant and drew 515,488, but friction developed between Schmittou and the Reds. Cincinnati didn't want to use the designated hitter, which every other team in the league employed. Despite that handicap, they won 83 games in the regular season, knocked off Memphis in the division playoffs, and beat Columbus for the title. Cincinnati would be replaced the following season by the New York Yankees. In its five seasons as the Yankees' Double-A affiliate, the Nashville Sounds would never have a losing record.

Steve "Bye Bye" Balboni arrived in Nashville in 1980, mashing 34 homers, driving in 122 runs and causing fans to arrive early to watch batting practice. "He was like Paul Bunyan," Farrell Owens said.

The next year, Don Mattingly was the Sounds' first baseman. Marveled Owens, "Mattingly was already a star. There was just something about him."

Brian Dayett inherited first base in 1982. At 5-10, 180, he seemed half the size of the larger-than-life Balboni, yet he still socked 34 regular-season home runs. His biggest homer, though, was a 12th-inning, two-run walk-off job in Game 4 of the Southern League Championship Series against Jacksonville, cinching the pennant.

In 1985, Larry Schmittou moved his Double-A franchise to Huntsville and brought a Class AAA team to Nashville. He wasn't finished in the Southern League, though. In 1993-94, after Charlotte moved up to Triple-A and the SL needed a site for its 10th team,

Schmittou opened Greer Stadium up to the Nashville Xpress, a Twins' affiliate.

It was also in 1993 that one of the minor leagues' iconic sights was unveiled. Schmittou had already incorporated a guitar into the Sounds logo, but wanted something bigger: a guitar-shaped scoreboard. He sketched a few designs on a napkin and shared them with a scoreboard manufacturer. They created the 117-foot-long board with the line score on the guitar neck and space on the body for outs, strikes, and, of course, advertisements. Said Richard Sterban, one of the Oak Ridge Boys and a Sounds owner, "It looks like Nashville. It has become the symbol of Music City."

The ballpark in which Farrell Owens sat on a July evening in 2013 was showing its age. Talk of a new stadium for Nashville has buzzed for a decade, but with NFL and NHL teams, pro baseball was less a priority for city fathers, despite the fact baseball frequently fattened the city coffers with its annual winter meetings.

"When we were there, it was like the Taj Mahal," said Baltimore Orioles manager Buck Showalter, who played for the Sounds from 1980-83. He was ambling alone toward his office in the home clubhouse at Camden Yards, not far from where his players were shooting pool and shooting the breeze between games of a day-night doubleheader against, ironically, Don Mattingly's Dodgers.

When asked for three minutes to talk about baseball in Nashville, Showalter said, "I could talk about that for hours." There were the half-million people who'd come watch in "a great baseball town." There were the nights when they'd play Memphis on quarter-beer night and "the whole park" was hammered. And there was the 1980 season when Showalter set a league record with 155 singles.

"A great minor-league player he was," said Owens. "He'd spray the ball. He was edgy. He'd get the other team mad."

Showalter recalled how he spent off-seasons working for a beer distributor and clearing land for the man who customized the Sounds' buses; the "who's who in the playoffs" in 1981 when the Sounds of Willie McGee, Don Mattingly, and Showalter swept Memphis, with Razor Shines and Terry Francona, before losing to Orlando, with Gary Gaetti and Tim Laudner in the championship round; and one other moment, which stood out more than anything else.

"I met my wife there," Showalter said. "That's the best thing that happened."

Angela Showalter was an usherette at Greer Stadium.

Let history note this: Farrell Owens introduced Showalter to Angela.

PENSACOLA, FLORIDA

Location, location, location

Bruce Baldwin was standing on the plush infield grass of Pensacola Bayfront Stadium, basking in a Ray Kinsella moment. Pensacola has built it, and they have come in droves.

Resting on a peninsula that juts into Pensacola Bay, Bayfront Stadium is a jewel. It is home to the Pensacola Blue Wahoos, who joined the Southern League in 2012. It's one of the most lovely settings anywhere in baseball.

A group judging the best stadium in baseball during that inaugural season visited Pensacola and noted they had recently toured Marlins Stadium in Miami. The group made a fuss over the Marlins' two 20-foot, 450-gallon salt-water aquariums behind home plate, which have become a source of controversy. To which Baldwin, the Wahoos' president, slyly countered, sweeping his arm theatrically across the bay, "We've got one bigger than theirs. And it was free."

Pensacola Bayfront Stadium won the award.

A cornfield becoming a field of dreams was nothing compared to the vision of team owner Quint Studer and city officials for this piece of property. This was a field of weeds, belted by a rusting fence. It was inhabited by vagrants. To declare the land an "eyesore," as long-time Pensacola sportswriter Bill Vilona did, is to employ kind understatement. The property featured civic monuments of ugliness, a sewage treatment plant, and empty tanks from an abandoned oil refinery. Cross two bridges and you can find some of the most beautiful sugary white beaches in the country, but downtown Pensacola wasn't overburdened with aesthetic appeal.

Bayfront Stadium has helped change that.

The stadium is the league's smallest, and that may be part of its secret. The fold-up traditional stadium seats number less than 4,000, but they are plentiful for those who wish to immerse themselves in the game. It also put a premium on the seats, making them a hot ticket. There is an oyster bar and three sun-splashed party decks where fans sit at shiny, high-top aluminum tables and bask both in baseball and the view, bringing the announced capacity to 5,038. The party decks are popular with the younger crowd that comes for the social aspect, a diversion from Pensacola's rustic beach bars and nearby hot spots like McGuire's Irish Pub, a funky establishment of dining rooms and catacombs, where more than $1 million in one-dollar bills have been stapled to the walls and ceilings.

Bayfront Stadium had 40 sellouts (out of 68 dates) in 2012, and the Blue Wahoos were the hottest story in town. They sold 3,000 season tickets, and kept that base for Season Two. Even if the novelty of a new franchise and new park first drew fans, the events and the operation—"we believe in taking the best and making it better" is a Baldwin credo—got the fans to come, and to come back.

"For a first-year ball club, we had too many neat things happen," Baldwin said. "Those are things you want to spread out if you can write the script." But nobody might have written a script that included a pitcher who'd finish with a .500 record, who'd never seen the eighth inning in his professional career, being part of a combined no-hitter that was caught by a backup catcher with six previous games in Double A, with the win assured by another player's first Double-A home run.

The day was June 16, 2012, with a sellout crowd on hand. Daniel Corcino, a 21-year-old right-hander from the Dominican Republic, started for the Blue Wahoos against Mobile, Pensacola's rival 50 miles to the west. His catcher was Chris Berset, a backup who'd be demoted to Class A six days later. It took a while, like a wave slowly building to a crest, for the fans to realize history was unfolding. Third baseman David Vidal kept the no-hitter alive with a great defensive play in the fifth. Then, as the Saturday night social crowd joined the baseball crowd in recognizing the no-hitter was in progress, the stadium grew tense. In the seventh, Corcino struck out the side. Vidal's first Double-A homer lifted the Blue Wahoos into a 3-0 lead going into the eighth, where Corcino whiffed two more.

In the bottom of the eighth, pinch-hitter Josh Fellhauer came up to bat for the pitcher, and the boos rained down on Pensacola manager Jim Riggleman. (The former big league manager had to explain later through the media that Daniel Corcino was on a careful pitch count and long-term development couldn't be sacrificed.) Happily, Wilkin De La Rosa, a journeyman reliever playing for his 10th different minor-league club, retired the side in the ninth to complete the combined no-hitter.

"We had the no-hitter. We had a Blue Angels fly-over, not once but twice," Baldwin said. "We had all the stuff. Bayfront Stadium. Forty sellouts. Boom! Everything. Then all of a sudden here comes this guy named Billy Hamilton."

On July 10, shortstop Didi Gregorius, arguably the Wahoos' fan favorite during the first half of the season, was promoted to Triple-A Louisville. To fill his spot, the Reds promoted the fastest man in baseball, a slender 21-year-old native of Mississippi.

In 1983, Vince Coleman set a professional baseball record with 145 stolen bases for Macon. Billy Hamilton arrived in Pensacola having already nabbed 104 bags at Class A-Advanced Bakersfield. He proceeded to swipe 51 more in Pensacola, topping Coleman's mark with a theft of third in the first game of an August 21 doubleheader against Montgomery.

None of this would ever happened without the vision of Quint Studer, a transplant from Wisconsin who made his fortune in the health-care business, and the guidance of Bruce Baldwin, who had cut his teeth in the Southern League decades ago at Savannah and Greenville. It was nearly a quarter-century in the making, in fact.

In 1987, Pensacola was examined as a potential site to which a struggling Southern League team might relocate, but the public support for a new stadium wasn't there. Studer bought an independent league team in 2002 that played on the campus of the University of West Florida, whetting the appetite for something bigger and better, especially as it might enhance downtown development. But Hurricane Ivan readjusted priorities in 2004, causing more than $6 billion in damage to the area.

After sufficient recovery, Studer revisited the downtown stadium options, looking at that ugly, abandoned property on the bay. Baldwin was enlisted first in a consultant role, then persuaded to take over leadership as president. Having been a part of previous new stadium construction at Greenville, South Carolina, Richmond, Virginia, and Gwinnett County, Georgia, he was a logical ally for Studer. There was resistance to spending money for the stadium, most of which went into the purchase and environmental improvement of the land, and it drew more than a few protesters. "Spotted-owl tree-huggers," Baldwin called them, a nod to his Pacific Northwest upbringing.

But approval was given in April 2009 and ground broken that September. A contest was held to determine the nickname, with Blue Wahoos winning out over Mullets, Aviators, Salty Dogs, and others. The logo and the mascot, a furry critter named Kazoo, were ingeniously unveiled during "Gallery Night," an annual event drawing thousands downtown.

All that done, "getting the team was the easy part," Vilona said. Studer arranged to buy the Carolina Mudcats, Cincinnati's Double-A club in Zebulon, North Carolina, for the move to Pensacola, leaving Zebulon to join the more geographically friendly Carolina League. "It was an arduous opportunity," Baldwin said, "but it was the only opportunity. Quint had to drop a lot of dimes, but he never wavered."

As Baldwin continued his tour, he came to the distant left-field corner. "Worst seats in the place, right?" he said, entering a gate that swung loose on the hinges. One imagined it'd be loose less than an hour before a worker made proper repairs. Baldwin climbed the steps through the stands to still another party deck, the one to be used by patrons in those seats. "Now look," he said. He gestured to a spectacular view of the bay, to his free aquarium, to a priceless panorama.

RICKWOOD
FIELD

Living history

It was a warm, glorious late May afternoon when they turned the clock back at Rickwood Field. The Birmingham Barons' staff wore skinny clip-on bow ties and vests. Broadcaster Curt Bloom was in suspenders and a hat, the houndstooth variety made popular in the area decades ago by Paul "Bear" Bryant. The umpires were in crisp white shirts and bow ties, the players of the Birmingham Barons and Tennessee Smokies were in white and gray faux flannel.

A band played "The Star-Spangled Banner" with a Tommy Dorsey/Swing Era flavor. There was almost a packed house, 7,200-plus, many keeping cool with cardboard church fans. If you drove up in a 2010 Toyota, you felt guilty for not wheeling into the lot in an Olds Coupe with running boards.

Ferguson Jenkins, the first modern-era Southern Leaguer inducted into the Baseball Hall of Fame, threw out the first pitch and acknowledged, "I was excited. I was only 19 when I first started [coming through with the Chattanooga Lookouts] and now I'm 70. It kinda wracks your brain to see it all again."

The Rickwood Classic is Birmingham's annual paean to anachronism, taking place in America's oldest minor-league ballpark, having opened in 1910.

Wayne Martin, a long-time sportswriter in Birmingham, trudged up to the Rickwood roof, where he spent so many evenings in a since-demolished press box, and where the writers would occasionally flaunt fire regulations and common sense by cooking steaks on a charcoal grill. He posed for a photo with the old-timey scoreboard in left field in the background, then trundled back downstairs to grab a seat in the next-to-last row of the grandstands, where he wracked his own brain.

He talked of old-time visiting baseball managers like Don Zimmer and Clint Courtney, "who'd wilt the grass" with their profanity. He recalled the opening night of 1967 when Rollie Fingers took a line drive to the jaw and was hauled off in an ambulance, only to have another ambulance called innings later when Art Miranda took one in the noggin while in the on-deck circle. He talked of Mamie van Doren, the buxom 1960s actress who was briefly married to Barons' pitcher Lee Meyers, a lefty with only a passing familiarity with the strike zone but was otherwise widely admired by his peers. Said Martin, "There would only be 200 people at the ballpark, and Mamie would show up dressed like a Hollywood starlet."

In some ways, Rickwood has gone the starlet route. It was a glamorous place, a stunning beauty in its youth, who sought to still remain gorgeous and relevant in old age. But adjustments and facelifts could only do so much, and the park fell out of the limelight. The Barons closed up shop at Rickwood and moved to suburban Hoover after the 1987 season. Ah, but through the grace of an organization called Friends of Rickwood, the grand old park still makes an annual appearance at the Classic and is still the site of amateur games and fantasy camps.

In its long history, Rickwood Field has had more grand openings and going-out-of-business moments than a discount furniture store. It resides in a decaying neighborhood, a description appropriate even a quarter-century ago before the Barons bolted to the suburbs. Owner Art Clarkson heard one day what he assumed was a car backfiring, only to look out of his office window and see one stranger chasing another down the street with a gun.

The historic ballpark sits at the west end of an elongated diamond-shaped path of Birmingham sports geography. To the east, at the cusp of downtown, sits the Barons' stunning $64-million stadium that opened for the 2013 season. To the north, easily spied from atop the spongy Rickwood roof, is Legion Field, home to countless historic football games. To the south is Elmwood Cemetery, where Bear Bryant was interred in 1983; others buried there include Negro Leagues icon Piper Davis and former major leaguers Ben Chapman, Spud Davis, Luman Harris, and Dixie Walker.

The Barons—shortened in the 1880s from Coal Barons—first played at a facility that opened in 1896. The field was known better by its unofficial name of the "Slag Pile," rather than West End Park. That team was purchased in February 1910 by A.H. "Rick" Woodward, against his father's wishes, and he made plans for a new concrete-and-steel stadium that would become something of his namesake.

On August 18, 1910, every major business in Birmingham shut down for the grand opening. The West Clothing Company on North 20th Street, advertised its $18, $20 and $25 men's wool suits for the drastic discount of $7.95, $9.95 and $11.95. The *Birmingham News* suggested that visiting team officials "will see sights never before presented in the Southern League, and which will never again be equaled." Other headlines proclaimed it was a "model of beauty and convenience [that] causes a dawn of new and brilliant baseball." The newspaper's Walter Harper was inspired toward verse:

> *"The sun was soft as woman's smiles;*
>
> *The air as crisp as new spring styles*
>
> *And peace lay on the land for miles*
>
> *Through all the vital forenoon*
>
> *But Rickwood saw another sight*
>
> *When the fan howled to see the fight*
>
> *And crowded center, left and right,*
>
> *On the grandstand and bleacher"*

The 10,000-plus crowd of that opening day saw the Barons beat Montgomery 3-2. Rickwood continued to draw massive crowds through the years. They drew more than 160,000 eight seasons in the 1920s. There were 20,074 there the night Ray Caldwell outdueled Dizzy Dean in the Dixie Series in 1931. Alas, success couldn't be maintained consistently. Woodward, battered by the Great Depression, had to sell the team in 1938. Pro baseball disappeared in 1962-63, returned in '64 for the new Southern League, left for Mobile after two years, then came back in 1967 under Charles O. Finley's leadership before moving to Chattanooga in 1976.

The University of Alabama-Birmingham baseball team, coached by Harry "The Hat" Walker, began using the stadium until Clarkson brought pro ball back in 1981. Birmingham reopened Rickwood on April 14, with a Tigers farm club transported up Interstate 65 from Montgomery. Mike Laga socked a two-out, 11th-inning homer into those right-field bleachers for a 6-5 win over Jacksonville before a crowd of 9,185. They closed Rickwood at 10:54 p.m. on Sept. 9, 1987, with manager Rico Petrocelli's team losing 5-4 to Charlotte in the second game of the Southern League championship series.

Rickwood Field was modeled after Philadelphia's old Shibe Park, including a most daunting and charming quirk: It is 90 feet from home plate to the backstop. Grumbled an old Barons' catcher, "A wild pitch and you gotta take a cab ride to go get it." The original distances to the outfield wall were two bus rides and a pleasant walk, then ranging 400 to left, 470 to center, and 334 to right. The light stanchions rose up inside the fences and thus in play. A covered grandstand section elbowed around the right-field foul pole. To the left sat another set of bleachers, now demolished. That was where all African-American fans were forced to sit prior to 1964.

There is now a plaque on the wall, marked with a big X, commemorating a 467-foot homer hit by Walt Dropo in the 1948 Dixie Series. The day after the homer, Dropo and sportswriter Alf Van Hoose strolled out to the wall it struck beyond the outfield fence and found where the ball hit, painting a white X to mark the spot.

The stadium seating once featured another note of interest. When the Polo Grounds was being torn down in New York, Birmingham officials bought seats and installed them at Rickwood, the NY logo etched in them looking incongruous in the Deep South. During the park's heyday, uncovered stands stretched all the way down the line in left. Once the team left in 1975, they fell victim to the elements. The Polo Grounds seats were torn out, many of them sold for scrap.

In its current incarnation, Rickwood's outfield signs and scoreboard are "period pieces," the creation of set designers to make the place look more authentic on film. The field has served as the location for several movies, including *Cobb* and *42*. Maintained Wayne Martin, "I don't think the movies made Rickwood famous. I think the movies came because Rickwood was famous."

Martin grew up in Chilton County, outside Birmingham, where his family followed the Barons in the old *Birmingham Post*. His sister created a scrapbook of Barons news. When Martin finally got to see Rickwood for the first time, it was a majestic place for a 14-year-old kid.

"The thing I remember most was walking out that tunnel on the third base side and seeing how green the grass was," he said while gesturing. "I don't know it was really that green, but it was shining. It looked like it glowed."

On a May afternoon when they turned the clock back, the grass glowed again. So did everything about this old gem, this dignified old starlet making her annual curtain call.

THE PLAYERS

Jose Canseco with the Huntsville Stars.

JIM BOUTON

Beyond "Ball Four"

There wasn't much in the budget for a ground crew at Savannah's Grayson Stadium, just a couple of guys provided by the city. They chalked the baselines and batters box, dragged the infield and mowed the grass, occasionally coming across smelly souvenirs left in the outfield by the tandem of guard dogs, aptly named "Grayson" and "Stadium."

Once a homestand in the 1978 season, the crew got an assist from a 39-year-old man who was spending his summer in Savannah. So precise and finicky was Jim Bouton that late at night on the eve of a start, or early in the morning of game day, he'd tend to the pitcher's mound the way a sculptor might caress and mold a work of art.

If it wasn't totally a masterpiece of a season, it was a magical one. Bouton, a pariah in the game after writing the groundbreaking, controversial *Ball Four* in 1970, a one-time fireballer with the New York Yankees left clinging to a capricious knuckleball and a low-caliber arsenal of breaking pitches, completed a stunning comeback and punctuated his baseball career as a pitcher/guru/father-figure for the 1978 Savannah Braves. He went 11-9, and his work ethic earned him the league's "Best Hustler Award," an honor more typically bestowed on base-swiping outfielders and dervish-like shortstops than 39-year-old authors.

"It was a key moment in a very important year in my life," Bouton recalled. "I was trying to come back from a career in the television business as a sportscaster, and as an author and actor in the sitcom, *Ball Four*. I really needed to get away from the studio. I needed to get away and see how far I could go playing baseball."

Bouton had alienated much of baseball's conservative power structure with the book *Ball Four*, a delicious diary of revelations that—gasp!—some of baseball's heroes might enjoy the occasional cocktail or behave in less than saintly ways while on road trips. He kept notes, dictated moments, and worked with Leonard Schecter to construct a diary of the 1969 season, when he played with the expansion Seattle Pilots and the Houston Astros. Having ruffled feathers, and featuring the maligned, capricious knuckleball as his primary pitch, he found himself out of the game in August 1970, released by the Astros after 29 appearances, sporting a 5.40 ERA.

However, Bouton had achieved fame—or infamy, depending on the viewpoint—and that notoriety carried him into the broadcasting business, and into acting, where Hollywood did what Hollywood often does, taking a good premise and turning it into a bad TV show. Baseball kept itching at him throughout these endeavors. As he poetically ended *Ball Four*, "You spend a good piece of your life gripping a baseball and in the end it turns out it was the other way around."

Bouton concocted a comeback in 1977, convincing the unconventional Bill Veeck to give him a shot in the White Sox organization. Bouton and his knuckleball went 0-6 at Knoxville, which prompted a lot of smiles behind the graybeards of the Southern League at the time. He bounced to Durango, Mexico, then finished at Portland, Oregon, at a Class A team. Fortune smiled on him there. Bouton and teammate Rob Nelson created "Big League Chew" while in Portland, selling shredded pink bubblegum in a chewing-tobacco-style pouch. Nelson had the idea, Bouton the influence, and soon it was being produced by the Wrigley Company.

The next season, Bouton approached Ted Turner, the Atlanta Braves' owner and a man who made Bill Veeck seem like a hopeless introvert by comparison. Turner, himself 39 years of age, was charmed by Bouton. As owner of one of the newfangled "superstations" bouncing signals off satellites, he saw Bouton as a ratings-getter should the comeback work. As Bouton would later write in *Sports Illustrated*, "Ted had promised me a fair chance, and I believed him. Now all I had to do was be sensational."

Hank Aaron, the Braves icon who was working as the director of minor-league operations, didn't find Bouton very sensational. He released him. But Bouton pleaded his case with Turner, who arranged for him to go to Class AAA Richmond as a batting practice pitcher. When Atlanta came to Richmond for an exhibition game, Bouton started for the minor-league club and struck out seven in seven innings. He was activated and assigned to Savannah. Before his first appearance there, general manager Dave Fendrick announced that anyone bringing a copy of *Ball Four* would be admitted free.

Before Bouton's arrival, Savannah manager Bobby Dews held a team meeting. There was no great celebration among the Braves when they learned a 39-year-old ex-big-leaguer was coming in. One of the Braves would have to be demoted or deactivated to make space on the roster. Nobody wanted to room with Bouton. "What the hell do we need him for?" they asked. "He's had his time. We want our chance."

Then Bouton mesmerized them with his work ethic and his personality, just as he mesmerized hopeless batters.

Roger Alexander reached out to become his roommate. Theirs became the gathering spot on many road trips.

"The players resented me a little bit, but they saw I was a hard worker," Bouton said. "In spring training I was running laps, I was ahead of everybody because I didn't want to look like an old man. After they put me into the (Savannah) rotation, I was pitching well. We were rocking and rolling. We'd sit in the hotel room with Roger and my teammates and they wanted to ask me questions, like 'Jim, what's it like in the big leagues?' 'What do you think we should work on?' Then they were asking me questions about their girl-friend problems. Sometimes they involved a number of girlfriends that needed to be sorted out and answers needed to be provided. I was the old guru. I was not just the old ball player, I was now somehow this psychologist. I had no training whatsoever, but I had a few years on me and somehow they thought I must have a lot of wisdom."

"He was a fun guy to have around," Fendrick said. "He was our best pitcher. He sold tickets. Having him there was a great experience for me. *Sports Illustrated* did a story, and *Sports Illustrated* coming to Savannah for Double-A baseball was a big deal."

For the magazine, Frank Deford wrote:

In the middle of his life, when all the children he grew up with have turned in their mitts and marbles, Bouton plays the boy again in the Class AA Southern League, starting every fifth day for the Savannah nine, throwing against the bats of certified prospects who can tell the correct time of life. One motive for this mad indulgence is, surely, a search for vanished youth.

The indulgence led Jim Bouton back to the majors. The Braves promoted him and assigned him a start on September 10 against Don Sutton and the Los Angeles Dodgers. Once again, controversy surrounded Bouton. Los Angeles was in a hot pennant race with Cincinnati and San Francisco. The other managers cried "unfair!", that the Dodgers could face this soft-tossing old geezer and they couldn't. Eventually Commissioner Bowie Kuhn, Bouton's old strait-laced adversary, ordered the Braves to pitch him against the Reds and Giants as well. (Bouton once noted Kuhn's office was "decorated in Early Authority.") The Dodgers defeated Bouton and the Braves, 11-5, with Sutton tossing a complete game.

On September 14, the Giants received their chance. Bouton beat them 4-1, allowing only three hits in six innings. San Francisco was left eight games behind Los Angeles.

Jim Bouton never won another major-league game. Fact is, the major leagues had lost their grip on him. "Those little cement boxes with nails [what passed for lockers in the Savannah clubhouse], it was very primitive. But it was just what I needed. It was great to put your house in order and go back to the basics, playing ball, and having fun."

JOSE CANSECO

The Ballad of Parkway Jose

On a partly cloudy, 85-degree fall day in central Florida, Jose Canseco experienced what Super Bowl-winning quarterbacks and beleaguered fathers from across the country have in common, taking his family on a trip to Walt Disney World. He also took a moment to indulge his Twitter addiction: "They should create a Jose Canseco characature [sic] for Disney."

Forgive the spelling and agree with the sentiment. From his first day in a Huntsville Stars uniform through the end of his controversial career, Jose Canseco was always part character, part caricature.

If Canseco wasn't the greatest talent and best prospect in the Southern League in its first half-century—many will argue that he was, among them the league's late president Don Mincher—he was on the short list.

Canseco was on the Huntsville Stars' inaugural team in 1985, winning the league MVP award despite playing only 58 games. In that time, he bashed 25 home runs and drove in 80 runs, batting .318. (That equates to 62 homers and 199 RBI over the course of a 144-game schedule.) On June 24, he hit three homers and drove in nine runs in the first game of a doubleheader at Birmingham. "I set so many records it was a joke," he wrote in his autobiography.

"Every time he went to the plate, you expected something big to happen," said David Sharp, then the Stars' batboy. "He could mash. Everybody watched when he went to the plate."

"It was unreal," said Larry Schmittou, the Stars' owner at the time. "He became a legend."

As Canseco would later say, in enormous understatement, "It was a great period in my early baseball career."

And, indeed, it was a great period in Huntsville's baseball life. The

Stars brought home the pennant in 1985, hitting 139 homers and scoring 729 runs. "They put on a show every night," said Bob Mayes, who covered the Stars for the *Huntsville Times*. Interestingly, for all of the Stars' power, the first home run at Joe Davis Stadium never left the park; Ray Thoma had an infield-the-park homer to center field in the first inning of the opener.

Huntsville, with Canseco joined by Oakland A's prospects like Terry Steinbach, Stan Javier, and Luis Polonia, won the pennant in a five-game series over Charlotte, with an extra-inning homer by crowd-favorite Rocky Coyle, long after Canseco had been promoted. "I told Don [Mincher, then the Stars' GM] this is the worst thing that can happen to Huntsville. You don't need to have the best team you ever had the first year," Schmittou said. No worries; the Stars won their division again each of the next two years.

(In 1986, Thoma was supplanted at third by a red-headed Southern Cal product named Mark McGwire. "Shame he never panned out and took advantage of that situation," Thoma joked. McGwire batted a mere .303 in 50 games, with 53 RBI and 10 homers.)

Joe Davis Stadium sits just off Memorial Parkway, which prompted a nickname for Jose Canseco. In the state where Alabama product "Broadway Joe" Namath is revered, Canseco became "Parkway Jose." Across the parkway was a lumberyard where second-shift workers listened to Stars' games, flashing a red light atop the building every time Canseco homered.

Despite the rumors to the contrary, the right-handed Canseco never reached the parkway located a football-field's distance beyond the right-field fence. But epic homers did become part of the Canseco legend. Schmittou swears he saw one travel at least 500 feet. Jimmy Jones, a former Huntsville player who roomed with Canseco at Triple-A, saw one at Tacoma that was still rising as it cleared a light-tower. Jones also recalled batting practices at spring training with Canseco and McGwire where they hit so many out at the minor-league complex into a cotton field, pitchers were dispatched outside the fence, keeping one eye on home-run balls, the other on rattlesnakes.

The cynic may well respond that these were homers produced via chemistry. Canseco finished his '84 season in Single-A as a lean, 6-3, 185-pounder. Bruce Robinson, an Oakland special instructor sent to work with him them, recalled a stubborn kid who had to be convinced that any changes were his own idea. One of Canseco's other ideas: steroids. He confessed to using them that off-season, showing up in camp at 230. "The players were walking around in awe," Mayes said.

He continued his juicing in Huntsville, a story later confirmed by the local gym owner where he worked out and purchased the performance-enhancing medicine.

For all that, and for the troubles that both pursued him and that he often pursued during his major-league career, Canseco could be a good friend and teammate. When he reached the majors, he often packed up boxes full of equipment to send to Jones to have him distribute among minor leaguers.

"One thing I can tell you about Jose Canseco, he played hard," said Jones, who keeps in contact with Canseco. "When he said something, it was always the truth."

David Sharp, the one-time Huntsville batboy, wrestles with a dilemma. He enjoyed a good relationship with Canseco in 1985. Now Sharp is the head baseball coach at Huntsville High School. (Small world: He inherited the job from Mark Mincher, Don Mincher's son.) "My impression of Jose has changed," Sharp said, sitting in his office next in the Huntsville locker room. "It doesn't mean I dislike him. But the situation I'm in now, I'm leading young kids. And I'm going to do what I can do and lead these kids in the right direction. Has it changed my opinion of him? Yes. But I know how he treated me individually."

When Sharp was the age of his players, he wore No. 33 in tribute to Jose Canseco. He carried 33 cents in change in the back pocket of his uniform. A Canseco poster was on his wall. He and the Stars' star had developed enough of a bond that on Canseco's final night in Huntsville, he grabbed Sharp by the arm and said, "Let's go play catch." Said Sharp, "He was one of those guys that just drew you to him."

As Sharp began his college-playing career at Montgomery's Faulkner University, he naturally shared Canseco stories with his teammates. And, equally naturally, they were skeptical.

In the fall of 1992, Jose made an appearance in court in Montgomery regarding an autograph show snafu. Sharp and a teammate skipped class and went to the courthouse; Canseco not only remembered him, he asked, "Hey, what are you doing tonight? I'm going to Montgomery Athletic Center to play wally-ball (volleyball on a racquetball court). Why don't you and some of your teammates come and play?"

So David Sharp and seven or eight teammates joined Canseco, skepticism firmly erased there in a 40×20 room with a character they'd only known from a distance.

JOE
CHARBONEAU

Super Joe's boast

The Spanish Trail Inn sat on the fringe of Tucson, a motel whose name might ring with some bit of romance but whose conditions would not bring to the mind the words "Ritz" or "Four Seasons." The rooms were large, the group rates generous, and the freeway nearby. It was a perfect locale for a baseball organization to encamp its minor leaguers.

On a March night in 1979, Joe Charboneau sat on a bed at the Spanish Trail Inn, conducting his first in-depth interview as a member of the Chattanooga Lookouts. There was an Ali moment in that interview. "I'm going to lead the Southern League in batting," he said.

It would later emerge that Charboneau was merely trying to entertain his roommate, Dave Rivera, but he made good on the promise. He batted .352 to lead the league, adding 21 homers and 78 RBI in 109 games. He was a postseason Southern League All-Star, though he was denied the league MVP award. (Danny Heep and Alan Knicely, from an 84-win Columbus team, were voted co-MVPs.)

It was Charboneau's outsized personality as much as his talent that made him stand out, both in the minors and in his meteoric major-league career. It was part of an era when "flake" was a cherished and loving compliment. Baseball had just been refreshed by the irrepressible Mark "The Bird" Fidrych of the Detroit Tigers, with his squirrely antics, talking to the baseball, manicuring the mound on hands and knees, and his quirky quotes. (Fidrych, who died in 2009 in a freak accident on his Massachusetts farm, was himself a

Southern League graduate; he was 2-0 with four saves in seven relief appearances for Montgomery in 1975, the season before his fabulous rookie year in Detroit.)

Baseball in the 1970s was a game remembered more for its multi-purpose, cookie-cutter, artificially turfed round stadiums that seemed to have alit on earth from a distant, and very boring, planet. The pastime received a much-needed charisma transplant with Fidrych. Suddenly it was OK to be a little different, a little flaky.

Charboneau fit that description in spades. He was surrounded on those Lookouts by more than a few other characters. The club was managed by a baseball lifer named Woody Smith, whose playing career topped out at Triple-A, and he fretted his players might make the same career-stunting mistakes he had made. He was once discovered by his players hiding out in a dumpster, with a folding chair and a six-pack, to detect curfew violators.

The second baseman was Kevin Rhomberg, who'd get a cup of coffee with the Indians. Rhomberg was uniquely superstitious and would not allow himself to be "touched last." Were a teammate to pat him on the back, Rhomberg would have to touch the teammate back. On more than one occasion, after stealing a base and being tagged in vain by an infielder, he'd call time-out and meander around, seemingly adjusting himself or brushing off dirt; he was actually going back to make subtle contact with the infielder.

Pitcher John Arnold once ventured into an all-night coffee shop on a road trip only to discover an angst-ridden server in a screaming fit with an over-served patron. When it became clear the patron was the mother of the server, and who seemed less than strict in her morals, Arnold said to a companion, "Give me all your quarters." He proceeded to play every song about mothers on the diner's jukebox, of which there was no small shortage at a 24/7 restaurant in the middle of nowhere Georgia.

Pitcher Robin Fuson joined the team in late-season. He owned a pet mole, embraced the label of "flake" and would candidly admit he began thinking of pitching a no-hitter "if I get the first batter out." In 1981, he was pitching a fall league game against "this $200,000 bonus baby for the Mets, back when $200,000 was a big bonus," Fuson recalled. The bonus baby was named Darryl Strawberry. Fuson struck out Strawberry twice, then plunked him in the helmet with a pitch in the last at-bat. Two decades later, Fuson was an assistant district attorney in Hillsborough County (Florida). Among the cases he prosecuted was one of Darryl Strawberry's drug arrests.

Joe Charboneau's major-league career was almost Fidrych-esque in its brevity. He was the 1980 American League Rookie of the Year, batting .289 and hitting 23 homers with 87 RBI, the season after he had fulfilled his prediction of a batting title at Chattanooga. He had no shortage of flaky antics. He could open a beer bottle with his eye socket. He could drink beer through his nose. He once sewed a gash in his own arm with fishing line. The media ate it up. He was the subject of a biography, by Terry Pluto, and a 45-rpm record, "Go Joe Charboneau." But back injuries stymied his career. He was out of the majors by the 1982 season, after only 201 games, even returning to Chattanooga for rehab work in '82.

For all the hype, and for a temper that could erupt like a geyser, he remained down-to-earth with fans and friends. Said the afore-mentioned Arnold, "He was something else. It was nuts, but he's got a big heart. He'd do anything for you." When a visiting journalist was headed to Cleveland, Charboneau demanded, "You're staying at my place." When the offer was refused, he countered, with obvi-ous awareness of the world of expense-account travel, "OK, there's a hotel near my house and I know the owner. You can stay for free and he'll give you a blank receipt."

To commemorate his batting championship, Charboneau agreed to a photo shoot for the afternoon newspaper. He was fitted for a powder-blue tuxedo with a frilly shirt—we did say it was 1979, after all—and posed in outfield behind a table with a red-and-white checkered cloth. A champagne bucket rested on the table and Char-boneau held a glass in the air. The iconic concrete LOOKOUTS sign, planted on an embankment inside the centerfield fence, served as the background. When he shed the tuxedo and climbed back into T-shirt and jeans inside the clubhouse, he grabbed his wallet. He was on a meager minor-league salary then, but he tugged out some cash and ordered, "Before you take the tux back, stop and buy some flow-ers for that lady at the tux place for being so nice to us."

When his career seemed to have ended, he was tending bar in Buffalo and awarded a small role in the movie *The Natural*, starring

Robert Redford. It was almost painfully ironic, with Charboneau himself having more than a passing similarity to Roy Hobbs.

The spring of 1984 found him in a motel-like dormitory room in Bradenton, Florida, sitting on a bed and wearing jeans and a University of Buffalo sweatshirt as a teammate re-strung a catcher's mitt and spat tobacco juice into a wastebasket. After three back surgeries, Charboneau was given the opportunity to make a comeback with the Pittsburgh Pirates. He laughed that "the craziest thing I've done lately is sign another pro contract." Some lines to an old Kris Kristofferson song, "The Pilgrim," were recited to Charboneau, about if "the goin' up was worth the comin' down."

"It is. It is. I've got to remember that line," he said. "Geez, you know, I really wouldn't change anything about that, either."

BILLY HAMILTON

History in a flash

"*Bil-ly! Bil-ly! Bil-ly!*"

The crowd at Pensacola's Bayfront Stadium came to life in unison. There was no one waiting in line for food. The restrooms were empty as a politician's promise. Those cooling inside at the oyster bar ducked outside, those on the party decks stopped their conversations and sat their drinks down.

Billy Hamilton stepped into the batter's box.

"*Bil-ly! Bil-ly! Bil-ly!*"

Hamilton reached first base. The crowd stilled in anticipation.

"When he got on base, everybody sat in their seats," said Blue Wahoos president Bruce Baldwin.

"He's always on first, then stealing second," said Huntsville Stars manager Darnell Coles.

And, sure enough, there he went.

"*Bil-ly! Bil-ly! Bil-ly!*"

From a lead at second base, third base is even closer. It's just as vulnerable.

Just as it was on Tuesday, August 21, 2012. It was still early, 40 minutes into the first game of a doubleheader. The usual 5,000-plus crowd hadn't yet filled the park. Hamilton singled off Montgomery pitcher Kyle Lobstein in the third, routinely stole second, then set out for third. Biscuits catcher Mark Thomas made an impeccable throw, but too late. With a headfirst slide, Hamilton was safe.

"*Bil-ly! Bil-ly! Bil-ly!*"

The crowd erupted even more than usual after a Billy Hamilton steal which, truth be told, had become routine as brushing your teeth in the morning. This one was different. It was his 146th steal of the season, achieved in a mere 120 games. He had broken the record for most stolen bases in pro baseball, set by Vince Coleman of the Macon Redbirds in 1983, with 145. Third base was lifted from the ground, all set to be shipped to the Baseball Hall of Fame in Cooperstown, New York.

There's already one Billy Hamilton there in Cooperstown. William Robert "Sliding Billy" Hamilton—not related to *"Bil-ly"*—was enshrined in 1961. Speed must come with the name; Sliding Billy ranks third all-time on the major-league list for most career stolen bases, his total of 914 from 1888 to 1901 ranks behind only Rickey Henderson and Lou Brock. Considering, then, the Hall of Famer's career preceded that of the current Billy Hamilton by more than a century—Sliding Billy died in 1940—it's not inappropriate to conclude that young Billy R. Hamilton of Taylorsville, Mississippi, is a once-in-a-lifetime talent.

Hamilton finished the 2012 season with 155 stolen bases, 104 of those coming before a July 10 promotion from Bakersfield to Pensacola. That, after 103 the previous year at Single-A Dayton. Said Hamilton, "I didn't come up expecting to be a record-breaker like this." He was initially a shortstop, but made the transition to center field during the 2012 Arizona Fall League en route to a 2013 promotion to Class AAA Louisville. The wordplay can't be resisted: the Cincinnati Reds had put Hamilton on the fast track. He is relatively small, at 6-foot, 160, but that still would let him tower over the stockier 5-foot-6 Sliding Billy.

Billy Hamilton, too, has impressed baseball experts not only with his speed, but his plate discipline and surprising pop in his bat. The Reds have transformed him into a switch hitter. From the right side he's more a free-swinger, from the left, he seeks to make contact to use his speed.

Regard this bit of baseball philosophy: "I have not watched many baseball games in the past years, because the players really didn't show me the fundamentals from day in and day out how to manufacture runs. ... Guys that steal bases have become obsolete. If I talked to Billy, I would let him know the game doesn't change, no matter what level you are at. Ever since I was eight years old, I thought I was Willie Mays, so you couldn't tell me there was something I couldn't do. He is in Double-A now, and I expect to see the same kind of progression, day in and day out."

That wisdom comes from a pretty good source: Vince Coleman, in an interview with Bill Vilona of the *Pensacola News-Journal.*

"This kid has world-class speed," Darnell Coles said. "If he hits the ball and it bounces twice, it's safe. Same thing with Deion [Sanders]." Coles, a 13-year major-league veteran, has compared Hamilton's speed with Sanders and Donnell Nixon, a former teammate in the Seattle organization who still holds the Southern League record of 102 stolen bases. Bo Jackson next comes to Coles' mind. "But Bo was a different kind of speed, strong, get-out-of-the-way speed. If he's stealing a base you're laying the tag down but you're laying it down gently and getting out of the way."

Billy Gardner, Jr., the Montgomery manager whose team was victimized for the record-breaking theft, figured the best way to get an out against Pensacola when Hamilton was on base was not to even worry about tagging him. "A lot of times, we'd just throw at the back-side runner (on a Blue Wahoos' double steal) and ignore him," Gardner said. "He could just fly. He made you very uncomfortable when he got on base. His approach was classic leadoff-type approach. He was going to work the count. He'd accept a walk. He knew what his role was. You just look to try to contain him. You're not going to stop him."

Even if baseball fundamentals remain pitching and defense, and even if Nike tried to convince us years ago that "chicks dig the long ball," Pensacola fans dug speed. They were enthralled by Hamilton, even though he played less than half the season with the Blue Wahoos, in their first year in the Southern League.

"He created a buzz in this town," said Vilona. "Everybody knew Billy Hamilton. That helped elevate the profile of the team and the whole experience."

"That might have been the first time in my career I have seen people come to a ball game to watch an individual," Baldwin said. "Every time he came to the plate, there was a buzz in the stadium. It was amazing. I never saw Mickey Mantle play, or Babe Ruth or Reggie Jackson, or Vince Coleman when he got on first base. But I think if Billy Hamilton makes it, he will be in that upper stratosphere.

"It was magic. It really was."

BO JACKSON

Incomparable

Professional baseball was returning to Birmingham on April 14, 1981, after a five-year absence. The Barons were opening the Southern League season at old Rickwood Field, the aging starlet of a ballpark on the city's decaying west side. The *Birmingham News* was giving appropriate sports-front coverage to the impending event.

But flip deeper into the section, to a page devoted to high-school sports. The newspaper was honoring its top high school athletes of the week. There, a two-column 42-point headline proclaimed:

VINCENT JACKSON WINS
NEWS' PLAYER HONOR

It was the story of a young baseball pitcher and shortstop at McAdory High who had thrown a three-hitter in one game, and delivered three hits and three RBI in another. His coach, Terry Brasseale, said, "He's an all-around athlete." Enshrine that one into the Understatement Hall of Fame.

Vincent Edward "Bo" Jackson had already established himself as a powerful running back and phenomenal hurdler at McAdory. Now, he was being introduced to the public for his baseball prowess, though Brasseale bemoaned that Jackson often missed baseball practice because of track practice and meets.

Below that story was the "Player of the Week" piece about another area of town, where Shades Valley outfielder Van Snider was being honored, with his .373 batting average and a recent 3-for-4 game.

McAdory and Shades Valley are separated by 20 miles or so, and even more distantly separated by lifestyle. Snider didn't know Bo. He soon would.

Five years later, Bo Jackson and Van Snider would not merely be on the same page, they'd be in the same outfield. Jackson, launching the most phenomenal (and phenomenally hyped) two-sport career in modern times, joined the Memphis Chicks and made his debut on June 30, 1986, wheeling into the parking lot in his Alfa Romeo, running late because he'd lost a hotel key. Snider was already established at Memphis where his brother, Rick, had been a three-year starter for the Memphis State football team. This was his third season with the Chicks during a 15-year pro career that would bring him some short cups of coffee in the majors with the Cincinnati Reds.

"The media attention was unbelievable. His first batting practice, there were credentials from everywhere," recalled Snider. "It was fun for everybody. Guys that hadn't gotten any attention, we were getting attention. It was fun."

Among the credentialed media who arrived to watch this Heisman-winning, first-round-draft pick tailback play outfield was Ross Newhan of the *Los Angeles Times*, whose son David would make his Southern League debut 11 years later as a Huntsville second baseman. Wrote Newhan, the hype "would have befitted a Jackson named Reggie. In fact, it was easily the most widely covered minor-league game in history. The cameras of ABC, CBS, NBC, ESPN, CNN and virtually every alphabetical combination in the USA were here."

Jackson had become a legendary running back at Auburn University. He rushed for more than 4,300 yards and 45 touchdowns. He won the 1985 Heisman Trophy. One can still raise a ruckus on Southern sports talk radio with a debate over who was the SEC's best back ever, Jackson or Georgia's Herschel Walker.

The Tampa Bay Buccaneers made Jackson the No. 1 pick in the draft. It seemed a given he'd play pro football. He did. But he also had something else in mind. The Kansas City Royals gambled their fourth-round draft pick on Jackson.

"He's the finest athlete and prospect of our time, maybe ever. I mean, there have been others, but never our time, maybe ever," Royals scouting director Art Stewart told Newhan. "I mean, there have been others, but never anyone with the overall talent, never anyone who combined the speed of a Willie Wilson, the arm of a Roberto Clemente and the power of a Mickey Mantle." Somehow,

Stewart neglected the whole "able to leap tall buildings in a single bound" and "faster than a locomotive" from the scouting report.

Jackson played 53 games for the Chicks before Kansas City called him to the majors that September.

"He was a good guy, a good team guy," Snider said, sitting in the cruiser he now drives as a policeman in Mayfield Heights, Ohio. "We all had a lot of fun. He elevated my game, I know that. Just his level of play, being there. It made the whole team lighter. For whatever reason everybody got life. Our team wasn't the best team. It seemed we played harder after he got there. He had an aura about him, a natural leadership ability and guys kinda gravitated to him."

Bo also elevated attendance like none other, at least until another Nike pitch man named Michael Jordan rolled around a few years later.

When Jackson made a homecoming at Birmingham's Rickwood Field, the Barons drew 37,377 for four nights. Said Jimmy Bragan, then the league president, "Not even The Chicken could do that. I don't know anyone other than Bo who could do that."

And who but Bo could become the first athlete to become an All-Star in two sports? He was an incredible physical specimen and natural talent. His former Auburn teammate Al Del Greco, who went on to a fine NFL career as a kicker, recalled Jackson hitting the top of the Superdome scoreboard with a pass. After ESPN rolled out its "30 for 30" series that boldly proclaimed Jackson the greatest athlete ever, Del Greco said, "Looking at it again years later I was still amazed at what he could do. The guy was an unbelievable athlete."

"Just his raw ability," Snider said. "The ability to swing the bat as hard as he did and still run a 3.6 (seconds to first base) was ridiculous. He just looks like a Greek god when he walks in. He's got bulges where most of us don't have muscles."

Jackson spent eight seasons in the majors, including four productive, healthy ones with the Royals from 1987-1990. He was the All-Star Game MVP in 1989. Yes, he led the A.L. in strikeouts with 172 in 1989 and batted only .250 for his career, but he was a highlight segment just waiting to happen every time he took the field, "a god-given gift to the bedtime sportscasters," as Steve Wulf wrote in *Sports Illustrated*. He was raw, but as Snider said, "If he made a mistake he was physically gifted enough to overcome it and make it look like it wasn't a mistake."

Football hovered. The Oakland Raiders spent a seventh-round pick on Jackson in the '87 draft—has any superstar ever been picked so deep in two separate drafts?—thinking he might give the NFL a second thought. Bo played in only 38 NFL games, with just 23 starts, but was a Pro Bowl pick in 1990. Then he injured his hip and the Royals ultimately released him. Though he attempted a comeback later with the White Sox and the Angels, Jackson never reached his full potential.

"I wish he had never gotten hurt," said Van Snider, perhaps speaking for millions. "It was a shame that happened to him."

In that widely covered debut in 1986 in the lineup with Snider, Jackson went 1-for-4 against the Columbus Astros, with an RBI single up the middle in the first, followed by a checked-swing strikeout, a grounder to the pitcher, and a strikeout looking in the ninth.

Jackson trudged to a tent that had been constructed behind the left-field fence at Tim McCarver Stadium to conduct his post-game interviews.

Someone asked Jackson if he retrieved the ball from his first hit.

He did not, the Heisman winner replied.

Why?

"My trophy case is already full."

JAKE
MARISNICK

Doubly grand

Not long after Jake Marisnick made history, his cell phone began filling up with messages. A couple came from Miami Marlins' manager Mike Redmond.

"He asked me if the wind was blowing out," said Marisnick. "If the mascot was pitching." To which Redmond explained to Miami media, "He wouldn't know what to do if I actually complimented him. I had to give him a bad time before I gave him a compliment."

The occasion was the night of May 30, 2013, when the Jacksonville Suns outfielder—"Big Fudge" to friends and teammates—launched grand slams in consecutive innings and drove in nine runs in an 11-2 win at Pensacola. "One of the better nights I've ever had," he told the *Pensacola News-Journal* in grand understatement. The nine RBI tied a league record held by four others, including Jose Canseco.

Marisnick's relationship with Redmond was forged in the previous two seasons, when Marisnick played for him at Lansing, Michigan, and Dunedin, Florida, in the Toronto Blue Jays' organization. Redmond, a journeyman backup catcher in the majors with impeccable defensive skills and remarkable baseball instinct, was hired as the Marlins' manager in November 2012. Less than two weeks later Marisnick also became part of the Miami organization, included in a 12-player trade that many South Florida critics labeled a salary dump, with the Marlins shipping off stars Mark Buehrle, Josh Johnson, and Jose Reyes for a slew of Jays youngsters. Marisnick was awaiting news of the trade while playing in the Arizona Fall League championship game, both Blue Jays and Marlins jerseys available in his locker.

He immediately hit a hiccup in the new organization, struck with a pitch by the Cardinals' Trevor Rosenthal in spring training that broke his left hand. "Kind of a bummer," Marisnick admitted. He spent a month on the disabled list, joining Jacksonville on May 1. Then he proceeded to add a historic bookend at the other end of the month.

Marisnick was 0-for-4 the previous night and had been focusing on timing issues at the plate. With one out and teammate Danny Black on second, facing Blue Wahoos' starter Daniel Renken, those timing issues were straightened out. The Californian drilled a pitch into a strong crosswind coming from left field that missed being a homer by only two feet, hitting high up on the wall for an RBI double. (He then stole third base, showing off his speed; he was considered Miami's No. 2 prospect by that point in the season.)

Renken got some measure of revenge, striking out Marisnick both to end the third and to open the sixth.

Pensacola manager Delino DeShields pinch-hit for Renken in the bottom of the sixth, though the right-hander had thrown only 86 pitches and allowed just four hits. His Blue Wahoos needed an injection of offense, still trailing 1-0 entering the seventh.

Reliever Chris Manno started the seventh for the hosts and immediately gave up a double, then a walk, and then the Suns' second run on a throwing error. Danny Black walked to load the bases, causing DeShields to yank Manno. The new reliever was Josh Ravin, a 6-foot-5 right-hander out of Chatsworth (Calif.) High, alma mater of Chips Swanson, who authored the Southern League's only nine-inning perfect game. Seven months earlier, Ravin celebrated with his Peoria Javelinas teammates when Marisnick, playing for Salt River, struck out in the ninth in the Arizona League championship game.

Ravin immediately got Marisnick into an 0-2 hole.

"Going into the at-bat, I was feeling OK at the plate," Marisnick said. "Timing is one thing I had been working on. The first time I get up and the bases are loaded, the last time I'm thinking was hitting a grand slam. I was down 0-2 and he threw me a curve ball that I was on. And I hit it pretty good. It ended up going out."

Then, because minor-league baseball, like 1960s family sitcoms, is developed around teachable moments, Jacksonville manager Andy Barkett first offered congratulations, then education. "Your swing was OK, but you were late on the fastball that at-bat," Barkett told him in the dugout. "Your timing was perfect for the curveball."

The next time up, Marisnick knew, "I needed to be on the fastball."

Fluky events took place in the Suns' eighth, presenting Marisnick with a shot at immortality. A walk and two singles loaded the bases for Christian Yelich, who hit a blast to right that Theo Bowe caught as he was colliding with the wall. The umpires ruled it wasn't a catch, but Yelich had thought otherwise. Not only did he round first and pass a runner on the base paths who had been waiting to tag up, he then U-turned to the dugout assuming it was an out. DeShields argued there should have been two outs, with the illegal passing of the runner and Yelich leaving the field voluntarily. The umpires disagreed.

Again the bases were loaded for Marisnick, and Ravin still on the mound. Said Marisnick, "When I was first walking I up there, watching everything that had happened, I thought, 'This is pretty crazy. The bases are loaded.' But I was thinking about what I was talking to Barkett about."

Ravin opened with a sharp breaking pitch that missed the strike zone, then came back with a fastball that Marisnick fouled back. But, "the next pitch I was on it. I put a good swing on it," and it cleared the fence in left.

Inform Mike Redmond: The wind was blowing in when Marisnick hit his second slam.

MATT MOORE

"The best stuff I've seen"

That June night in 2011, Matt Moore said he felt "like I had cooties or something." The Montgomery Biscuits dugout at Mobile's Hank Aaron Stadium was rife with tension. Moore was crafting a magnificent no-hitter and superstition kicked into high gear.

"Nobody was saying anything about it," manager Billy Gardner Jr. said. "Everybody was sitting in the same spots, doing the same things they'd been doing all game." That meant not speaking to Moore, a 6-foot-3 left-hander two days shy of his 22nd birthday. He didn't even realize he had a no-hitter going until the seventh, when a fan hollered at him.

Who'd have thought pitching a no-hitter wouldn't be the highlight of Matt Moore's season? One-hundred-seven days after his June 16 gem in Mobile, Moore started for the Tampa Bay Rays in the first game of the American League Division Series, beating the Texas Rangers 9-0 with seven innings of two-hit ball. Said Rays manager Joe Maddon, "What he did … was spectacular." Moore had made his major-league debut barely a week earlier, striking out 11 New York Yankees in five innings of shutout work.

Maddon didn't tell Moore he'd be the Game 1 starter until 24 hours before the first pitch. As Moore told reporters then, "They didn't give me a whole lot of time to get nervous and to think about it a lot." But, with an air of confidence, he did tell his father, Marty, "Dad, they're not asking me to do anything I'm not good at." He mowed down Ian Kinsler with a 95-mph fastball for a strikeout to begin the game and struck out five more opposite a Rangers offense that was the most potent in the American League.

Moore was a lifesaver for a tired, emotionally drained Tampa Bay team. The Rays had trailed Boston by nine games with 3½ weeks remaining in the season but earned the playoff spot on September 28, a night many consider the most dramatic in baseball history. They trailed the Yankees 7-0 going into the bottom of the seventh, only to rally behind a three-run Evan Longoria homer, a two-out, game-tying homer in the ninth by pinch-hitter Dan Johnson, and a Longoria walk-off homer in the 12th. On the same evening, Baltimore shrugged off a long rain delay to dramatically beat the Red Sox and knock Boston from playoff contention, while the hopeful St. Louis Cardinals, 10 ½ games out of first in late August, watched from afar as Philadelphia extended Atlanta into extra innings, eliminating the Braves on a broken-bat single in the 13th.

"A lot of times you'll see pitchers come up with this great stuff," Maddon said after Moore dazzled the Rangers. "You'll see 95, 97, 98. That's wonderful. But you have to be able to handle the moment. You have to have the right pulse or the right heartbeat. He does."

Alas, Moore would pitch only three more innings in the postseason, appearing in relief in Game 4, a Texas win that clinched the ALDS and propelled the Rangers into the World Series.

There is a tattoo on Matt Moore's left shoulder of St. Michael. He's the patron saint of battle, Moore explained. Patron saints are nice; ninety-five-mph fastballs are even better. That's what he took into battle against the Rangers on that final day in September 2011—and against the Mobile BayBears on June 16, 2011.

The no-hitter couldn't have come with more sentimental value. Moore was born in Fort Walton Beach, Fla., just 100 miles away from Mobile on the Gulf of Mexico. But he was a child of a peripatetic military family, living in Japan for four years, then settling in New Mexico. His father, mother, brother, and sister-in-law arrived in Mobile that day; only his father had seen Matt pitch that season. Said Moore, "That makes it even more special. They don't get to see me throw too often and, when they do, I usually don't throw very well."

"The thing I remember most is how dominant Matt was," Gardner said. "He had everything going. It was impressive to watch him pitch. Any time you're on the side of a no-hitter, it's a pretty good deal, and Mobile had a pretty good lineup to go through to get it."

Dave Eiland, the Rays' roving minor-league pitching instructor, was alongside Gardner in the dugout, monitoring Moore's pitch count. So efficient was Moore, the pitch count never became a factor. He threw only 106 pitches, 76 for strikes, retiring 11 batters by groundout and 11 by strikeout.

"That's the best stuff I've seen," Mobile manager Turner Ward said. "He threw everything for strikes. He threw it where he wanted. When he missed, he missed where he wanted to miss. He had command of his pitches."

When Moore struck out Daniel Kaczrowski and Jake Elmore to open the ninth, then got A.J. Pollock on a bouncer to the mound, he wrapped up the 8-0 win over the BayBears for the first no-hitter of his life and his first professional complete game. It was the first no-hitter in Biscuits' history, the first for a Montgomery pitcher in the Southern League since Steve Trella and Sheldon Burnside threw no-hitters in 1976.

"Right after the last out, it felt like a flashback," Moore said. "Did that just happen? Am I dreaming? It was just an unbelievable feeling."

It opened up an explosive celebration. Catcher Nevin Ashley bolted to the mound for an embrace, then came a flood of teammates. "We beat the crap out of him" in celebration, second baseman Shawn O'Malley told the *Montgomery Advertiser*. "We were all out there screaming at him and congratulating him." The party continued in the clubhouse, where they flung the half-dressed Moore into the showers. Perhaps that helped wash away the cooties.

MANLEY JOHNSTON

The 20-win slugger

Manley Johnston, a towering figure with a huge, strong right hand that could smother a baseball, was sitting on the edge of a bed, scanning the roster of the 1964 Lynchburg White Sox. With a soft laugh, more accurate than immodest, Johnston said, "I had such a good year I could have been mayor of Lynchburg. Everything I did was right, hitting and pitching."

Johnston won 20 games for the Lynchburg club that year, the inaugural season of the Southern League. No pitcher has won 20 since; in fact, between 1991 and 2013, only two pitchers even surpassed the 15-win total. "That's a long time ago," he said. "I'll be damned. I didn't think that's possible [to retain a record] through all the years." Johnston led the league with a 2.46 ERA. He started 29 games and twice appeared in relief, throwing 227 innings. (As a point of contrast to modern-era pitch-count concerns, that's 66 1/3 innings more than the most overworked Southern League pitcher of 2013.)

A half-century later, though, what still delighted Manley Johnston was his hitting. He batted .292 with seven homers—two in one game—and drove in 30 runs. Said Johnston, "Some years things go for you, and some don't. It seemed like everything that year went my way." That included a pennant for Lynchburg for which he was instrumental. In 1964, Johnston collected five wins against the Birmingham Barons; his White Sox edged the Barons by one game for the division. Groused Barons manager Haywood Sullivan, who was raised only a few miles from Johnston, "If it hadn't been for [Johnston], we'd have won easily."

On a hot, overcast summer morning, Johnston was in his room at a nursing home in Graceville, Florida. A fellow resident was across the room, *Andy Griffith Show* reruns on his TV, the volume cranked up. Johnston was a bit timid in his walking, the legs giving him some problems in recent years, but he was blessed with a good memory—and good memories.

Graceville sits in the muggy, piney flatlands of the Florida Panhandle, just south of Dothan, Alabama. It was the setting years ago for some wonderful baseball semi-autobiographical fiction, Paul Hemphill's under-appreciated classic, *Long Gone*. A quick tour proves that progress has not infringed much on Graceville since Hemphill played there in the Alabama-Florida League in the 1950s and drew inspiration for his book. There is a slight twist of symmetry. Hemphill retired from baseball and enrolled at Auburn, where he'd write for the school newspaper... and cover the exploits of Manley "Shot" Johnston and his teammates.

Johnston grew up in Ashford, just outside of Dothan. His dad always called him "Hot Shot" and when a classmate heard it, the nickname stuck. "Somehow," Johnston said, "the 'Hot' got dropped." He earned a scholarship to play baseball and basketball at Auburn, playing there two years, first on the freshman teams, then the varsity. Auburn won the 1958 Southeastern Conference baseball championship, and one of Johnston's teammates was Lloyd Nix, who had quarterbacked the Tigers to the national football title the previous fall.

Truth be told, "I really loved basketball better than baseball," said Johnston. "I thought I was a better basketball player." But after watching him in a summer baseball league, the Chicago White Sox dangled a $50,000 contract in front of him. He signed, then bought a brand new white Chevrolet Impala and banked the rest. "I never had any money," he said, "so I didn't know how to spend it."

Johnston was signed to play outfield. He hit .352 with 18 homers his first full season in 1959, then amassed 26 homers and 105 RBI the next year. In 1962, the White Sox opted to make him a pitcher. He learned an effective slider in spring training and they sent him to Class A Savannah, where his teammates included future big leaguers J.C. Martin and Don Buford and future NBA star Dave DeBusschere. There he won seven games in a row. Before taking to the mound in search of an eighth straight win, Johnston was told of even greater significance. This was an audition, he was told. Win this, you're headed to Chicago. Instead, Portsmouth-Norfolk lit him up. "I couldn't get 'em out," he said. "Maybe it was the pressure, knowing I was going up."

He spent 1963 as a pitcher and part-time outfielder at both Lynchburg and Class AAA Indianapolis, setting the stage for his unmatched 1964 season. There was his three-homer game, which even drew notice from Dizzy Dean on the next Saturday's "Game of the Week" telecast. No, Manley Johnston "wasn't one of those 95, 100-mile-an-hour throwers," but he dominated the league—especially Birmingham.

Johnston was 18-7 as the White Sox faced the Barons at Rickwood Field on September 2. Birmingham had been in first place for 96 days, but hit a stretch of eight losses in 10 days. Johnston and Lynchburg made it nine defeats out of 11 with a 10-8 Lynchburg triumph, tying the two teams atop the SL standings.

The White Sox and Barons both traveled to North Carolina for the next four games, Lynchburg playing in Asheville and Birmingham at Charlotte, before what Birmingham sportswriter Alf Van Hoose called a "Hollywood-type, season-climaxing, three-game series" at the Sox' hitter-friendly City Stadium. The Barons had ended their skid, winning three in a row when the rivals met on September 9, the teams' records deadlocked at 79-58.

Birmingham put two men aboard with a hit and error in the first, but a base-running error and two strikeouts killed the rally. Johnston found his groove, encouraged by the occasional "War Eagle!" cry from Lynchburg fans, honoring his Auburn background. He finished with a six-hitter for his 20th win, an 8-1 White Sox win.

It seemed almost a formality the next night when manager George Noga's club clinched the pennant, beating Birmingham 10-3 thanks to a nine-run second inning, notable for a pair of Deacon Jones homers.

Manley "Shot" Johnston moved up to Indianapolis, going 11-11 in 1965 and 18-7 in 1966. The scuttlebutt was that the Orioles were looking at him. But the innings had taken their toll. He had started 139 games and completed 33 of them. His arm was constantly sore. He doubted himself, "question[ing] my arm being good enough to pitch in the majors." The scouts had similar questions. By then, Johnston was 25 and raising a young family. He retired to Dothan, working at a paper mill, then getting involved in real estate.

"All I'd ever done is play ball," he said. "I didn't know anything but ball. Once you get out of baseball and get an 8-to-5 job, you can never get used to it. It'd have been best if I stayed in sports."

As Johnston talked, he pored over a stack of photos retrieved from the top shelf of an armoire. They took him a long way from a nursing home in the Panhandle, back to the days when everything he did was right, and when what he did made history that would live a half-century or more.

MICHAEL JORDAN

His Airness joins the Barons

Every evening, the phone would ring in the press box, somebody calling long distance. "Are the Barons going to be home?" on such-and-such date was the inevitable question.

It was the summer of 1994, and the best basketball player to ever play in the Southern League was packing them in everywhere.

Birmingham drew 467,868 that season. Five of the Barons' biggest 14 crowds at the Hoover Met were in '94. "Going to the ballpark, you never knew what you were going to see, witness, or meet," recalled Jonathan Nelson, Birmingham's current general manager who was then in his first season in the group sales department. The combined attendance in the league was a record 2,596,340, nearly 190,000 more than the previous season.

Give credit for that increase to a long, tall right fielder with a .202 batting average named Michael Jordan.

Give credit, too, to Michael Jordan for handling things with as much class and dignity as possible for a man under a constant microscope and scrutiny.

Yes, he lived in a mini-mansion in the exclusive, gated Greystone community and drove a black Porsche. But, said the Barons' radio broadcaster Curt Bloom, "He tried so hard to be an ordinary guy, tried to find quiet time in the locker room. He respected his team-mates." Jordan made a point to swing by the front office and say hello to the staff on occasion and once jumped to the rescue and helped the grounds crew pull the tarp.

He could be seen occasionally pumping his own gas or hanging out at T.J.'s Sports Bar watching games or, every now and again, at

Sammy's, an establishment featuring dancing ladies who were less than scantily clad. Heck, the first time Wayne Martin, who covered the Barons for the *Birmingham News,* sat down to interview Jordan during spring training in Sarasota, he was eating lunch from a McDonalds' bag. "They pay me," Jordan reminded.

Jordan had already won three NBA championships with the Chicago Bulls and established himself as one of the most recognizable figures on the planet. However, after his father James was murdered in 1993 on a North Carolina highway, Jordan sought release in a new challenge at age 31.

The critics were many: "Bag It, Michael!" *Sports Illustrated* proclaimed on its March 14, 1994 cover, with "Jordan and The White Sox Are Embarrassing Baseball" blared underneath. Steve Wulf wrote in the cover story that "Michael Jordan has no more business patrolling right field at Comiskey Park than Minnie Minoso has bringing the ball upcourt for the Chicago Bulls." (The story was the genesis for a long-running disdain for the magazine by Jordan, who typically refused comment to *SI* writers.)

Michael Jordan made a point to be one of the guys and never sought special treatment. Special treatment still followed, naturally. There were two boxes for incoming player mail: One for Jordan, one for the rest of the players. The black Porsche was parked in a special space to facilitate quick, safe escapes after games. But he traveled every mile on that bus with his teammates, took early batting practice, and shared dressing quarters. He was not immune from teammates' teasing, and he was occasionally found guilty in the team's Kangaroo Court. He also spent the majority of his clubhouse socializing time with his manager, Terry "Tito" Francona, just four years Jordan's senior.

While attendance numbers related to Jordan were more impressive than numbers that would go on the back of a baseball card, he had his defenders, Curt Bloom among them.

"I always look at it as a success," Bloom said, kicking back in a reclining office chair a few minutes before air-time for a mid-summer broadcast. "There has never been one day that I ever looked at it as a failure. When you look at what Michael did, there's nobody on earth at his age, with the lack of baseball in his career, that could have done what he did. I look at .202. I look at three home runs.

I've got guys on this team that won't hit three home runs. He stole 30-some odd bases. You can't take that away. You've heard Tito Francona talk about it. Nobody ever considered it a failure. It was a success."

Jordan didn't play in the season opener—the White Sox had him in Chicago that day for their Windy City Classic exhibition game against the Cubs, after which Jordan flew to Birmingham and proceeded to get lost en route from the airport. He made his debut on April 8 with a pair of strikeouts and a flyout in front of 10,359 at the Hoover Met. He moved comfortably into the home team's big-league style clubhouse with a bit of whimsy above his locker: a bumper sticker proclaiming "Barkley for Governor," a nod to Charles Barkley's claim he'd run for Alabama's highest office.

After a stretch of four consecutive strikeouts amid an 0-for-8 start, Jordan collected his first regular-season professional hit, a looping single to center on Sunday, April 10, at 2:39 p.m. It came off Knoxville pitcher Joe Ganote, with whom Jordan had played a round of golf in Sarasota during spring training. Asked how his first hit compared to his first NBA basket, "This was a little better," Jordan said. "When I started basketball, everybody knew I would get at least two points." The breakout afternoon triggered a 13-game hitting streak.

The Barons took to the road a few days later in a custom-made bus that Jordan inspired—contrary to urban legend, he didn't buy the bus (see Chapter 51)—to travel to Chattanooga. You *can* blame Jordan for the Barons' loss that night. He drew 13,416 fans into ancient Engel Stadium. Because of the anticipated huge crowd, Chattanooga officials cordoned off part of left field, normally 360 feet down the line. Lookouts hitters plopped two homers into the crowd beyond the temporary fencing.

"Oh, man," said Bloom, "the first half it was absolutely insane. We were the traveling sideshow like I've never seen before or since."

By July, Jordan's average still hovered around .200, and Chicago media was reporting rumors he'd make a basketball comeback. He vehemently denied it, saying he was committed to baseball. "Nobody expected me to hit .300," he said, "except maybe myself. And a lot of the baseball purists said I couldn't succeed. But nothing has changed since spring training. ... I'm happy where I am, and I'm happy with what I'm doing. I don't see myself being back in the game [of basket-ball] at any time in the near future. ... I just don't like to say 'never.' I don't like to close doors. But if you want me to say it, OK, "never." I will never play basketball again, except recreationally."

Michael Jordan finished his first Double-A season with a .202 average, with 17 doubles, one triple, driving in 51 runs and stealing 30 bases. He committed 11 errors in the outfield and struck out 114 times in 436 at-bats. A clutch player in basketball, he did lead the Barons with RBI with the bases loaded (11) and with runners in scoring position with two out.

Oh, and as Bloom remembered accurately, Jordan finished with three home runs. (Pitchers Kevin Rychel of Carolina, Jeff Ware of Knoxville, and Glen Cullop of Chattanooga have something to tell their grandchildren.) The first homer came on his 354th at-bat of the season, on July 30. He dedicated it to his late father.

Jordan's "never" was erased when Major League Baseball cooked its own goose with the strike of 1994, canceling the World Series and wiping out much of the early 1995 campaign. He returned to pro basketball and to a second run of three consecutive championships.

"Nobody can say with certainty that he would have made it (to the majors)," Francona said. "But I don't think you can find somebody who would definitely say he would not have made it."

"Had he started paying baseball early," said Wayne Martin, "he could have been as good as he wanted. He could have been an impact player."

Martin ran into Jordan two years later in Atlanta when the Bulls came to play the Hawks. Jordan reflected upon his baseball career, saying, "Nah, I'll never try again. That part of my life is passed." He then added, as if it could be any other way, "I appreciate the people in Birmingham remembering me."

DERREK LEE

And on the sixth day...

For the entire 1996 season, Derrek Lee's performance was outstanding—but for six games in June, he was unprecedented.

The youngest player in the league at 20, Lee was also its Most Valuable Player. Overall, he led the circuit in homers (34), extra-base hits (75), and equal opportunity; Lee homered against every team. And from June 2 through June 8, he belted a home run in every game, a Southern League record still standing as the league reached the half-century mark.

"A tremendous, tremendous talent," said Ed Romero, a journeyman utility infielder in the majors for a dozen years who was the Memphis Chicks' manager in 1996. "Derrek was a hard-working guy that went about his business."

During a season when Memphis had the best record in the league, Lee's business was hitting longballs.

He was the son of Leon Lee, who played as high as Triple-A, and the nephew of Leron Lee, who made the big leagues. The Lee brothers played professional baseball in Japan and were the inspiration for the Max "Hammer" Dubois character, played by the baritone-voiced Dennis Haysbert, in the movie *Mr. Baseball*. (Haysbert also played the mercurial Pedro Cerrano in *Major League*. He is far better known now for his Allstate insurance commercials and his TV role as President David Palmer on *24*.)

"A lot of Americans who go over there try to go against the system, but my dad adapted and didn't try to defy it," Derrek Lee told the *(Memphis) Commercial Appeal*. "He pretty much had the respect of the people of Japan."

The brothers were also inspiration for young Derrek. His father played 10 seasons in Japan, and Derrek joined him there for three of those seasons. "'He came to Japan a couple of times on his own and learned how to find his way through airports," the elder Lee told the *Commercial Appeal*. "I remember once when we were in Tokyo, he flew to California to play in a little league all-star game, then flew back to Tokyo, all on his own. He learned early to adapt to things."

Derrek was equally talented in basketball (his favorite sport, he maintained) as he was in baseball, signing to play both sports at North Carolina. Those plans were derailed when the Padres made him their No. 1 pick in the 1993 draft, signing him for a reported $600,000. It was a first-round draft class that included Alex Rodriguez, Jason Varitek, Trot Nixon, Billy Wagner, and Torii Hunter.

At 17 years of age, Lee had already hit his first home run in the Class A California League. He played for Rancho Cucamonga in 1994-95, honored as the league MVP in 1994. His manager was Tim Flannery, the perfect man to handle the callow youngster. When Derrek was late arriving in spring training, the skipper ordered him to buy pizza and wings for his teammates. He could afford it, Flannery figured. Lee continued to work out and pack on muscle onto his lithe 6-foot-5 basketball player's frame, putting up astonishing numbers in '95. The Padres stayed patient and opted not to promote him. The teenager wasn't quite so patient. He admitted to being immature and falling into "a funk," telling the *Commercial Appeal*, "I figured, why can't I have the same success in Double-A that I had [in Class A]? I think the minor leagues is about progression, not staying in one place to build your confidence. I didn't think I should have been put on a timetable."

"A lot of people questioned at that time his demeanor and the way he went about his business," Romero said. "That's the way he was. That was his personality. He was kinda laid back."

The timetable would speed up. He enjoyed his record-breaking season in Memphis, then after starting the 1997 season at Triple-A Calgary had a brief call-up to the Padres. At season's end, he was a piece of the Florida Marlins' fire sale, sent to Miami in a deal that brought Kevin Brown to San Diego. His 15-year major-league career, with 331 home runs, was underway.

But the 1996 season began for Lee with a frosty April, not quite the Double-A success he was expecting. He was batting .119 with only two homers before his bat started to sizzle, delivering 10 homers, 36 RBI, and a .364 average over the course of May. The month saw Lee homer in four consecutive games; he just missed a fifth when a double hit the top of a fence and bounced back in play. Entering the initial days of June, he had notched base hits in 15 of 17 games. Then The Streak was born:

Game One: Sunday, June 2, Tim McCarver Stadium, Memphis. Chicks 7, Carolina 6: Lee had a solo homer in the fourth inning, but his most crucial hit was a 10th-inning RBI single that drove in Gabe Alvarez with the winning run.

Game Two: Monday, June 3, Tim McCarver Stadium. Carolina 8, Chicks 5. Lee homered to lead off the sixth inning in rain-delayed game that saw the Chicks fall behind 8-0, commit five errors and end a five-game winning streak.

Game Three: Wednesday, June 5, Tinker Field, Orlando, Florida. Chicks 12, Orlando 6. The Chicks' Jorge Velandia had two homers and Lee cracked his 15th of the season in what had been anticipated as a pitcher's duel between Heath Murray and Jeremi Gonzalez.

Game Four: Thursday, June 6, Tinker Field. Orlando 3, Chicks 2. No tension here about extending the streak. Lee homered in the first to stake Memphis to a 1-0 lead that oozed away.

Game Five: Friday, June 7, Tinker Field. Orlando 5, Chicks 4. Lee tied the record of homers set in five consecutive games, set by Memphis outfielder Chito Martinez in 1989 (and most recently matched by Khris Davis, with five in a row for Huntsville in 2012). Lee again avoided any tension, with a two-run homer in the first. Troy Hughes had two homers to life Orlando to the win.

Game Six: Saturday, June 8, Tinker Field. Chicks 10, Orlando 6. Lee homered in the fourth on a 3-0 pitch from the Cubs' Al Garcia. He made reference to the early four-game streak and the near-miss double in the fifth game. "I didn't even know about the record at the time," Lee said. "My teammates and coaches were telling me about the record, but I didn't think too much about it. But I wasn't about to let it pass me by again."

The record run ended in a Sunday at Jacksonville's Wolfson Park, in a 6-4 Memphis win. In an interview later that season, Lee said, "Anywhere you go you're going to have hot streaks and cold streaks, and you just try to keep the cold streaks as short as possible."

For Derrek Lee in the summer of 1996, one game was a cold streak.

MIKE REINBACH

The Triple Crown Bruin

Mike Reinbach was going to be the next great UCLA quarterback, the guy to pick up the legacy of the Heisman Trophy winner Gary Beban. Thing is, another half-dozen freshmen had the same idea when he arrived in Westwood in 1968.

Soon, Reinbach was a defensive back. Not long after after that, he was concentrating solely on baseball.

Good choice.

The decision led Reinbach to the Southern League MVP award in 1972, the only player in the first 50 years of the league to win the Triple Crown. If you were following the "Player Periscope" that the *San Diego Union-Tribune* used to track local talent, you knew he batted .346 with 30 homers and 109 RBI for the Asheville Orioles.

"A great athlete and a hell of competitor," said friend and former UCLA player Earl Altshuler.

"He was a driven young man who had a great year for us," said Al Harazin, the Asheville general manager and future GM of the New York Mets. "We had about half that 1972 team that had at least a cup of coffee in the big leagues, with some who had big careers [Al Bumbry, Doug DeCinces]. I always thought Mike would make it, too."

Alas, with an Orioles outfield that included Don Baylor, Merv Rettenmund, and Paul Blair, with Bumbry and Tommy Davis in reserve, it'd have been easier to break into Fort Knox with a bobby-pin than to break into that outfield. Reinbach instead became a star in the Japanese Baseball League, then remained in the country for a while after his retirement, working as a banker. He was back in the United States, looking for a fresh start, when he attended a reunion of old UCLA players. He looked to still be in playing shape.

On May 20, 1989, Reinbach's car sailed off a cliff on a treacherous, winding road outside Palm Desert, California. Though no cause of the accident was made clear, Altshuler had often ridden with him in Reinbach's "muscle car" during his UCLA days and knew he loved to drive fast.

Mike Reinbach was 39 when he was buried at El Camino Memorial Park in San Diego. His grave marker reads:

In Loving Memory
A Friend and a Father

The figure of a baseball player is on the marker, poised in a right-handed stance at an imaginary home plate. Reinbach, it can be gently observed, was a left-handed hitter.

After giving football a go during his freshman season at UCLA and separating a shoulder, Mike helped the Bruins reach the College World Series for the first time in school history, playing on a team led by future star Chris Chambliss.

"I had told myself that if I ever got hurt [playing football], I'd go to baseball," Reinbach said in *The Sporting News* in 1972. "I knew I could play football, but I felt I had a better chance in baseball."

He and UCLA baseball coach Art Reichle didn't always see eye-to-eye, so Reinbach made himself available in the January draft of 1970 and the Orioles drafted him in the first round. He spent a full season at Miami in the Florida State League, moving up to Dallas-Fort Worth in 1971 in the ill-fated Dixie Association (see Chapter 3).

When the Orioles relocated to Asheville, with a short right-field fence at McCormick Field, it was one big Christmas gift wrapped up for Reinbach. His greatest performance came in a 17-1 win over Columbus on June 12, 1972, going 6-for 6 with nine RBI.

Asheville was indeed a gift for many of the Orioles: Royle Stillman had 23 homers and 83 RBI, DeCinces 10 homers and 60 RBI, and Jim Fuller 23 homers and 70 RBI.

Managed by Cal Ripken, Sr., the O's won 81 of 139 games and scored 707 runs, 42 more than the next-most prolific team.

Reinbach spent the '73 season at Triple-A Rochester, and then opened the 1974 season with the Orioles at age 24, making his debut on April 7 as the designated hitter, batting between Brooks Robinson and Blair in the lineup. It was only a temporary stay. Reinbach played in just 12 games, with 23 at-bats, hitting .250. He was optioned back to Rochester, but refused to report, instead returning to San Diego to work in the construction business when the Orioles informed him his salary would be cut from $15,000 to $8,800. After three weeks at home, he agreed to return to Rochester. "That working for a living isn't what it's cracked up to be," sportswriter Dick Young wisecracked in his nationally syndicated column.

Mike Reinbach played again in Rochester in 1975, then became part of a growing migration of American players to Japan. Only once in five seasons did he hit below .284 and he had career numbers of .296 with 94 homers and 324 RBI in 565 games for the Hanshin Tigers in the Japan Central League.

"One of the most competitive guys I ever played with in my life," Alshuler said. "He played with every amount of heart an athlete could possibly have. Not everybody understood him all the time, but I liked the guy. I liked his demeanor. Everybody should play like he did."

CAL RIPKEN, JR.

The Forging of the Iron Man

As a child, he had to literally dodge bullets in the Southern League. As a young player, he had his confidence buoyed by his time in the league. As a balding, graying icon of the game, he enjoyed the most memorable victory lane in baseball history, credited as the man most instrumental in removing the tarnish from the sport.

Calvin Edward Ripken, Jr., arrived at Charlotte late in the 1979 season, just long enough to acclimate himself in Class AA. That prepared him for 1980—which then prepared him for 3,001 major-league games, 2,632 of which came consecutively.

When Ripken arrived in Charlotte for an opening-night appearance after his retirement, he echoed what he often told interviewers about the 1980 campaign: "On the field, it was the season that really made me believe that I could play in the big leagues."

A lot of others believed as well.

"He had a decent year the year before, but you could really see his confidence growing by leaps and bounds as the season went on," said Stan Olson, who covered the O's for the *Charlotte News.* "He became their most consistent hitter, the guy everybody was afraid of in the middle of the order."

Ripken, unsurprisingly, played in all 144 O's games, batting .276 with 25 homers and driving in 78 runs. His .933 fielding percentage was the best of all SL third basemen, though he did play 25 games at shortstop, a foreshadowing of where he would spend most of his major-league career. He was the anchor in what Owen called "a great slugging team," hitting alongside Dan Logan and Drungo Hazewood.

Cal Ripken, Jr., is one of seven members of the National Baseball Hall of Fame to have come up through the Southern League in this half-century, accompanying his Baltimore teammate Eddie Murray (Charlotte, 1976) as well as Ferguson Jenkins (Chattanooga, 1964), Rollie Fingers (Birmingham 1967-68), Reggie Jackson (Birmingham, 1967), Tom Glavine (Greenville, 1986), and Frank Thomas (Birmingham, 1990).

(Ryne Sandberg had a brief rehab stint at Orlando late in his career and managed at Tennessee in 2009.)

Cal Ripken Sr. was a baseball lifer, a winner of more than 1,000 games as a minor-league manager. He had a gruff voice and countenance, but had universal respect inside the clubhouse, strict as he might be. One day in the minors, he discovered a pitcher, Dave Johnson, had snuck his golf clubs onto the bus. Ripken ordered the bus emptied, grabbed a brand new box of golf balls Johnson had in the bag, and Johnson's 5-iron. He proceeded to launch the balls into the woods behind the stadium.

Cal Sr. was eventually called upon to manage in Baltimore, inheriting a team that was almost AARP-eligible at most every position, save for its double-play combination, the 22-year-old Billy Ripken and the 26-year-old Cal Jr. Those Orioles finished 67-95. Six further losses into 1988, and Cal Ripken, Sr., was fired. Ever loyal, he agreed to remain on the Baltimore coaching staff.

Upon the elder Ripken's death in 1999, Thomas Boswell of the *Washington Post* wrote, "that moniker—Cal Ripken—will be remembered, and respected, as long as baseball is played. For some of us, the name will always evoke memories of two fine men, not just one."

Cal Ripken Sr. was manager of the Asheville Orioles in 1972 at age 36, already his 11th season as a manager. The team won the Eastern Division by a game over Savannah, led by guys like league MVP Mike Reinbach, Al Bumbry, and Doug DeCinces, and pitchers like Mark Weems, who could pitch with either left or right hand, but drowned the following off-season in Venuezuela while playing winter ball.

The team's general manager was Al Harazin, who had been a lawyer in Cincinnati but bought the Asheville club out of his love for the game. He moved up the ladder of the Orioles system and eventually became the general manager of the New York Mets.

"Cal Jr. was a skinny Little Leaguer who hadn't hit his growth spurt yet. His younger brother Billy was our clubhouse boy," Harazin said. "Cal Sr. was a true 'baseball man,' always willing to help his players improve. He was a 'what you see is what you get' guy. You always knew where he was coming from. I learned a ton from him and still use some of his expressions."

Cal Ripken, Jr., became the Orioles' bat boy, just as the author Thomas Wolfe and North Carolina basketball coach Roy Williams were in their teen years. Early arrivals to McCormick Park might find Senior pitching batting practice to Junior. "You could tell he was going to be good," said Jim Baker, who covered baseball for the *Asheville Citizen-Times.*

Before a game one night, a teenager in a house neighboring the ballpark broke into his parents' gun closet and starting firing a gun into the air from the porch of the house. Young Ripken was playing catch with Doug DeCinces.

"Cal was like a shadow of mine. He would take ground balls with me every day," DeCinces said. "We're halfway up the first baseline and I threw a ball and I heard this pop. All of a sudden there was a whiz and the ground exploded next to me, maybe 10 feet away. I could hear the bullet go by. I was in the Air National Guard and had gone through boot camp and everything registered with me. Like 'Holy crap, that was a rifle shot.' And just as that happened I turned and I grabbed Cal on his uniform right at his neck and and started to run off the field. I hear another bang and this time the bullet went about four feet in front of me. It was so close. I don't think Cal Junior ever touched the ground. I went flying into the dugout."

"You could hear the bullet," Ripken told the *Winston-Salem Journal* years later. "And then you could see it [when it landed]. And I wasn't sure what it was, just a very fast flying object. But DeCinces immediately knew what it was. I don't know if it was that close to us or not. I didn't necessarily think I was at risk, but Doug grabbed me and put me in the dugout. Then I paid him back by taking his job."

Two-thousand, six-hundred, thirty-two, games later after Ripken took that job, there wasn't much chance for DeCinces to get it back.

Actually, it was Floyd Rayford who was the Orioles' third baseman in the second game of a Monday, May 29, 1982, doubleheader, DeCinces having been traded that off-season to California for Dan Ford. Ripken was back in the lineup on Sunday, going 0-for-2 in a loss to Toronto. It would be 16-plus years before Cal Jr. took another day off.

The signature moment of Ripken's streak was September 6, 1995. Baseball was under dark clouds. A work stoppage cut short the 1994 season, canceling the World Series. The 1995 season began with replacement umpires. Attendance was down 20 percent. Baseball needed somebody to gallop to the rescue, like some gallant hero untying the damsel in distress from the railroad tracks in a hokey old movie.

Cal Ripken, Jr., stepped to the forefront. His work ethic, and certainly his good health and good genes, enabled him to pass Lou Gehrig's record of 2,130 consecutive games played on a night of unprecedented celebration at Oriole Park at Camden Yards, that lovely poster child for retro ballparks.

After things became official, the 0 in 2,130 was replaced by a 1 in the row of banners hanging from the warehouse beyond the right-field wall, looming over Boog Powell's barbecue stand in the concourse. The crowd rose as one in a standing ovation. Uncharacteristically, ESPN's Chris Berman remained mute for more than 22 minutes, letting the pictures and crowd noise tell the story. Ripken was coaxed from the dugout a half-dozen times, once handing his jersey and cap to wife Kelly and children Rachel and Ryan. In perhaps the most poignant moment, encouraged (and all but shoved) by teammates Rafael Palmeiro and Bobby Bonilla, he embarked on a lap counterclockwise around the warning path of the stadium.

Some would say the victory lap began at the Orioles dugout. Others might suggest it began in Charlotte in 1980.

THE MOMENTS

Joe Charboneau in Chattanooga.

FOUR SWINGS

1969

Fran Kalafatis was in Montgomery in March 2012, doing advocacy work on behalf of the Bristol-Myers Squibb Foundation. She stopped in a pharmacy, trying to find something to ease a nagging back pain that has been exacerbated by constant travel. The pharmacist, noting she was visiting town, asking how she liked the city, and she responded that she had once lived there.

As she handed her credit card to the pharmacist, he stared at it and paused.

"George Kalafatis. Left-handed first baseman. He could hit the heck out of the ball," he said.

"I just looked at him," said Fran. "Of all the drug stores in Montgomery, and he knew him immediately. It gave me shivers up my spine."

It had been merely 43 years since Fran's late husband had played for the Montgomery Rebels.

Kalafatis never created memories as explosively as he did on July 1, 1969, when he hit four home runs against the Birmingham Barons, an accomplishment no other Southern League batter matched in the league's first half-century.

"Greatest thing I've ever seen and it couldn't happen to a nicer guy," Rebels catcher Jim Leyland, who has gone on to see pretty great things as a major-league manager, told the late Jack Doane of the *Montgomery Advertiser*.

"It was magical," Fran recalled decades later, cooking dinner in the kitchen of her Cleveland, Ohio, home. "It was hit after hit after hit after hit."

"I just hit them and they went out," Kalafatis told the *Advertiser*.

Kalafatis was a 6-foot-5 Goliath, yet deft enough around the bag to lead Southern League first basemen in fielding in 1969. He had a robust minor-league career, but with Norm Cash entrenched at first for the Detroit Tigers, Kalafatis never had a big-league appearance. He was a free-swinging power-hitter whose stats were further complicated by poor vision. Said Fran, "He could walk into a wall. He had to put on glasses just to get out of bed." Glasses were too awkward to wear while playing and the hard-lens contacts of the day were troublesome because of infield dirt and the poor lighting of a minor-league park.

They were an odd couple to the community, New Yorkers with a funny name, "and people assumed we were Jewish." There was George with rich, deep olive skin, and Fran with a resemblance to Cher, her long, straight hair parted down the middle, and "elephant pants," as he called them, a look that had not entirely caught on in the Deep South. In those days, players' wives had their duty as set decoration in the stands. "We were part of the show," she said. They were expected to wear skirts and pantyhose, something at which Fran often balked.

She arrived late, if not totally fashionable, "dragging myself not to get there too early," on a typically hot and humid night at Paterson Field, two-year-old daughter Lara in tow. Everyone she saw caught her up. "You just missed a home run from George," they told her.

It had been a solo homer in the second inning against Don Buschhorn, hitting atop the right-center fence and bouncing into the kudzu-covered bank behind the fence. Kalafatis touched up Buschhorn again for a two-run homer in the fourth and drove in another run with a single in the fifth. In the sixth, he took reliever Kelly Prior deep with a teammate aboard.

That seemed like it might be Kalafatis's last at-bat, especially when Nicky Curtis, a right-hander with six years of experience in the Southern League, struck out Hagan Andersen and Larry Groce to open the eighth. But Pete McKenzie singled. Said one fan, "If he hits another one, he could be elected mayor tomorrow." Sure enough, Kalafatis mashed his fourth homer, launching it over a fence sign sponsored by a local clothing store to earn himself a free sports coat.

The Rebels wrapped up the 13-0 win, eight of the RBI provided by Kalafatis. (The league mark is nine, co-owned by Tommie Reynolds, Mike Reinbach, Jose Canseco, Butch Garcia, and Jake

Marisnick.) The team headed out to a player's home to celebrate. Fran can't remember exactly which player hosted the bash, only that it was "one of the single guys because the place was filthy."

In February of 1995, at age 50, George suddenly died of a heart ailment.

He had become a prominent sports agent, first with International Management Group, then with his own company, Omni Sports International, representing athletes from basketball, baseball, and football. He left behind Fran and two children, Lara and Christopher.

In a dinner-table conversation with friends in Toledo one night, the "what's-after-baseball?" conversation arose, and Kalafatis, with a degree in marketing management from Long Island University, noted he wanted to help players who weren't as well prepared to face the "real world." He was encouraged to attend law school and, in fact, was studying for the LSATs while playing winter ball in Venezuela. While in Venezuela, Kalafatis contracted a virus that caused him to lose more than 20 pounds. He continued his law studies and baseball career, eventually joining Mark McCormick's famed IMG when partners there noticed how well-connected Kalafatis was in baseball. Said Fran, "He could never remember my birthday but he knew the phone number of every locker room in the United States."

George Kalafatis purposely kept his own company relatively small when he left IMG so he could devote as much personal attention to each client as possible. He was a soft touch. He dispensed free advice. He'd try to salvage things after star-crossed players went through agent after agent. "He never tried to make a ton of money as an agent," Fran said. He never flaunted his prominence or name-dropped his clients, in public or at home. One day when son Christopher was asked in school what his father did for a living, he replied, "He gets on airplanes and he goes to lunches."

What no one knew was that the virus he got in Venezuela lay dormant in his body for years. It eventually caused cardiomegaly, an enlarged heart. It proved fatal, even though he was in the prime of life and apparently in perfect health. "Most people said, 'Of course George would die of a big heart,'" Fran said softly.

Kalafatis was of a generation that was paid little to play, under conditions that were more primitive and grueling. Said Fran, "They played for the sheer love of it."

One night, George and Fran went to the musical, *A Chorus Line*. There is a powerful song in the show called "What I Did For Love," about the dancers' sacrifices and about turning toward the future. Fran turned her head slightly to look at her husband. He understood. "It resonated with him," she said. There was a tear in George's eye.

THE MAESTRO

Unexpected perfection

Next time you're enjoying one of those TV nostalgia nights, watching some classic old show, notice when the credits roll around. The name Chips Swanson will likely appear on the screen. It might be at the end of *Cheers* or *Wings* or *Frasier*, or any of the other 100 or so TV shows on which Swanson worked as music editor.

You'll also see his name in the Southern League record book, albeit listed incorrectly:

PERFECT GAMES

August 14, 1970   Chip Swanson, Montgomery (vs.)
Savannah   W, 3-0

Swanson is the only pitcher in the first-half century of Southern League play to have authored a nine-inning perfect game. Birmingham's George Lauzerique, in 1967, and Orlando's Chad Gaudin, in 2003, both had seven-inning perfect games, the latter in his Southern League debut. Both pitchers are listed beneath Swanson, tagged by asterisks.

"That's amazing. You'd have thought there'd been a few of them by now," Swanson said, relaxing on a late afternoon in his Southern California home he shares with wife Ginny and a couple of dogs, one of which was playfully barking as Swanson talked.

"It didn't set in that night," Swanson said. "It took a couple of days before I realized what happened." Rather than a massive celebration after his teammates had carried him off the field on their shoulders, he went to a friend's house for dinner, politely refusing a couple of TV interview requests. He didn't think to collect and store any mementoes from the win. Happily his mother collected a scrapbook of various clippings and Ginny has the scrapbook stored somewhere, "but if you asked me to go and get it, I couldn't tell you where to look for it," he said.

There was the usual superstition going on in the Rebels' dugout, avoiding Swanson between innings as if he were contagious. He recalled that Tim Hosley was his catcher that night and, in understatement, Swanson said, "Everything seemed to be OK."

"Every pitch was right on the black, just perfect," Hosley told the *Montgomery Advertiser.* "He had tremendous stuff and control on every pitch."

The day before, Swanson and other Montgomery pitchers were lolling about in the bullpen and Swanson thought aloud to his teammates, "I wonder if anybody is going to pitch a no-hitter in the league this year?"

"He said he just felt it for some reason that someone was going to pitch one real soon," teammate Bill Gilbreth said.

Swanson, 22 years old at the time, needed just 87 pitches to blow away the Indians. It took a mere 1:29 to finish the game, played in a near vacuum at Paterson Field in front of just 556 fans.

After his 1-2-3 top of the first, Tom Grayson homered for Montgomery, the only run Swanson would need. Defense was another matter; he needed the split-second reflexes of shortstop Chuck Scrivener in the third inning when a Vic Correll line drive hit Swanson in the foot and ricocheted away. First baseman John Young made a nifty play in the fifth, then Swanson went 3-0 on Correll in the sixth before coaxing a grounder to third.

Swanson and Hosley mixed things up to keep the Savannah hitters off-balance, with a steady dose of sliders to right-handed hitters and curveballs to lefties to complement his fastball. The breaking pitches weren't always a part of his arsenal. He was primarily a power pitcher when the Braves drafted him in the second round of the 1967 draft out of Los Angeles Valley College. Paul Richards, Atlanta's revered general manager, suggested to Swanson after his second minor-league season that if he developed a curveball, he could be in the majors the next year. But rather than prolong Swanson's career, that likely shortened it.

"Unfortunately I went home and tried to learn it on my own and I screwed up my arm," Swanson said. "I never threw that hard again." Eventually, once Swanson moved to the Tigers' organization, Dr.

Bob Kerlan and Dr. Frank Jobe did surgery on his arm. "Dr. Kerlan told me I'd never throw as hard as when I signed. I became a better pitcher because I learned control and how to finesse." But scouts seldom stick their necks out for the guys whose velocity drops from 98 to 89.

The final blow: Just as Swanson was on the cusp of a call-up to Detroit in 1974, his Evansville team got into a brawl with Wichita. Somebody stepped on Swanson's pitching hand during the battle, putting him briefly out of action. By this point, he and Ginny had two sons, David and Brian, and baseball life was starting to grow more difficult. He stuck it out one more season, pitching again at Evansville in 1975.

Chips Swanson—his given name is Charles—already had a fallback position after baseball. His father Bob was an Emmy-winning film editor and producer on such 1960s classics as *The Untouchables* and *The Fugitive*. (It was Bob Swanson who nicknamed his son and requested the "S," often dropped in historical records, be attached to it.) Chips had made contacts in the TV industry through his father and was working studio jobs in the off-season, working in the music editorial department.

Though he "had no music background," Swanson had some sort of preternatural abilities when it came to music selection.

"Basically, what I did for the studio was two jobs," he explained. "One, I would work with a composer where I would go through a show and decide where the music goes, relay that to the composer and we would talk about it and he would write the music and I would put it in. The other side of the job, they would send me a show and from libraries I would go through and find music for the shows and put them in the show, cut them and make them fit."

His first credit was with *Laverne & Shirley* in 1976; he was music editor for 144 episodes, according to *IMDb.com*. "Laverne & Shirley was fun. I would be doing that show and [producer] Garry Marshall would call and say there was a tough *Happy Days* coming up and would I mind doing it? They told me at the time, 'Here's the show, you do whatever you want to do and we won't get involved.' "

With the help of *Baseball-Reference.com* and *IMDb.com*, you could almost put together some back-of-a-baseball-card sheet for Swanson:

Charles D. "Chips" Swanson

Born: Dec. 13, 1947

Bats: Right   *Throws:* Right
Height: 6'2   *Weight:* 200 lb.

1976-83: Laverne & Shirley, 144 episodes
1977: Happy Days, 2 episodes
1979: The Bad News Bears, 12 episodes
1983-93: Cheers, 248 episodes
1990-97: Wings, 170 episodes
1993-2004: Frasier, 250 episodes
1995-97: Almost Perfect, 19 episodes
1999-2002: Becker, 6 episodes

"I guess what I have," Swanson said, "it's not that I can write music. What they liked was I had a sense of the way, as they would describe to me, what should go where and what fit musically as far as moods or atmosphere or whatever. They said I had a pretty good sense of feel for the show, and I had a pretty good sense of where to start and end music."

Swanson is now retired, a scratch golfer dealing with the challenge of an aching back that's threatening to add a few strokes to his scorecard. He and Ginny get to travel. David, who played basketball and ran track, and Brian, who played football at UCLA, are both doctors.

You can't help notice the coincidences. Of two of the greatest shows for which he worked, *Frasier* and *Cheers,* one features two sons who are doctors and the other centers around a retired baseball pitcher.

Television credits that roll by quickly are not a place where everybody can know your name. Now, should you spot Chips Swanson's name at the end of a rerun, having added the perfect subtle atmosphere to the show you've just watched, you can connect it to a night of perfection on a baseball diamond in 1970.

A TALE OF TWO NO-NOS

1971

Two no-hitters, separated by a week, delivered for an anemic team for which even a no-hitter wasn't guaranteed to win, twirled by two teammates soon to be going in opposite directions: One would become a principal in one of the most famous and dramatic games ever played. One would never pitch another regular-season professional game.

On August 29, 1971, Columbus Astros right-hander Pat Darcy threw a no-hitter against the Charlotte Hornets, winning 2-0 at Columbus's Golden Park.

On September 5, Astros left-hander Dan Evans threw a no-hitter at Jacksonville, winning 3-0 on the penultimate day of the season.

The next day, the Astros staggered home with a 51-91 record, 41 games out of first place, the worst season in Columbus baseball history.

It was after those no-hitters where the similarities and parallel paths ended for Darcy and Evans.

Pat Darcy's destiny led to the big leagues. Pitching for the Cincinnati Reds, he surrendered the epic, perpetually replayed 12th-inning, game-winning Carlton Fisk home run in Game 6 of the classic 1975 World Series. Darcy's Reds overcame the loss, triumphing over the Red Sox in Game 7.

Evans reported to spring training in 1972, was released, and never pitched again.

It was a sleep-deprived Darcy who took the mound for a 1 p.m. Sunday afternoon game in front of 279 fans. The Astros' bus broke down near the small burg of Daisy, Georgia, following their Saturday night game in Savannah. After the driver and some mechanics spent an hour and a half trying to fix it, they found the solution.

It had run out of gas.

It was a metaphor for the Astros that year, and a metaphor even for Darcy, who recalled, "I was tired. Everybody was tired." In a display of absurdist humor, he told fellow pitcher Roy Bethel before the game he was going to pitch a no-hitter. Replied Bethel, "I'll be in to relieve you about the sixth [inning]."

Worse yet than the dog days biting, it was Charlotte who was coming to visit.

"I think we only beat those guys once or twice that season. Asheville and Charlotte were the two best teams," Darcy said.

Pat Darcy was pitching well in the second half of 1971, finishing the season with a deceptive 5-10 record and a skinny 2.56 ERA. But, he said from his Tucson, Arizona office, "I got on a good roll there." Relying mostly on fastballs and sliders, he struck out 10 Hornets, retired 10 in a row in one stretch and allowed only three walks—one intentional—and a hit batsman. Third baseman Dave Grangaard saved the no-hitter with a deft play on a Jerry Terrell bunt in the third, one of those defensive gems that seems to always crop up to preserve a no-hitter. Darcy struck out the nettlesome Minnie Mendoza to lead off the ninth and dispatched Glenn Borgmann on a routine fly to left to end the game.

The Astros traded Darcy to Cincinnati three years later for veteran infielder Denis Menke, and he pitched 44 games in the majors, all for the Reds.

He was a rookie, at the end of his first full season, when manager Sparky Anderson called on him to relieve Will McEnaney in the bottom of the 10th in the thrilling Game 6. He retired the first six men he faced—including Hall of Famer Carl Yastrzemski—on three groundouts, a pop-up, strikeout and routine fly. But after the Reds left a pair of runners on board in the 12th, Fisk launched Darcy's second pitch down the left-field line, clanking off the foul pole. (It is now a part of network television lore that the dramatic instant-replay footage of Fisk waving the fall fair was captured only because the cameraman had become distracted by a Fenway Park rat that had crawled into his space, and he neglected to move his camera to follow the flight of the ball.)

There is no discomfort in being the answer to a trivia question, even in a negative role. Said Darcy, "It was a great game, one of the greatest games ever played. And we won the World Series. It was OK. I see Pete [Rose] every now and again, and he's said it was the best game ever played. I was privileged to play in a game like that."

Upon retirement, Darcy dove into the real-estate business in Tucson. When major-league teams began investigating the area as a potential spring-training site and a new complex was being planned, Darcy was enlisted by the city as its point person with the Colorado Rockies. That civic involvement led him to contemplate a run as mayor, but he opted not to campaign.

He had lunch in the middle of the 2012 season with an old Columbus teammate, Greg Gross. Gross was serving as the hitting coach for the Diamondbacks' Triple-A club, bringing him to Tucson. The two former ballplayers reminisced about the horrendous bus rides, peculiar hotels, and other memories of the '71 season.

It was Gross who made the defensive gem that saved Dan Evans' no-hitter, occurring in the first game of a doubleheader at Jacksonville's Wolfson Park. (Teams, by the way, played nine-inning games in doubleheaders in those days, rather than the current seven. Evans' no-hitter still sped by in a swift 1:40.)

Right fielder Ed Armbrister was playing close to the line, with Greg Gross slightly shaded to right against left-handed hitting Jim Norris. Evans hung a slider and "the minute it went off the bat, I looked at where it was going and I just started running for third base," the pitcher remembered. "I thought it'd hit the wall. The only person who had a ghost of a chance was Greg. He got the greatest jump."

Gross dove and the caught the ball in the webbing. Even from 350 feet away, "you could see three-quarters of the ball like an ice cream cone," said Evans. The outfielder remained motionless on his belly, afraid to move lest the ball drop. Armbrister had arrived by that time and reached down to pluck the ball out of Gross' glove.

Evans wrapped up the no-hitter with six strikeouts and only three walks, working well with catcher Dale Weatherford. It was merely his second win of the season for Columbus, the other coming on a two-hitter against Birmingham. The key to his recent success was a devastating forkball that he learned from manager Dick Bogard in his second year in the pros. It wasn't an easy education. "First time I threw it," Evans said, "it went 20 feet up the backstop."

He was tall and gifted with big hands, and the forkball helped compensate for decreased velocity after suffering an arm injury in 1970. But it wasn't enough to keep him in baseball the following spring.

When the Astros released him, "It wasn't a crushing thing. I'm not throwing 94 any more. They looked at the future. I was getting older and they made room for a younger, better pitcher."

Evans joined the Church of the Latter Day Saints and embarked on a mission to Australia. He enrolled at Brigham Young, where he met his future wife Sharon at a church function. Their first date, they went horseback riding. "She could outride John Wayne," Evans said. As for Evans' equestrian skills, "Me and horses still haven't come to any synergy." He graduated with degrees in journalism and history, but he had been working part-time for the BYU police force and chose to stay with them. He remained in law enforcement until 1990; he now counsels high-school and college students in the LDS faith.

While Darcy still has the last-pitch ball from his performance, the final-out souvenir from Evans' no-hitter is long gone.

Late in the game, a young fan, perhaps 10 years of age, stretched out flat across the dugout roof, leaned into the Columbus dugout and said, "Hey, Lefty, are you going to get a no-hitter?" That, of course, goes against all superstition. Columbus outfielder Larry Mansfield, a 6-foot-8 former basketball player at the University of Tennessee who socked 33 homers that year, heard the boy and growled at him. "The kid looked crestfallen," Evans said, "like 'I've done something wrong.' I just said, 'I hope I come through with this.'"

Evans recorded the final out and a teammate tossed him the ball. As Evans reached the dugout, he spied the boy and yelled to get his attention. Evans then rolled the baseball across the dugout roof and into the kid's waiting hands.

SIX HOURS IN SAVANNAH

1973

Columbus Astros manager Wayne "Twig" Terwilliger pronounced that "it was amazing," but, really, what did he know? After all, he had been ejected from the game 16 innings earlier in what would stand alone for a quarter-century as the longest game in Southern League history.

It was only the second game of the 1973 season when the Astros began play on Saturday night, April 14 at Savannah. It would be two-and-half games' worth of play before Columbus erupted for six runs in the top of the 23rd inning in the wee hours of the morning, assuring a 10-4 victory in a six-hour, 14-minute affair. Not until Greenville would beat Huntsville 10-7 in August 1998 would any Southern League game last as long.

Aside from the managerial ejection, the epic contest also featured a triple play, an 0-for-11 batting line, 33 men left on base, four Columbus runners picked off first base, and a Savannah player whose sibling was a year away from making baseball history himself.

The Astros took the field for the scheduled doubleheader wearing uncharacteristic orange caps. They traditionally wore blue caps with a "C" on the front, but the cap manufacturer goofed and didn't deliver the caps to the Columbus sporting-goods store through whom the Astros ordered their caps. General manager Jim Koger scrambled and had a supply of Houston's orange caps shipped by bus to Columbus, just in time to make the road trip.

They took a 2-0 lead in the sixth when Jerry Moxey tripled home Nate Pettaway, then scored on an Al Leaver fielder's choice. However, Alvin "Junior" Moore tied the game with a homer off Paul

Siebert, the ball sailing over the concrete left-field stands (since torn down) and into a grove of pine trees.

The next inning, left fielder Moxey charged in for a sinking line drive. The umpires ruled he trapped the ball after a short hop. Moxey disagreed, as did Terwilliger. The umps briefly conferred and stuck with the original ruling. Terwilliger would later remind the *Columbus Ledger*'s Cecil Darby, "I don't usually have anything to say to the umpires unless I'm sure I'm right."

Twig was an ex-Marine who served in the Pacific during World War II, then kicked around the majors for nine years as a good-field, no-hit second baseman. He became immortalized with the phrase "Terwilliger bunts one" in Annie Dillard's memoir, an announcer's description that captivated Dillard's mother. That same phrase later turned into the title of Twig's autobiography. He coached in the majors once his playing days were through—he was Ted Williams' right-hand man when Williams managed the Senators—and managed 13 seasons in the minors, the last with the Fort Worth Cats in 2005. Twig was a mere 80 years old then.

Terwilliger and Moxey, continuing to plead with the umpires, even pointed out the lack of a grass stain. There soon would be, though. The irate Terwilliger, having lost his case and his temper, snatched the ball and "heaved it as far as I could into left field," he said.

The score remained 2-2 into the 11th, when Moxey singled and took second when a pickoff throw eluded Tommie Aaron. (The following April, Tommie's older brother, Henry, would surpass Babe Ruth's home run record.) It was one of 11 errors, but also one of the few times it seemed that Savannah pitchers failed to nab Astro runners, with four picked off base. Moxey scored on a Pastor Perez single. Another Leaver RBI single followed, making it 4-2.

Freddie Velazquez opened the 11th with a double, then a walk and infield single loaded the bases against Ron DeJean. Toy McCord grounded into a fielder's choice for one run, then Jose Salas committed a passed ball to let Savannah tie the score at 4-all, with pinch-running Bahamian pitcher Percival Edmund Wentworth "Wenty" Ford hustling in from third. Columbus threatened in the 16th after a pair of errors from pitcher Pablo Torrealba, who pitched 11 innings in relief of starter Jamie Easterly. But Bob Blakley hit a line drive to

Aaron at first, who stepped on his bag to double up one runner, then threw to second to nail the other for the triple play.

Things plodded along scorelessly from the 17th through the 22nd. After the latter, the anxious workers at the *Columbus Ledger* had to finally roll the presses, leaving their Sunday morning readers hanging with "Astros tied in 22nd." There was no Internet to help, no @TwigTweets to tell the story of the 23rd, not until a day later.

That was when the Astros apparently had enough of this tomfoolery. Perez tripled off Ken Alfred, making his unlucky 13th professional appearance since being drafted from Nicholls State. Leaver walked, and Steve Gardner, an outfielder who would play in only 16 more professional games before a distinguished career in college coaching, hit a two-run triple for a 6-4 lead. Blakley added a three-run homer to assure there'd be no Savannah comeback.

"I think," Terwilliger said, "our kids just outlasted 'em."

As the final stats were compiled, abbreviations of long names were probably preferred by many of the game's principals. The hitless futility of the Astros' Jesus de la Rosa and the Braves' Marian Murphy, for instance, was cryptically disguised:

d la r'a 1b 11 0 0 0

and

Mur'y cf 10 0 0 0

But the number that stood out most vividly in the box score was on the very last line: T – 6:14.

PLAYOFF GEMS

1993, 2005, 2007

Paybacks are hell, they say.

On June 21, 2007, Huntsville pitcher Corey Thurman surrendered a two-run homer to Tennessee pitcher Mark Holliman in the first game of a doubleheader, a 3-0 Stars' loss. But that was only the second-best thing Holliman did that night. He completed a seven-inning no-hitter, retiring the final 15 Huntsville batters he faced.

A little more than two months later, on September 7, 2007, Thurman turned the tables. He and two other Huntsville pitchers combined for a no-hitter to beat the Smokies in the first round of the Southern League North playoffs. Said Thurman, "After Holliman threw his no-hitter, I was thinking tonight, 'I'd much rather do it now.'"

Thurman, a well-traveled pitcher out of Texarkana, Texas, and the owner of a miniature Doberman named Tyson, threw the first six innings. Dave Johnson handled the seventh and eighth before handing off to closer Luis Peña. The latter hit 100-mph four times on the Stars' radar gun and literally loosened the strings on Lou Palmisano's catcher's mitt.

The Stars' team no-hitter was one of only three postseason no-hitters in the Southern League since 1993, when the league began keeping playoff records.

Mike Hostetler of Greenville beat Knoxville 2-0 on September 8, 1993, in the only complete-game no-hitter, played in front of a mere 511 fans at Greenville's Municipal Stadium in the opener of the Eastern Division playoffs.

Chad Billingsley and Jonathan Broxton of Jacksonville no-hit Birmingham 2-0 in the first game of the South Division playoffs on September 8, 2005.

There was some hellish payback for Jacksonville to enjoy in its no-hitter over Birmingham. The Barons and Jacksonville met eight times in the final 11 games of the regular season before this post-season rematch, and the Barons had won six of those, including a home-stadium sweep that earned the division title. However, one of the Jacksonville wins in that span was a seven-inning, one-hit shutout by Billingsley on August 26. He would tell Jeff Elliott of the *Florida Times-Union* that his fastball was off that night and he "could have been better."

Indeed, he *was* better on that Thursday night at the Baseball Grounds in Jacksonville, mowing down the Barons for seven innings before turning it over to Broxton. Billingsley had been the dominant pitcher in the league in the final half, going 9-2 with a 2.03 ERA in his 13 starts prior to the no-hitter.

So it was the hottest team, and hottest hitting team with a league-best .279 average, vs. the hottest pitcher when Billingsley took the mound. He walked a couple of men early, but retired 10 in a row at one stretch and saw his no-hitter preserved on a running catch in center by Todd Donovan in the seventh.

"I got ahead of a lot of hitters and that allowed me to throw a lot of breaking balls," Billingsley said. "I was going after the hitters early with my fastball, but in the last couple of innings, I was able to keep them off balance by mixing in the breaking stuff. When you're throwing strikes with your fastball and breaking balls, it really keeps hitters guessing what you're going to do."

Then came Broxton with 100-mph fastballs in relief, striking out two, including Casey Rogowski, who was thrown out arguing the called third strike. Perhaps it sounded a little low.

"Those two guys would have beaten a lot of major-league clubs tonight," said Birmingham manager Razor Shines.

The ultimate payback for Jacksonville was a three-game sweep in the series on the way to the Southern League pennant.

Two years later, Huntsville manager Don Money was leaning on the batting cage at Joe Davis Stadium, watching his club in a final workout before the playoffs against Tennessee. "The key for us," said the former Brewers great, "is to keep them off base and from stealing bases. But we have to play our own game. We have to do the simple things for us. We've got to get men on and move them around and get two-out base hits."

Clearly, the true key—albeit, not quite a simple thing—was to not let Tennessee get any hits. Money and pitching coach Rich Sauveur, who later admitted he watched the final inning of the no-hitter "with a tear in my eye," opted to start Thurman. Good choice. A year earlier, he pitched Huntsville to a playoff-opening shutout win, outdueling Chattanooga's Homer Bailey (who now boasts two big-league no-hitters).

Thurman said he had a "nervous, anxious energy" all day, but began the game cautiously. He walked two batters in the first rather than serve up hittable pitches, he said. Then, he pretty much threw zero hittable pitches, retiring 16 in a row. But after six innings, his pitch count was high. The Stars were up 2-0 in the bottom of the sixth with the bases loaded. Corey Thurman was no Mark Holliman, let alone Babe Ruth. He was 1-for-14 for the season. Money called on pinch-hitter Mike Goetz, a recent call-up from rookie-level ball who was 0-for-4 in his only other game. But Goetz hit a Super Ball chopper over shortstop to drive in two runs. It would be the only hit in Class AA ball in Goetz's career.

Thurman hustled to the clubhouse and encased his arm in ice, then hid in a breezeway outside the Stars' clubhouse watching Johnson and Pena wrap things up.

"I didn't want go back down to the dugout and do anything different and jinx it," said Thurman.

Mike Hostetler and the Greenville Braves were equally aware of superstition and custom. During his 1993 postseason no-hitter, he sat in the same spot, at the far end of the first-base dugout, each time the Braves were batting. "I had my spot and everybody stayed away. There was three or four feet around me and nobody got in my space," Hostetler said. "I had the whole corner to myself and nobody broke silence the last two or three innings."

He enjoyed a near-perfect connection with catcher Brad Rippelmeyer, whose signals Hostetler shook off only twice. "The only thing I saw was the glove," Hostetler said. "Rip and I were on the same page with the pitches we wanted to throw, and every time he put the glove up, I seemed to be able to hit my spots. When I got behind, I was able to throw a quality pitch and get an out on it."

"I remember being on the same page with him," Rippelmeyer said. "I loved catching Mike. He pitched what we called 'backwards' a lot. He threw off-speed stuff early in the count and when he was ahead in the count. When ... he got ahead 0-2, 1-2, he threw fastballs."

Or, as Knoxville first baseman Tim Hyers told the *Knoxville News-Sentinel* with some bit of disdain, "He kept throwing a lot of junk."

It was the second pro no-hitter for Hostetler, who was a 21st-round pick out of Georgia Tech. He was part of a four-person no-hitter the previous April while at Class A Durham, with a third-inning walk the only flaw. He reached Triple-A the next season but ultimately a pair of arm surgeries ended his career. Now a financial planner—as is Rippelmeyer, who is in business with their former Greenville teammate, Blase Sparma—Hostetler also helps coach Mt. Paran Christian School and youth league teams involving his son, Michael, also a pitcher.

Being around baseball, he has found himself on a bench watching one of his players make a no-hit bid. "It's much easier when I've got one going as a pitcher because you can at least control the execution of what's going on," Hostetler said. "Sitting on the bench trying to call pitches and hope we're on the same page about how we're trying to set up the hitter and I'm watching as the pitcher is trying to execute the pitch, it's more nerve-wracking to be in that situation."

The Braves' defense kept it interesting, making four errors to keep Hostetler pitching from the stretch, but outfielders Pat Kelly and Mike Warner made diving catches to prevent hits. Hostetler retired Hyers to lead off the ninth, then went backward against the dangerous Carlos Delgado, the league MVP with 25 homers and 102 RBI. Hostetler fell behind 1-0, threw a pair of changeups, then froze Delgado with a fastball for a called third strike. The future All-Star dropped his bat and helmet at the plate and was summarily ejected by umpire Bob Brooks; Smokies' manager Garth Iorg also eventually got the heave-ho. After nearly five minutes to settle that mess, Hostetler retired Howard Battle grounder to short.

Alas, Knoxville took a 2-1 lead in the series before nine walks by Knoxville pitchers in Game 4 necessitated a fifth game. Hostetler started and was tagged for 10 hits in 6 2/3 innings. The Braves' bullpen failed him in the seventh, leading to a four-run Knoxville rally in a 5-0 series-clinching win for the Smokies.

You think pitchers have superstitions when it comes to no-hitters? Consider Knoxville pitcher Huck Flener, who allowed only five hits in eight innings in Game 5. He had a horseshoe hanging in his locker that had been presented to the Smokies for good luck by students from the Chilhowee Intermediate School. And, for payback's sake, Flener had been the Knoxville starter when Hostetler threw the no-hitter. You know what they say about payback.

SUPERSTITIOUS AND STREAKING

1987

> *"The root of all superstition is that men observe when a thing hits, but not when it misses."*
> **– Francis Bacon**

The Tennessee Highway Patrol was hiring. To Greg Tubbs, it seemed the ideal solution.

He was at a low point in his baseball career, nearly 25. The Braves had just passed him up for promotion. Then they started tinkering with his batting approach, turning him from aggressive to passive, demanding he go deep into counts and look for walks to take advantage of his speed.

When the Southern League adjourned for its midseason All-Star break, the league's best players convening in Greenville, South Carolina, for an exhibition against the Triple-A Richmond Braves, Tubbs bolted Greenville to return to his home in Smithville, Tennessee., up on the Cumberland Plateau in middle Tennessee.

"I almost called it quits," Greg remembered, but his mother, Jean Biles, would have none of that. "My mom told me to get back there and battle."

Mom knew best. Tubbs, to use a pet expression, "was on fire" after the All-Star break. On July 28 against Columbus, he notched the hit that provided the first spark. By the time his bat cooled off, on August 29, the penultimate game of the season, he had compiled a Southern League record hitting streak of 33 games. The streak broke the previous mark of 30 set in 1974 by Asheville's Kim Andrew, and it still stands today at the conclusion of the Southern League's 50th season.

Greg Tubbs collected 49 hits during the streak, 13 for extra bases. He had the occasional close call. On the night he tied Andrew, he was 0-for-2 going into the seventh. Another time he was 0-for-4 and hustled out a grounder to deep short, reaching as the throw sailed into the stands. The official scorer awarded him the hit, recognizing that with Tubbs's speed and the hurried throw, it would have been a bang-bang play at first.

Thinking back on the streak, Tubbs believes he "didn't get serious about it until I got to about 15 games." That was when superstition kicked in. "I didn't shave. I wore everything the same," he said. "I didn't change up anything. Same socks, same T-shirts, I cleaned my shoes the same way before every game."

He was not a regular tobacco chewer, but realized he had been chewing some when the streak started. So before his first at-bat, he'd put in a chaw and quickly spit it out as soon as he got his first hit.

When both streak and season ended, he was not chosen for the Southern League Postseason All-Star team. Greg Tubbs had but a .269 average, a good indication of just how miserable that first half of the season had been. Like many hitters, too, he had always been more of a warm-weather player, putting up his best numbers from late June until season's end.

There must have been something tricky in the cosmos in 1987. It was The Year Of The Streak. Future Hall of Famer Paul Molitor strung together a 39-game hitting streak for the Milwaukee Brewers, seventh-longest all-time. Rookie catcher Benito Santiago hit safely in 34 consecutive games for the Padres. At the college ranks, future All-Star Robin Ventura hit in 58 consecutive games for Oklahoma State, an NCAA Division I record; the string was finally ended in the Cowboys' third game of the College World Series, a win over Stanford. (The opposing starting pitcher was Jack McDowell; two years later, McDowell and Ventura would be teammates with the Chicago White Sox, the club Ventura was hired to manage in 2012.)

Greg Tubbs's 33-game streak didn't halve the minor-league record of 69, set by Joe Wilhoit in 1919 for Wichita of the Western League. You could win a bar bet by knowing the second-longest streak in minor-league history: 61 games by 19-year-old Joe DiMaggio for the San Francisco Seals in 1933, eight years before his major-league record of 56. "Baseball didn't really get into my blood until I knocked off that hitting streak," the Yankee Clipper would later say.

Tubbs had batted .319 and .317 his first two seasons in the minors, climbing the Braves' prospect list. He hit .269 in 1986—the exact same average as the streak season—and that's when Atlanta started tweaking his approach at the plate. The Braves traded him to Pittsburgh in 1990, hardly the opportune time or place for a young outfielder with Barry Bonds, Andy Van Slyke, and Bobby Bonilla ensconced in the Pirates starting lineup. After two Triple-A seasons in the Pittsburgh organization, Tubbs was granted free agency and was signed by Cincinnati in 1993.

He was at his apartment in Indianapolis, sorting through laundry, when his phone rang on a Saturday. It was his manager, Marc Bombard, telling him to be on a plane to Cincinnati the next morning at 6:30. A month shy of his 31st birthday, he was finally going to the majors. He spent a nervous night, tossing and turning, and then slept through his alarm, missing his flight. He called Bombard in a dither. Said the manager, "It's an hour and a half drive." Tubbs sped to Cincinnati, arriving at 9:30 a.m. to an empty clubhouse. But there was already a locker with his name on it and a pristine Reds jersey with his name on the back above the numeral 51.

Manager Davey Johnson stopped by and told him he'd be in the starting lineup that day against San Diego. Tubbs ducked into a restroom with a towel and covered his mouth, screaming in excitement. Facing Andy Benes in his first major-league at-bat, he singled to center. They retrieved the ball for a souvenir. "Unbelievable," he said. "To relive it now still gives me goosebumps."

He played in 35 more games that season, batting .186. "But I hung in there," he said, "and I finally got my shot."

When Tubbs ended his career, he returned to his Tennessee roots, settling in Cookeville, which straddles the roller-coaster Interstate 40 between Nashville and Knoxville. He went to work at Cookeville High, working with special-needs students and serving as the baseball team's hitting and outfield coach; two of his former players are sons Darien, a 2013 signee of the University of Memphis, and Demond, who played at Roane State. Tubbs had been influenced by a number of notable baseball men—Luke Appling, Hank Aaron,

Willie Stargell, Barry Larkin, Bill Virdon, Ray Knight, and Bobby Valentine, to name a few. "A big list of people touched my career and now I'm giving all that back to kids."

As Greg Tubbs sat at his desk, nearby were some scribbled sheets of football plays. The special-needs students were beginning to participate in some competitive activities, like flag football. "I had to do some research and learn how to adapt and work with these kids," he said. "Every year it's something different. Every year I'm in this, the more I love interacting with them.

"I grew up in a little ol' town. I was a good player, but I didn't realize how good until I went out there. I dreamed. And these kids dream, too. I feel like it's my place to give back to those kids."

THE GREENVILLE MARATHON

1998

This was not starting out to be Adam Johnson's night. A couple of early outs in one of those games that erodes a little of your soul, coming in the crushing heat of August where time drags along as slowly as it can manage.

This Thursday night date between Johnson's Greenville Braves and the visiting Huntsville Stars, "started out like a typical game, a nondescript day in August," said Steve Kornya, the Stars' radio broadcaster. In fact, to steel themselves against the dog-day doldrums and to enliven their broadcasts, Kornya and Greenville's Mark Hauser agreed to do a dual broadcast, both in the same booth, sharing the play-by-play and simulcasting on their respective flagship stations. Little did they know that would turn out to be a lifesaver.

Little, too, did Johnson know he'd U-turn from a slow start to have four straight hits, that he'd become a part of history, that this nondescript game would, as Kornya put it, "keep going and going and going and going and going and going...."

Thursday night, August 6, 1998, turned into Friday morning, August 7, "and everybody was saying, 'When is this going to end?' " Johnson remembered.

Curfew arrived, and the game was still going.

The next afternoon, after a 16-hour hiatus, it was still going.

Finally, with one out in the 23rd inning, Johnson socked a three-run homer off Huntsville reliever Jeff D'Amico to end what should be recognized unofficially as the longest game in Southern League history, with the formula of time and distance.

The 23 innings matched a previous marathon (Columbus at Savannah, April 14, 1973), though the six-hour, 26-minute duration was shorter, by a comparative hiccup, than an 18-inning game Huntsville played in Birmingham in 1989 that lasted 6:37 or—poor Huntsville, again—a Stars game at Memphis in 1991 that took 6:32 to play 20 innings.

Huntsville took an early 3-0 lead, ignited by a two-run Jose Ortiz home run, but the Braves tied it at 3 in the third. It remained that way until the 12th when Huntsville plated a pair of runs, only to have Johnson extend the game with a two-out, two-run double.

As grueling as it was on the playing field, it had gotten a little slap-happy in the radio booth. Hauser admitted, "Once we got past the 13th or 14th inning ... we started looking in record books for the longest league game by innings, longest by time. We thought, 'As long as we've gone this far, let's make it worth something.' We got to the point of absurdity where we might as well stick around and do something people will talk about."

Danny Ardoin ripped a two-run homer in the top of the 20th for a 7-5 lead, only to see Greenville make it 7-7 in the bottom half, tying the game on Jake O'Dell's wild pitch. The game was then suspended at 1:13 a.m. EDT, according to a Southern League rule that mandated no new inning could begin at 12:50 a.m.

The next afternoon, R.W. Jacobs held the Stars hitless in the top of the 23rd. George Lombard opened the Braves' at-bat with a double to left that missed only by a few feet from being the game-winner. After a sacrifice bunt failed, Mark DeRosa walked, setting up Johnson's homer. Said Johnson, "I don't remember the double at all. I remember hitting the home run [which cleared the right field fence]. It was one of those no-doubters." The clutch situation appealed to Johnson throughout his career. "Everybody always jokes that if you could go back and play one more game, I'd love to be up in the bottom of the ninth, with a tie game and the winning run on second."

Both teams used seven pitchers and 18 position players. Batting averages took a severe beating. Ortiz, for instance, who began the game so successfully, finished with a 2-for-11 showing.

It was even worse for the Stars after the 23-inning game was completed. There was still the regularly scheduled nightcap to play. Bruce Chen, one of the Braves' top prospects, was sent back down from Triple-A to make the start; his Richmond club was on a trip to Canada and he didn't have the proper visa. He left with a comfortable lead en route to a 14-6 Greenville win. This affair also proved historic: Mike Eaglin—still a Facebook friend of Johnson's—went 6-for-6 for Greenville, tying a league record shared by 10 others. Braves' reliever Eric Olszewski found an ignominious spot in Southern League record book by walking six batters in a four-run Huntsville seventh inning. Greenville manager Randy Ingle's hands were tied, having used up most of his relievers through the course of two days and the previous 30 innings.

The Stars-Greenville marathon was still considerably shorter than the longest professional baseball game ever played which, coincidentally, was started by a Huntsville native. "I'm the answer to a trivia question," said Dan Parks, who went the first of 33 innings in a Class AAA International League game his Pawtucket Red Sox won over the Rochester Red Wings, 3-2.

That game began April 18, 1981, in temperatures so cold, Rochester outfielder Drungo Hazewood told author Dan Barry, "that when you opened your eyes, the inside of your eyes got cold." Pawtucket tied it 1-1 in the bottom of the ninth, then after Rochester scored to open the 21st inning, Wade Boggs evened the score again with an RBI double in the bottom half. Finally, at 4:03 a.m. on April 19, the umpires suspended the game after 32 innings, having stubbornly refused to do so earlier because of a misunderstanding of league bylaws. The teams completed the game June 23, Pawtucket winning in the bottom of the 33rd inning—in only 18 minutes of playing time.

Adam Johnson, a 55th-round draft choice out of Central Florida, never made it to the majors, eventually a victim of a numbers game and his own burn-out. His career was not uneventful, though. In a game at Knoxville, teammate Lonell Roberts collided with him while chasing a fly ball, knocking out three teeth and opening a gash in his lip. He was ferried to a local hospital by a Knoxville intern and as he arrived at the emergency room he pulled out a wad of bloody gauze. The intern got one look "and all I remember is her running out the door, throwing up," Johnson chuckled from his office in Naples, Florida, where he runs a moving business that's been in his family for more than a century.

Winning a 23-inning game with a home run is one thing—but Johnson knocked an even more memorable home run later in the season at Birmingham (where, by coincidence, he'd finish his Southern League career as a Baron in 2000-01). The Barons had a promotion that any player who homered in the fourth inning would win an SUV from Long-Lewis Ford, a local dealer. Johnson was the DH and went to the bullpen to loosen up before his at-bat. His teammates there were talking about the promotion. One of them grabbed his bat, a fresh Troy O'Leary model bat that had just arrived, and slammed it against his cleats. "Now you're ready for that home run," he told Johnson.

The second pitch from the Barons' Jason Lakman, "I leaned back and swung and when I hit it, I knew it was gone." He also knew what it meant.

"I tripped over first base because I was watching it as I was running," he said. "I got up and told the second baseman, 'I just won a truck! I just won a truck!'"

GAUDIN'S PURSUIT OF PERFECTION

2003

Chad Gaudin was a bloody mess at home plate. A foul ball had ricocheted off his own bat and socked him in the face. He'd later tell the *St. Petersburg Times* he knew he was all right " 'cause my eye wasn't popped out of my head." It was 2001. He was the starting pitcher for Crescent City Baptist High in the New Orleans suburb of Metairie, and he was one inning away from completing a perfect game.

Still, Gaudin retook the mound for the final inning. He retired the first two batters—and then yielded a flare for a single. He responded by striking out the final hitter. A Tampa Bay scout named Benny Latino would tell the *Times* of Gaudin's courage, "It was the greatest thing I ever saw."

Four years later, on May 16, 2005, Gaudin was pitching for Class AAA Syracuse against Columbus in the International League. He had another perfect game, this time through eight innings. But Ryan Hankins, a journeyman who would bat only .258 that season, ripped a single to left field to lead off the ninth and ruin things.

Roughly halfway in between those heartbreaks, Chad Gaudin, a slight 5-10, 185-pound right-hander, did find a way to achieve perfection. He did so under circumstances to pop everybody's eyes out a little bit.

The Orlando Rays needed pitching help. Matt White, 0-4 and struggling in his final season of pro ball, went on the disabled list with a bum right shoulder. Gaudin was 5-3 with a 2.12 ERA at Class

A Bakersfield when the Rays summoned him cross-country to fill White's spot.

Gaudin pitched a seven-inning perfect game in his Southern League debut, beating Jacksonville in the first game of a double-header on July 15, 2003. He was only 20 years old. When he called home and told his mother what he'd done, Gaudin would tell the *Orlando Sentinel* his mother was "not the brightest in the baseball world" and "I had to tell her what it was. She was proud of me."

It was only the third perfect game in Southern League history. Birmingham's George Lauzerique had worked a seven-inning per-fect game against Evansville on July 6, 1965, in the second half of a doubleheader. Chips Swanson of Montgomery (see Chapter 41) boasts the only nine-inning perfect game, achieved on August 14, 1970.

Gaudin needed only 78 pitches, 56 of them for strikes. He only had a three-ball count against one batter, future big-league standout Shane Victorino, the first batter he faced.

He needed a bit of defensive help, too. The perfect game was saved in the fifth on a diving stab by first baseman Dan Grummitt, and in the sixth when Jesus Feliciano, a former Jacksonville Sun, made a diving catch of a Tony Soccaras line drive. Said Gaudin appreciatively, "I tried to be aggressive and stay in command of my fastball and everything worked out well today. But give credit to my defense, I couldn't have done that without their effort."

The Suns, meanwhile, were giving full credit to Gaudin.

"He pitched a helluva game in his first start," Jacksonville manager Dino Ebel told the *Florida Times-Union*. "We've been swinging the bats well, and he put pitches where we weren't looking. ... He's got an advantage in that we didn't know anything about him, and he had great command of his pitches tonight."

The Suns' Reggie Abercrombie echoed, "He used all his pitches very well and never got behind on the count on any of us. In his first start like that, he didn't have anything to lose. He just pitched his game, didn't appear to be nervous and he had us off balance. ... We'll have a better idea about him if we face him again."

Abercrombie wouldn't have to worry about facing Gaudin and having "a better idea." The Devil Rays, smitten with Gaudin, pro-moted him to the majors. He debuted on August 1. Heady stuff for a kid who was a 34th-round draft pick, spurning a scholarship offer from LSU to sign for a $132,000 bonus.

The Rays traded Chad Gaudin to Toronto in 2004, beginning a peripatetic major-league career in which he'd wear nine different uniforms by the end of the 2013 season, spent with the San Francisco Giants.

On September 6, 2013, Gaudin was present at San Francisco's AT&T Park when Giants teammate Yumerio Petit took the mound against the Arizona Diamondbacks. That night, Petit lost a perfect game with two out in the ninth inning.

Perfection, Gaudin might well advise Petit, doesn't come easy.

PEAVY VS. PRIOR

2002

The game and the outcome had become a fuzzy memory. But as Jake Peavy stood at his locker on a mid-summer Sunday, wearing a fading, threadbare, sleeveless T-shirt and uniform pants more than a decade later, what he could remember was "there being a lot of hype around it."

That's a bit of 20-20 memory.

It was the kind of hype rarely seen in the minor leagues, where typically stardom is something yet to be achieved.

On late morning of April 17, 2002, in Mobile, the stars were aligned. It wasn't the Mobile BayBears vs. the West Tenn Diamond Jaxx. It was one of those games you could imagine in the bold, unique font of a boxing promotional poster:

PEAVY

vs.

PRIOR

If there was ever a much-ballyhooed, heavyweight pitching bout in the Southern League, this was it.

"Probably the biggest start of my career up to then," Peavy said.

In one corner, there stood Mobile's pride and joy, Jake Peavy, the right-hander from St. Paul's Episcopal School, already on a fast track to the majors. He'd eventually be given his own "day" in Mobile and presented the key to the city.

In the other corner, there was Mark Prior, the "Can't-Miss Kid," with the fireplug calves and 95-mph fastball, the second overall pick in the previous year's draft.

The two pitchers would eventually become friends, and briefly even teammates during spring training with the Padres. Said Peavy, "I think the world of him. He's a class, class act." Peavy even belonged to the same country club in San Diego as Prior's father, Jerry. He'd occasionally see Mark on the golf course.

They weren't yet acquainted when this main event rolled around, an occasion for which the *Mobile Press-Register* promised, "The eyes of the baseball world will be on Mobile today." Perhaps the world would be watching, too. But with an 11:35 a.m. start, only 2,479 were in attendance at Hank Aaron Stadium when Peavy came to the mound to face West Tenn center fielder Nic Jackson.

This was a familiar mound for Peavy. He was in his second season at Mobile, having become so synonymous with the BayBears, he worked in the team's front office in the off-season.

Peavy grew up as an Alabama fan but Crimson Tide coach Jim Wells "broke my heart" and didn't offer him a baseball scholarship. "It wasn't meant to be," Peavy shrugged. Instead, Hal Baird at Auburn "treated me like royalty" on a visit and Jake committed. "I wanted to go to Auburn and beat Alabama." But the Padres drafted him in the 15th round after his senior year at St. Paul's (13-0, 0.82 ERA, 151 strikeouts, .443 batting average) and they ponied up more than the usual 15th-round bonus. Peavy was off to pro baseball—and soon back home in Mobile.

After spending 1999 at the rookie levels, he spent all of 2000 at Class A Fort Wayne, with 164 strikeouts in 133 2/3 innings. He began 2001 at Lake Elsinore in the A-Advanced California League and was promoted to Mobile in August of that season.

This was only the third professional start for Prior, who began his college career at Vanderbilt, then transferred to Southern California, where he was All-America and named the top college player of the year in 2001. He completed his degree at USC and was even invited in 2004—by then he was in the majors—to speak to the graduating class of the USC business school. In his talk, he noted that Cubs teammate Greg Maddux told him, "Boy, you're overqualified for this job."

Prior spent the months after ending his USC career playing for

Team USA and in negotiation with the Cubs, finally agreeing to a $14-million deal that included a $4-million bonus, the highest in team history.

On the eve of their matchup, Prior said, "I'm looking forward to a good, old-fashioned pitching duel."

It was far from that. Though Mobile columnist Tommy Hicks rightly called it "one of those 'I was there' moments," Peavy gave up a homer in the second, then loaded the bases in the fourth before Prior, a .242 hitter in limited college experience, skied out to deep left-center. Peavy gave up walks to Mickey Lopez and David Kelton in the fifth—Peavy would complain later he was "squeezed" by the home-plate ump—and manager Craig Colbert went to the bullpen, which let things grow worse. Peavy's line was four innings, five hits, three runs, two walks, five strikeouts.

"Jake was nitpicking in the strike zone instead of going after them with his good stuff," Colbert said after the game. "He's gotten into a little thing the last couple of outings of trying to make too-good pitches. His stuff is good enough where he can go right at the hitter."

"He pitched better than I did," Peavy would say years later. "It was a big matchup for both of us. We were both prospects. He was Mark Prior—the biggest thing in baseball."

Prior pitched seven strong innings, allowing only two hits and striking out eight. But, as Hicks wrote, "Those are the stats. The reality is he would blow away a hitter with his 95-mph fastball on one pitch, stymie the hitter with an 88-mph curveball on the next pitch and leave the batter motionless with a 76-mph change-up on the next pitch. There was a lot of guessing in the batter's box, only a couple of them being correct."

"A lot of big-league guys are going to have a tough time with [Prior]," Colbert said. "It was an impressive outing by him. He's a very mature kid on the mound. His presence is very good on the mound. That's just a God-given thing that he has."

Peavy was promoted to the majors on June 22 of that season. Two years later, he'd win the National League ERA title and in 2007 was the unanimous Cy Young Award winner. He returned to Mobile in 2004 for a one-game rehab start and lost; it'd take him a dozen years from his Double-A debut to level his Southern League career record at 7-7, winning a rehab assignment for the Birmingham Barons at Huntsville in 2013.

Prior made the majors exactly a month earlier than Peavy, having gone 4-1 in six starts at West Tenn and 1-1 in three appearances at Class AAA Iowa. He finished 6-6 in Chicago as a rookie. The next year, he went 18-6 for the Cubs and seemed indeed on the verge of becoming the biggest thing in baseball. He was on the mound on October 14th, 2003, and owning a 3-0 lead in the eighth inning of Game 6 of the NLCS when he induced Florida Marlins second baseman Luis Castillo to hit a long foul ball down the left-field line. It appeared left fielder Moises Alou might have a leaping chance to catch it in the narrow foul territory of Wrigley Field, but a fan named Steve Bartman got his glove on the ball. Given a reprieve, Castillo drew a walk and Ivan Rodriguez cracked an RBI single. When shortstop Alex Gonzalez booted a double-play grounder by Miguel Cabrera, Cubs Nation was in the throes of still another curse. The Marlins won Game 6 and won again the next day, ending Chicago's season.

Prior's career seemed equally cursed. He suffered a litany of injuries, from shoulder to Achilles tendon to a broken elbow after being hit with a line drive. After winning 18 in his first full season, he'd win only 18 more games in the majors. Said Peavy, "Mark was an outstanding talent but, unfortunately, his career in the big-league level was so short."

Peavy vs. Prior would never happen again. They never met in the majors. But when Peavy was the Padres' ace in the mid-2000s, San Diego offered Prior a shot in spring training.

"Who wouldn't hope this was the year that Mark got healthy and you could recapture that," Peavy said. "I know he was so close to breaking back through, but not to what he once was. But there for a little while, he was good as anybody we've seen in the game."

ALL BY HIMSELF

2013

The night before, Eric Jokisch got some news that broke his heart and opened his eyes in at the same time. Kevin Rhoderick, his close friend and road roommate with the Tennessee Smokies, was handed his release a mere two weeks before his 25th birthday.

Tough as the parting may have been, Rhoderick was in good spirits as they sat up late talking at the Hyatt Regency overlooking Jacksonville's neon-spangled riverfront. An exceptional golfer, he wondered if the door closing on baseball might open another in golf. Said Jokisch, "He was pretty excited for his future." In turn, Eric Jokisch had an epiphany of his own, observing, "I had put a lot of pressure on myself to be good, get better and move up and try to get to Chicago. When that happened with Kevin, the world wasn't over. It was a relief for me. I saw that it wasn't that bad. I decided to go out and pitch for the fun of the game again. That was something I lost a long time ago."

Rhoderick's release left a spot open on the roster for an August 6, 2013, game in Jacksonville against a Suns team that had won 11 consecutive games. Filling that spot in a parole from the disabled list was Eric Jokisch. And what fun he had, pitching—and hitting—in the Smokies' 10-0 romp at the Baseball Grounds of Jacksonville in front of 3,860 fans.

Jokisch hurled a no-hitter, the first in the league in more than two years, while striking out eight. He retired the first 10 batters he faced and walked four, one of them quite strategically. He also supplied a pair of hits, including an RBI single.

Jokisch is one of those players, as Smokies general manager Brian Cox said with a laugh, "you're intimidated to talk to." The valedictorian of his senior class in Virginia, Illinois, Jokisch was wrapping up work on his degree from Northwestern University. Valedictorians are not exactly as prevalent as sunflower seeds in pro baseball dugouts. Shrugged Jokisch, "I went to a really, really small high school."

The proud Knoxville/Tennessee franchise had supplied the first no-hitter in modern Southern League history. Fittingly, Jokisch's no-hitter was the last individual no-hitter in the first 50 years of the league. (Five Mobile pitchers combined to no-hit a punchless Huntsville team eight days after the Jokisch gem.) It had been more than 28 years since a Knoxville pitcher threw a nine-inning no-hitter.

Doug Gallagher, a lefty out of Ohio who had gotten two starts with the Detroit Tigers two years prior, had the first Knoxville no-no, a seven-inning win over Asheville on May 3, 1964, with the league less than a month old. He pitched only eight innings total innings in three games for the Smokies before being summoned to Class AAA.

It would be 20 years before another one, and Knoxville didn't even win the game. David Shipanoff, Mercedes Esquer, and Tim Rodgers combined for a no-hitter the Smokies lost to Charlotte in 1984.

In 1985, Scot Elam pitched a nine-inning no-hitter to beat Memphis, 2-0, before 7,495 witnesses at Bill Meyer Stadium. He was in his third season with what was then the Knoxville Blue Jays, having endured a 16-loss season there in 1982. Elam's control wasn't exactly perfect, walking eight batters, including three in the eighth inning. Jeff Neuzil bounced a chopper over Elam's head, but second baseman Orlando Blackwell stabbed the ball, kicked second for a force and threw off-balance to first for a double play. The Chicks' Joe Citari reached in the ninth on a scorching liner off third baseman Chris Shaddy's glove that was ruled an error, but after a walk, Elam retired Joe Jarrell on a strikeout.

Fiver years later, Rob Wishnevski, who overslept and arrived disheveled at the ballpark for the first game of a June 4, 1990, doubleheader, no-hit Charlotte 3-0 in seven innings. Teammate Pete Blohm performed an abbreviated six-inning job against Greenville two months later; there were five no-hitters in the Southern League in 1990.

Leo Estrella was a right-hander from the Dominican Republic acquired by the Blue Jays from the Mets for Tony Phillips. He had already earned a niche in history as having thrown the first pitch (and allowed the first home run, one pitch later) in Smokies Park history. On a rainy May 27, 2000, in Sevierville, he held Orlando scoreless in a six-inning victory. Three weeks later, in his debut for Triple-A Syracuse, Estrella pitched a seven-inning perfect game in the front end of a doubleheader at Indianapolis.

Mark Holliman beat Huntsville with a no-hitter on June 21, 2007, hitting a two-run homer to boot. He would later be the losing pitcher when a Stars' trio combined for a no-hitter against the Smokies in the '07 playoffs.

Jokisch's teammates made it easy for him to add his own name to the list in one sense, though they stressed him in another way. They scored five runs in the top of the first, a foreshadowing of an active offensive performance. What was the trouble? "I was constantly coming up to the plate," Jokisch said. He led off the seventh never intending to swing the bat, hoping to take three strikes and sit down, but he was walked on four pitches. In the ninth, he told plate ump Jose Esteras, "I'm taking three pitches. Anything close, please call it a strike."

Meanwhile, the Smokies' defense was a lifesaver. Matt Szczur made a tough catch in center early in the game and John Andreoli made a diving snag in left. When Jokisch hung a change-up on the first pitch of the ninth to Isaac Galloway, third baseman Christian Villanueva came up with a sterling play, followed by shortstop Javier Baez, ranked the No. 3 prospect in the league in 2013, snaring a liner by Chris Gutierrez inches before it hit the ground. "You're going to have a lot more special moments in your career," Jokisch told Baez, "but you gave me one."

With two outs and Derek Dietrich coming up, Jokisch noticed Suns pitcher Pete Andrelczyk on deck. Jacksonville had already spent its bench with four pitching changes and three double-switches. He yielded "an intentional unintentional walk" to Dietrich, bringing up Andrelczyk. After one vicious swing and miss, Andrelczyk hit a bouncer that nearly handcuffed Villanueva at third before he threw across for the final out.

"It was only something that happened because of the teammates playing behind me," Jokisch said. "To have it work out, I still get goosebumps thinking about it. It was honestly a team thing." So much did Jokisch want to share the credit, when Smokies owner Randy Boyd asked to take him to lunch upon the Smokies' return to Tennessee, Jokisch asked if he could bring along catcher Rafael Lopez.

Jokisch was made aware of the Smokies' no-hitter history, knowing his was the first nine-inning no-hitter since Elam's performance 28 years earlier. What he didn't know until after the season was that Elam pitched for the University of Michigan, a Big Ten rival to Jokisch's alma mater of Northwestern University.

"It's good to get those Michigan guys out of the way," he said, "and get a Northwestern name out there."

THE LIFE

Gov. George Wallace and crew.

DIAMOND JESTERS

Chickens, clowns, and Zooperstars

Max Patkin was wearing casual clothes, sitting alone behind a couple of crab cakes on his plate. It was the specialty of the house in the press lounge at Baltimore's old Memorial Stadium. He saw a familiar face and rasped, "C'mon kid. Sit down."

It was a September Saturday in 1977, and Patkin was as out of place as a kindergarten teacher at a biker's bar. He was there to visit, not entertain. Baseball season was still going on. But Patkin's season was over. "The Clown Prince of Baseball" was a man of the minor leagues, not the majors.

Minor-league baseball has always needed performers and promotions to help spike the gate. Indeed, major-league baseball has offered a similar stage to those who'd make fans laugh and spin the turnstiles. The leisurely pace of the game and the breaks between innings leant themselves to goofiness.

Al Schacht was the original clown prince. After a modest three-year career in the majors, he became an entertainer, performing on diamonds from 1927 through 1952. Patkin picked up where Schacht left off. Then, as minor-league baseball's popularity hit a resurgence in the 1970s, along came various intrepid souls like Captain Dynamite, who'd crawl inside a coffin and explosives would go off underneath the box, sending it into splinters. (Kids, don't try this at home.) From the human clowns like Schacht, Patkin and the shell-shocked Captain, emerged The Chicken and the Zooperstars! It was a reverse Darwinian process of evolution, from man to bird to all manner of (inflatable) animals.

The Zooperstars! may be characters, but Patkin was a caricature.

Everything on his big, ugly, lovely, rubbery face seemed an exaggeration. He was a master of expression underneath a cap cocked sideways. There did not seem to be a bone in his body, such a contortionist was he. And he was goofy, no question. Like all the entertainers, he had his schticks, spewing water, mimicking the umpires, and bellowing loud quips to the stands. He wore a baggy uniform long since washed and worn past its original color, with a question mark on the back in place of a numeral.

If you traveled by bus in the Southern League in the season of 1977, before spying Patkin in the Memorial Stadium press box, you'd swear you saw the act a half-dozen times, from Engel Stadium to Paterson Field to Wolfson Park to Grayson Stadium. You've heard of players' managers? Patkin was a players' clown. In those days, when dressing-room space was tight, Max would often dress in the visitors' clubhouse. He'd occasionally suffer the sophomoric pranks—analgesic balm in the jockstrap, things like that. But the players respected him and he respected the game. His humor and vocabulary was salty enough to make him feel at home in a stevedore bar, much less a minor-league clubhouse.

A 12-year-old kid named Dominic Latkovski watched Patkin from the first-base stands in Louisville, inspired by "watching him coach first base and trying to figure out how he's doing it. Thinking how cool it was that he was there. And that everybody's eyes in the stands were on him and he was doing his corny, funny, dirty act, whatever he's doing, and people are laughing their butts off. I was thinking that would be a cool way to make a living, doing your thing, people laughing at you, and travelling around the country."

Patkin's career does help solve a mystery of life: Which came first, a good egg or The Chicken?

In 1974, a diminutive young man named Ted Giannoulas climbed into a chicken costume sewn by his mother, Helen, as a publicity stunt for a San Diego radio station. He soon became an international sensation. (As Giannoulas once quipped before an appearance in Mexico, "All those people see me, in that colorful costume, and they think I'm a walking piñata.") The KGB Chicken became The San Diego Chicken, mascot of the Padres. Now he is simply The Chicken or The Famous Chicken, filling ballparks with laughter and hatching a hundred bad puns, from his "fowl humor" to "poultry in motion." (The Chicken, by the way, was never popular with Patkin.)

As he reached the quarter-century pole of his performing career, The Chicken had become Jimmy Buffett in feathers, playing to the kids of the kids he used to entertain. One day, the Pirates' former All-Star catcher Jason Kendall stopped The Chicken to tell him of a photo that showed Kendall, at age 2, with his head caught in The Chicken's beak at a San Diego game, where Kendall's father, Fred, was playing.

"Laughter," Giannoulas told interviewers, "never gets old."

The hottest act as the 21st Century arrived was the Zooperstars!—and the fulfillment of Dominic Latkovski's childhood imagination.

Dominic was first hired as Billy Bird, wearing a costume sewn by Helen Giannoulas. In those days, Giannoulas was making $8,500 a game, not exactly chicken feed. Latkovski was making $35 a game as Billy Bird and envisioning a greater opportunity for himself.

A perfect storm of exposure approached, with the Triple-A All-Star Game coming to Louisville in 1991, the Baseball Winter Meetings in 1992. Dominic and brother Brennan leveraged the opportunity, expanding and marketing their act. The Zooperstars! were formed, inspired by the "shenanigans" of the entertainers that were their ancestors.

"Those laid the groundwork and the foundation for everything that's out there today," Dominic Latkovski said, riding south on Interstate 39, heading from one gig to the next. "You see a lot of teams that have adopted a lot of those different acts and concepts. And some teams are using what we started.

"The game is important to the players and to the major-league teams and to die-hard baseball fans. But, honestly, the game is not that important to most of the fans at the game. It's about having something to do. It's about having a beer or a hot dog or taking the kids out, hoping to catch a foul ball. It lends itself to the goofy entertainment. There's got to be entertainment to draw fans, and I think that's why minor-league teams draw so well now."

The Zooperstars! characters were based on familiar names for a newer generation of fans. The Latkovski's father Andy dreamed up the first, Harry Canary. Then came an entire menagerie. Shark

McGwire. Cow Ripken, Jr. Monkey Mantle. Mackerel Jordan. Ken Giraffey, Jr. The Zooperstars! entertained people who weren't around in the days when players' names sounded like Zooperstars instead of the other way around. Think: Catfish Hunter, Ducky Medwick. Hawk Harrelson. Goose Goslin. Mudcat Grant.

Many of the new generation, left in stitches by the Zooperstars! act, know Max Patkin's name only from *Bull Durham*, released in 1988, eleven years before the great clown's death on October 30, 1999. The movie, a baseball classic, was the brainchild of Ron Shelton, who played in the Orioles' minor-league system. The movie showed some of Patkin's act, then even included him in a bar-room scene with Kevin Costner, Susan Sarandon, Tim Robbins, and others. You could hear him even now, what he'd say after being in the movie: "Did you see me, kid? I finally got to dance with the pretty girl."

ON THE ROAD

Why They Call it a Bus League

He was accustomed to charter travel, jets with specially designed seating to fit him and his Brobdingnagian teammates. His coach even once called it "our flying limousine." They taxied to exclusive spots at airports and onto waiting buses, with dutiful valets waiting to handle their baggage.

That was how Michael Jordan traveled in the National Basketball Association with the Chicago Bulls.

It was not how Jordan learned he would be traveling in the Southern League with the Birmingham Barons.

Life on a bus was not something Jordan had pondered when making his drastic career change in 1994. His manager, Terry Francona, recalled in the book, *Francona: The Red Sox Years*, "We had major bus trips everywhere. The shortest ride was three and a half hours. It was 16 or 17 hours from Memphis to Orlando, and we did that. I told him we bused everywhere. He came back later and said, 'What if I can get us a better bus?'"

That led to the most famous bus in Southern League history. Urban legend holds that Jordan purchased the bus the Barons used that season, but it isn't true. "Michael never bought the bus," said Barons broadcaster Curt Bloom. "His name helped arrange the lease that three companies got together. He had heard in spring training about bus rides. He didn't know we took buses. He thought we flew. 'Bus. Bus? I'm 6-foot-6.' His name helped arrange a lease to help get a new bus."

Even though the bus was more roomy than most, Jordan would still work his way to the front of the bus, sitting near Francona and the driver as often as possible, giving him even more room for his long legs frame.

Buses have long carried moonlighting basketball stars, baseball millionaires-to-be, grizzled veterans, and hopeful prospects across the ever-changing map of the Southern League for a half-century. "It was always a bus league," said Wayne Martin, who covered the Barons that year for the *Birmingham News.* "Until 1994, it was a bad bus league. Then they got the nice buses."

The number of trips by plane you could count on both hands. Railway travel had brought a bit of romance to minor-league baseball, prompted more than a few journalistic ambitions. As the late Atlanta columnist Lewis Grizzard once wrote, "I had but one ambition, and that was to be the guy who covered the Atlanta Crackers, home and away, rode trains, and got paid for it." But the trains were replaced by buses in the 1950s.

The math is impossible to calculate with any amount of accuracy, but here's a decent estimate: Southern League teams traveled, city-to-city, more than 3.7 million miles by bus in 50 years, based on an annual average of 8,000 mile per team. That's nearly eight round trips to the moon.

The buses have thankfully evolved and the trips have improved. Individual screens for movies and TV are above the seats. Some have beds. There is wi-fi. Seats are more comfortable. Players heading into the next half-century of the Southern League owe a great debt of thanks to technology—and, just a little bit, to Michael Jordan.

The old-timers at least were able to, well, hydrate a little on those buses. Before organizations began to outlaw the practice of drinking alcohol on buses, concessionaires at many parks on getaway games would have six packs of beer iced down in plastic bags for traveling players to purchase. Combined with the fast-food hamburger, it was a different sort of seven-course meal.

Barely does any extensive conversation with a former Southern League player go more than 10 or 15 minutes without a bus story, usually offered with the same tone of a person who has trudged barefoot across the Sahara.

Manley Johnston, the league's only 20-game winner, was awash in memories one morning in Niceville, Florida, when buses were brought up.

"Don't mention that," Johnston said, screwing up his face in a sour-lemon look. "If I told you the truth you wouldn't believe it.

We'd get through with a game and you wouldn't even take time to eat. Then, 10, 11, 12 damn hours and have to play that night. And [no other cities] were close. That was as minor leagues as you can get." Indeed, if GPS tells you now it's nearly nine and a half hours from Lynchburg to Birmingham, imagine the days before every site was connected by interstate highways and there were 100 towns along the way with two stoplights and one eager constable.

"When I played there, we had trips from Mobile to Evansville," said Rene Lachemann, a former player and manager in the Southern League. "You're on the bus 14 hours with the same guys, it'd drive you nuts."

"I think our average trip was eight hours," said Ed Romero, who managed Memphis in 1996. "We had trips to Carolina that were 12 or 16 hours. Guys would get there and have colds and sore backs. It'd take two days to recover. You'd look back in the bus and guys were stretched out in the luggage racks and on the floor trying to sleep."

Pat Darcy recalled the grueling 1971 Dixie Association season, when Southern League and Texas League teams played interleague games that necessitated even longer travel. Darcy's Columbus team had a bad ride to begin with, "this old Greyhound bus where some of the seats had the springs out. In the summer, it'd get real cold or [the air conditioning] wouldn't work. You'd go from wearing a jacket on the bus, then having to take it off. You always had a sore throat by the end of the road trip. You get home and you get better, then you get back on the bus again."

Not only was the bus bad, but the driver was not exactly gifted with an impeccable internal GPS system. The Astros were once traveling from Columbus to Little Rock, Darcy remembered, and "it was four in the morning and somebody said, 'Hey, this is the Mississippi River.' About 10 minutes later, 'It was, 'Hey, it's the Mississippi River again.' We got in the wrong direction somehow. He was always doing that."

Teammate Dan Evans recalled Darcy as an elegant dresser who was wearing a yellow alpaca sweater on one trip. The bus broke down and the driver commanded the players to get out and push the bus. "The driver popped the clutch and when the bus started it belched diesel smoke everywhere," Evans said. "It covered the whole team. It ruined Pat's sweater."

While Michael Jordan helped get a bus hired at the dawn of April, long-time front-office maven Syd Thrift got one fired. He happened to be riding along for the Chattanooga Lookouts' inaugural road trip in 1976, and the bus driver seemed more appropriate to be driving the Grateful Dead's bus than a minor-league baseball team; perhaps, even more appropriate to be in the Grateful Dead. When the bus was stopped by a North Carolina trooper, the driver couldn't produce all of the necessary paperwork. Thrift was on the phone to the Chattanooga front office the instant he reached the hotel, and a new bus was found for the next trip.

Doug DeCinces, the former Orioles and Angels' third baseman, recalled a short bus trip long on memories. His Asheville club had just seen a two-game lead against Savannah evaporate in the final series of the season. The team bus pulled into a McDonald's after a loss and manager Cal Ripken Sr., general manager Al Harazin, the bus driver, and trainer went into a full-service restaurant across the parkway while the players went to McDonalds', then had to wait on the bus for the others to return.

"We were getting rowdy and Tim Nordbrook stands up and he goes, 'If I knew how to start this thing I'd drive it. This is brutal. Anybody know how to start this?' I go, 'Yeah, I do,'" DeCinces said. "I went up and started it and now the bus is running. Nordbrook is pressured into driving it because he had popped off. And we took off down the street."

Nordbrook made a U-turn at a traffic light, then passed by the restaurant just as Ripken and others were coming out. The others piled into Harazin's orange VW Beetle and take off. Naturally, "we got lost," DeCinces continued. "We finally get to the right street and the motel and there is Cal, standing out there waiting. Everybody files off and Rip is just standing there, cold-faced. He's giving us the evil eye, because we're now tied and we have one game to play. He just lays into Nordbrook and fines him like 600 bucks. And we're only making 500. He said, 'I better have that money before team curfew tonight.'

"Nordbrook is going, 'I don't have that kind of money' and 'I've just thrown my baseball career away.' Then everybody started walking by his room and guys were throwing him 20s and just giving up cash. At the end of the day," DeCinces said, "he ended up making money.

"And," he added,"we went out and kicked Savannah's but the next day."

RED TAPE FOR THE BOYS IN BLUE

A Season On the Road

The umpires were up way past their bedtime the night before. First, a rain delay before the game could start. Then a marathon of bad pitches, hits, runs and the sort of dawdling pace that accompanies a game in 90-degree temperature and the sort of humid air you wear like a sweater. Then there was an ejection of a player. That meant submitting a detailed report to the league office, the drudgery of a cop filing information on a six-car pileup.

Jonathan Bailey, the crew chief, and partners Alex Ransom and Garrett Patterson piled into their van, heading for their first meal of the day, a 2 p.m. lunch meeting at a sandwich spot they had discovered. By the most remote coincidence, their lunch companion had in his car a bobblehead doll of the ejected player, obtained from a game two weeks earlier. "Got a little gift for you," he said, handing it to Bailey as Ransom and Patterson roared.

"Get him to autograph it," it was suggested.

"Yeah," Bailey said. "I'll say, 'Write on there what you called me last night.'"

Ejections are no fun. Read an umpire's report: It'll erase the notion that they love tossing players and managers. Heave-hos make nights go longer. Sometimes, they foul up the most intricate plans.

Earlier in the season, Ransom had flown his girlfriend to Pensacola for a series. As he had confided to Bailey and Patterson, he planned to propose to her on a particular night at a postgame dinner at a restaurant on the beach. Then up popped an unruly player who required an early exit. Romance took a back seat to paperwork. A determined Ransom still headed to the deserted beach and, at 1:30 a.m., popped the question.

Their jobs are hardly all about running players. It's about running a game smoothly and consistently. It's about being a professional, respected decision-maker and maintaining poise. It's about their own improvement and advancement, a share goal with the other uniformed personnel on the field. This is where they hone their craft, gain experience, and gain exposure. Except their lives are more difficult, their odds more challenging. There are only 68 major-league umpiring jobs, and it's not a profession with an enormous attrition rate.

"You have to have great timing on top of great timing on top of great timing," Bailey said.

Many umpires who have worked in the Southern League have made the jump, from relative newcomers like Jordan Baker, who found himself catching grief in print for his ritual of throwing his used chewing gum into the outfield grass each inning, to the veteran Joe West, who reached the major leagues in 1977, the year after he famously tried to eject Chattanooga Lookouts' organist Charlie Timmons from the park for playing "Three Blind Mice."

For Southern League umpires, their daily lives are even more challenging than players. There are no home games. There's nobody cheering for you. It's 12,000-15,000 miles a year in a van shared with two other guys, every night in a hotel, living off a per diem and a salary in this league that averages somewhere around $2,500 a month for a six-month period. This is a routine that, if not careful, can become a rut. Wake up, find a local gym in which to work out, eat, relax, drive to stadium, dress, work a game, eat postgame, file a report, fall asleep when nothing is on TV but infomercials. Wash, rinse, repeat—except on those getaway nights when a game ends in Jackson, Tennessee, at 10:30 p.m. and you've got a 7 p.m. game the next night in Montgomery and you pile in the van to drive half the night, bickering over who gets control of the radio.

"I think it's a gift," Bailey said. "A lot of people think it's simple. I challenge them to do it."

"Absolutely," chimed in Patterson.

Said Bailey, "To love it enough to keep getting better is tough."

Each umpire's story is unique, yet there is a thread woven through each of their stories, as consistent as an ideal strike zone. They are dedicated to what they do. They are imperfect in a game that demands perfection from them—but where 30 percent perfection at the plate puts a batter in the majors. They typically started umpiring at an early age. They can't explain, to a layman's ears, why on God's green earth they'd ever subject themselves to the lifestyle and abuse and steep odds against them.

There is also this common sensation: Bailey worked the 2012-13 winter league in the Dominican Republic. He felt "lost." He said "the closest I felt at home was on the ballfield." That's universal, whether in the Dominican Republic or the heart of the South.

Bailey, Patterson, and Ransom are unique as a crew, but they're also representative of the five crews that criss-cross the South as the league's umpires each year. Bailey, 29, is the veteran. He was selected as crew chief for the league's mid-season All-Star Game. Patterson is 26, Ransom 23.

Jonathan Bailey grew up in Marietta, Georgia, where his father officiated and was in charge of the local umpires' association. Bailey began umpiring at 13, then worked all the way through high school, where he played football and wrestled. He found himself umpiring games in which former baseball teammates were playing. "You feel a little nerdy at first," he admitted. It was good money for a high-school kid, then somebody said, "Are you going to go pro?" The family looked into the Wendelstedt Umpire School and he was accepted, then eventually hired for minor-league ball in 2006.

Garrett Patterson, with the shoulders and arms of an NFL fullback, is a Phoenix native who started umpiring at 13 because his father was in charge of the local association. The family's next-door neighbor was Gary Darling, a veteran major-league ump. Patterson worked his way through the University of Arizona by umpiring baseball and officiating football and basketball. "The only job I've ever had is officiating sports," he said.

Alex Ransom—"my dad was *not* the umpire-in-chief in my Little League"—was born in Canada and raised in Boise. He played baseball but got burned out on playing. There was still an interest and his father mentioned the Wendlestedt school. Ransom is not merely a graduate. He's an instructor there in the off-season.

They arrive at the park an hour or two before the first pitch, depending upon the facility, and casually dress for work. Bailey sets a photo of his wife and son on the shelf of his locker. They spend a lot of their early time simply busting each others' chops with teasing humor. "Gets our skin a little thicker before we go out there," Bailey said. There's not a lot of formal meeting, as a football crew would hold. These guys are together enough, the reminders are constant. There might be some discussion if they're walking into a bad-blood scenario, where batters were being hit and retaliation was made. There is frequent communication with other crews, advising of past controversy they'd seen between the two teams, helping be proactive.

It is routine as they hit the field. The bobblehead player bobs his head in silent acknowledgement to Bailey, then later stays silent as a mime when he is picked off base. Carrying a grudge, on either side, can be fatal. Tempers are inevitably going to erupt. Passion is a facet of all sports. There is a photo on the wall in the man cave at Bailey's Marietta home, with a manager nose-to-nose with him. Bailey and the manager had trouble all season. Yet the final game, Bailey arrived in the umps' locker room to find the framed photo, inscribed by the manager. "It's part of the game. Good luck and hope to see you in the big leagues."

This was another three-hour game, with Patterson behind the plate and pitchers on the mound who couldn't have found the strike zone with a $300 GPS.

At postgame, they were eating out of Styrofoam boxes, cutting into slabs of meat and dishing up veggies with plasticware, the feast provided by a clubhouse attendant. The crew reviewed the evening's events. They were pleased with the seamless "rotation" on a couple of plays, where three men had the challenge of covering four bases. They were perfectly set for one play, when it looked as if a throw from the outfield might become a bang-bang play, and sounded disappointed the play didn't materialize. There was another ejection, and they discussed that with the strong confidence and almost benign arrogance that must accompany people in charge of maintaining order.

The frustrated losing catcher, who had seen two batters cross the plate with bases-loaded walks, couldn't stand it any longer. He barked at Patterson, then crossed the line. There was no choice. So, again, another long night, another report to file.

This ejected player, for the record, had yet to be immortalized by a bobblehead.

GEORGE WALLACE AND THE LOOKOUTS

The Ways of a Master Politician

Author's Note: While the following chapter may not illustrate some integral part in Southern League history, I hope you'll indulge a little personal memory that may at least shed some light on idle time-killing by minor-league players as well as a brief look at one of the South's most polarizing figures during the last part of the 20th Century. The memory includes Brian Kingman, a Lookouts pitcher who went on to both make the cover of Sports Illustrated *and attain a measure of dubious history; Bruce Robinson, a catcher who developed a hinged shoulder pad for chest protectors, adding cushion over the previously exposed right shoulder, a prototype of which is now in the Baseball Hall of Fame in Cooperstown; and Governor George Wallace. Kingman is now a businessman in Phoenix. Robinson is retired, dividing his time between San Diego and Idaho and occasionally writing songs and performing as a singer-guitarist.*

This is a column I wrote for the Sept. 15, 1998, edition of the Huntsville Times.

On the surface, a dubious baseball record and the death of a legendary political figure would seem to have nothing in common.

But when I heard about the death of Gov. George Wallace, my first thought was about my old friend, Brian Kingman. In 1980, Kingman lost 20 games for the Oakland Athletics. No one has "accomplished" that feat since, though some pitchers seemed poised for a run at the record this year. Their "pursuit" drew some new-found attention for Kingman. *Sports Illustrated* wrote about him; so did some other publications.

Let's go now into flashback mode, where the screen goes fuzzy and wavy, and the characters eventually emerge in focus with embarrassing wardrobes, an abundance of hair and enviably youthful looks.

It was August 1976. Gov. Wallace was still in the national spotlight. I was covering the Chattanooga Lookouts on a road trip in Montgomery and had hooked up with Kingman and catcher Bruce Robinson for lunch. They were two of my closest friends on the team. I think—and a photo seems to bear it out—we were all unshowered and unshaven.

We walked through downtown, killing time. We found ourselves at the state capitol and, with nothing better to do, went inside. Almost immediately, we encountered a young, cute tour guide named Wendy.

After only brief conversation, Kingman demanded, "We want to meet George."

Not "the governor." Not "Mr. Wallace."

"George and my dad are old friends," Kingman continued. "They played baseball together. George told my dad any time I was in town I was supposed to come see him."

You buy that? Didn't think so.

But Wendy did. And—wouldn't you know it?—her dad and The Gov actually were close friends. Kingman cajoled her into taking us to Gov. Wallace's office to see if he was meeting any visitors.

Robby and I were already starting to sense where this was headed, a tiny fib exploding into a nightmare, like some sitcom episode gone bad. But Brian was as determined as the tour guide was gullible.

Wendy escorted us to an elegant waiting room. Inside was Harvey Glance, the Auburn track immortal who had just returned from the Olympics. He had his gold medal and let each of us try it on for size.

Glance was ushered into Gov. Wallace's private office for a few minutes. When we left, an aide beckoned us to come inside. It felt as if we were going into the principal's office. We're busted. A governor can commute a death sentence, but can he make you write on the blackboard 100 times "I won't lie to a tour guide ever again?"

Gov. Wallace sat behind his cluttered desk in his wheelchair.

Wendy hugged him and made the introductions, the two minor-league players and the sportswriter. Since my old newspaper's editorial philosophy made *Mein Kampf* seem almost liberal in comparison, Gov. Wallace was intimately familiar with it and spoke highly of its work.

He spoke of his love for baseball, and regretted that "since the accident"—which is how he referred to the assassination attempt—he didn't get to as many Montgomery Rebels games as he'd like. He talked about playing baseball on the freshman team in college.

Wendy chirped in, looking at Kingman, "Is that where your father played with him?"

Turning to the governor, she said, "Brian said you and his father played baseball together and you told his father to have him come see you."

Robby and I looked at each other, trying not to laugh or choke. OK, Kingman. Pitch out of this jam.

Gov. Wallace asked Kingman his father's name, then looked deep in thought.

"Yes, I vaguely remember him. But I meet so many people, and since the accident, my memory isn't what it should be," the governor responded.

He beckoned his official photographer, had an official photo taken and we said our official goodbyes. As we left, Gov. Wallace told Kingman with a wink, "Be sure to tell your father I said hello."

At that moment, I realized George Wallace may not always have been a good governor. He may have had views that I would never share.

But I knew then the man was a master politician to the core.

THE SOUTHERN LEAGUE GOES HOLLYWOOD

The Ultimate Movie Sets

Associate producer Frank Pace was surrounded by dozens of civilians who had auditioned for spots as extras in his new movie. "The first day on a movie set will be the most exciting day of your life," Pace promised. "The second day—and every day after that—will be the most dull days of your life."

Indeed, the extras wearing the flannels of the Memphis Chicks and Chattanooga Lookouts (including a one-time local baseball prodigy wonderfully named Ted Williams May) would be numbed by the constant waiting as movie equipment and egos were meticulously adjusted.

Lights...

Camera...

Inaction...

Southern League stadiums have been transformed into sound stages for Hollywood invasions numerous times, involving local actors and extras and providing authentic backdrops for historical baseball pieces.

A Winner Never Quits, Pace's production, was filmed at Chattanooga's Engel Stadium in the summer of 1985. It was the story of Pete Gray, the one-armed outfielder who earned a war-time promotion to the St. Louis Browns in 1945. Such is the gift of Hollywood mythmaking, movie director Mel Damski turned the irascible, bitter Gray into a rather likeable chap as portrayed by Keith Carradine, who himself was a rather likable chap who'd occasionally chat up the extras. It was a 40-year-old idea for a movie. Gray had been approached about playing himself in the 1940s—but balked at Hollywood's request he wear a toupee.

The music video of the Alabama song "Cheap Seats," still a ballpark staple, was filmed at Engel as well. To this day, Lookouts radio voice Larry Ward is occasionally recognized by fans as the umpire in the video.

The Chattanooga ballpark received a starring role in *42*, the 2013 Jackie Robinson biopic, transformed to resemble Brooklyn's Ebbets Field from the 1950s.

Macon's Luther Williams Field, which housed the Macon Peaches of the Southern League in the 1960s, was also used for *42*, with additional credits including *Trouble With The Curve* and *The Bingo Long Traveling All-Stars & Motor Kings*.

Birmingham's Rickwood Field, the oldest minor-league ballpark in the country, was used for *42*, *Cobb*, and *Soul of the Game*, an HBO production about the Negro Leagues. Several Alabamian actors earned roles in *42*, including Lucas Black as Pee Wee Reese, Linc Hand as Pirates' pitcher Fritz Ostermueller, and Andre Holland as sportswriter Wendell Smith. Hundreds of others showed up for work as extras or simply as fans in the grandstands, able to register via a website.

In Chattanooga in the summer of 1985, the word was spread the old-fashioned way, on print and television, and extras were asked to report to Engel Stadium, one of several sites in the area where filming of *A Winner Never Quits* would take place. There was be a tryout camp of sorts for baseball players to serve as Gray's teammates and opponents. Warned Pace, "The more handsome they are, the more of a deterrent it is. We're looking for guys with good character, guys who look like they've been rubbing their noses in the dirt for the last 15 years."

They would have to shave beards and mustaches and have their hair trimmed; the movie company had a barber set up in the stadium to take care of that on-site. The visiting clubhouse was turned over to the wardrobe department, which filled it with 1940s area civvies and baseball uniforms. The uniforms had previously appeared in *The*

Natural, with "Chicks" and "Lookouts" stitched where "Knights" had been.

The clean-shaven, undeterred, unhandsome baseball extras spent much of the two days in ennui, waiting for action. They told stories, sweated in the sun, chewed tobacco, and had some bit of quality time with a few actors. They took infield practice as the cameras rolled, the backdrop to Carradine's surprising arrival, this one-armed curiosity trying to play the game. A long-time local sports figure named Jim Morgan hit the longest fungo in baseball history. He launched it at home plate in Chattanooga... and it came down as Carradine caught it weeks later on a Los Angeles soundstage.

Proving that Pete Gray took no guff from anyone, a fight scene was blended in. It was precipitated by a hard slide into second base on a steal attempt. A stunt professional choreographed Carradine's fake fight against a supporting actor with all the precision of Operation Overlord. The meticulous work was necessary since Carradine's right arm was lashed to his chest underneath a baggy jersey and care had to be taken how he might hit the ground.

The tussle ignited a bench-clearing brawl that involved the extras. Spurred to action, they bolted from the respective dugouts, found opponents coming from the other side and went at it. It was the bedlam of junior high in the middle of the Engel Stadium diamond, with wrestling and tugging and fake punches and stifled laughs behind fierce looks. After the detailed instructions for Carradine and his fight, the director had words for the extras before the brawl.

"Just act like you're fighting," Damski said, "and make sure you don't hit the stars."

SOUTHERN
LEAGUE CITIES

Asheville, North Carolina

Teams: Tourists, Orioles

Affiliates during the Southern League era: Pittsburgh (1964-66), Cincinnati (1968-70), Chicago White Sox (1971), Baltimore Orioles (1972-75)

Stadium: McCormick Field, opened in 1924 (326' LF, 373' CF, 297' RF)

McCormick Field, still in use by the Tourists of the Class A South Atlantic League, is one of the oldest parks in professional baseball. Tucked into a hilly area of Asheville, it has quirky dimensions that contractors wisely chose to keep sacred during renovations in 1959 and again in a massive rebuild in 1991. Because it is less than 300 feet from home plate to the right field foul pole, a 36-foot-tall fence looms like Asheville's version of Fenway's Green Monster.

Top graduates from the Southern League era:
Eddie Murray
Dock Ellis
Bernie Carbo
Sparky Anderson (manager)
Cal Ripken, Sr. (manager)
Dave Concepcion
Al Bumbry
Doug DeCinces
Mike Flanagan
Rich Dauer

Notable: The final team for which the fictional Crash Davis played in "Bull Durham" was the Asheville Tourists, and some scenes were shot at McCormick Field. Among the Tourists' batboys in the past were author Thomas Wolfe, University of North Carolina basketball coach Roy Williams, and Cal Ripken, Jr.

Birmingham, Alabama

Teams: A's, Barons

Affiliates during the Southern League era: Oakland (1964-1975), Detroit (1981-85), Chicago White Sox (1986-current)

Stadiums: Rickwood Field (321' LF, 393' CF, 332' RF), Hoover Met/Regions Park (340' LF, 405' CF, 340' RF), Regions Field, opened in 2013 (320' LF, 400' CF, 325' RF). Regions Field, in downtown Birmingham near the campus of UAB and a cornerstone of an aggressive urban redevelopment plan, is the Barons' third stadium since their return to pro baseball in 1981. They played at Rickwood Field, the oldest stadium in minor-league history, until moving to the suburban Hoover Met in 1988.

Top graduates from the Southern League era:
Frank Thomas
Rollie Fingers
Reggie Jackson
Terry Francona (manager)
Vida Blue
Mark Buehrle
Darrell Evans
Joe Rudi
Robin Ventura
Bert Campaneris
Mike Cameron

Notable: For all the ex-Barons who have gone on to sensational major-league careers, the most famous former Baron still has two pages dedicated to him in the Birmingham media guide. It's a 6-foot-6 right fielder who batted just .202. Guy by the name of Michael Jordan.

Charlotte, North Carolina

Teams: Hornets, Orioles, Knights

Affiliates during the Southern League era: Minnesota (1964-72), Baltimore (1976-1988), Chicago Cubs (1989-1992)

Stadiums: Clark Griffith Park, later Crockett Park (340' LF, 410' CF, 330' RF), Charlotte Knights Stadium, opened in 1940 (325' LF, 400' CF, 325' RF), BB&T Ballpark, opened in 2014. The stadium most connected to Charlotte's Southern League history was the classic old wooden structure in the leafy neighborhood of Dilworth. It was named for Clark Griffith, the owner of the Hornets and the Washington Senators, for which Charlotte was the long-time farm club. It was purchased by Jim Crockett in 1976 as he brought baseball back to the city after a three-year absence. On March 16, 1985, the stadium was burned to the ground, with investigators ruling it was caused by juvenile vandals. The team eventually moved into a new park in suburban Rock Hill, S.C.

Top graduates from the Southern League era:
Eddie Murray
Cal Ripken, Jr.
Mike Boddicker
Curt Schilling
Graig Nettles
Rick Dempsey

Notable: The Crockett Family was primarily known for its promotion of professional wrestling; indeed, its property was eventually purchased by Ted Turner as fodder for his fledgling WTBS network. The famous wrestler Klondike Bill served as a groundskeeper at Crockett Park in between his ring gigs.

Chattanooga, Tennessee

Team: Lookouts

Affiliates during the Southern League era: Philadelphia (1964-65), Oakland (1976-77), Cleveland (1978-82), Seattle (1983-1988), Cincinnati (1989-2008), Los Angeles Dodgers (2009-current)

Stadiums: Engel Stadium (325' LF, 471' CF, 318' RF), AT&T Field, opened in 2000 (325' LF, 400' CF, 330' RF). Located atop what was once known as "Hawk Hill," the site of a high school football stadium, AT&T Field overlooks downtown Chattanooga and the Tennessee Aquarium. It replaced Historic Engel Stadium, which sits a few miles away. Engel Stadium had cavernous dimensions—announced measurements ranged from 360 to 377 down the line in left to 451 to 471 in dead center. Engel Stadium had enormous, eight-foot metal Coca-Cola bottles spaced atop the wall, a tribute to a product that was first bottled in Chattanooga.

Top graduates from the Southern League era:
Ferguson Jenkins
Mike Marshall
Dwayne Murphy
Steve McCatty
Edgar Martinez
Alvin Davis
Mark Langston
Trevor Hoffman
Joey Votto
Adam Dunn
Homer Bailey

Notable: Former owner Joe Engel once drew thousands for an "elephant hunt" that turned out to be a hoax, but owner Frank Burke, who led the move into the new ballpark above the Chattanooga skyline, had a pair of camels, Lumpy and Larry, in the final two seasons at Engel Stadium.

Columbus, Georgia

Teams: Confederate Yankees, White Sox, Astros, Mudcats

Affiliates during the Southern League era: New York Yankees (1964-66), Chicago White Sox (1967), Houston (1970-90)

Stadium: Golden Park, opened in 1926 (330' LF, 415' CF, 330' RF)

Golden Park was built adjacent to the Chattahoochee River in downtown Columbus. After the Astros departed for Carolina in 1991, the park hosted a South Atlantic League team. The stadium underwent renovations in preparation for the 1996 Summer Olympics in Atlanta, with Golden Park hosting the softball competition.

Top graduates from the Southern League era:
Luis Gonzalez
Roy White
Ken Forsch
Cesar Geronimo

Pat Darcy
Mike Easler
J.R. Richard
Terry Puhl
Glenn Davis
Ken Caminiti

Notable: The white cinder-block walls of the visitors'clubhouse for years was covered with graffiti and lists provided by the various players. Among the lists: Nominees as the ugliest player in the Southern League.

Evansville, Indiana

Team: White Sox

Affiliates during the Southern League era: Chicago White Sox (1966-68)

Stadium: Bosse Field, opened in 1915 (315' LF, 408' CF, 315' RF). Bosse Field is the third-oldest U.S. pro baseball stadium in regular use, behind only Fenway Park in Boston and Wrigley Field in Chicago. It was built for a cost of $65,000. It hosted teams in a variety of leagues before joining the Southern League in 1966, the team moving from Lynchburg, Va. After the park sat empty in 1969, Evansville landed at Class AAA American Association club.

Top graduates from the Southern League era:
Bill Melton
Ed Herrmann

Notable: Bosse Field was used as the primary setting for the movie, *A League of Their Own.*

Greenville, South Carolina

Team: Braves

Affiliates during the Southern League era: Atlanta (1984-2004)

Stadium: Municipal Stadium, opened in 1984 (335' LF, 405' CF, 335' RF). The Braves moved their franchise from Savannah to the new park on the outskirts of Greenville and the city enjoyed a long string of top-flight Atlanta talent. However, the stadium location and its age began to impact attendance and the Braves moved to a new park in Pearl, Miss., a suburb of Jackson, in 2005. That sparked a drive to build a stadium in downtown Greenville that hosts a Class A South Atlantic League.

Top graduates from the Southern League era:

Chipper Jones
Tom Glavine
Andruw Jones
Javier Lopez
David Justice
Adam Wainwright
Ron Gant
Mark Lemke
Mark Wohlers
Ryan Klesko
John Rocker
Steve Avery
Rafael Furcal

Notable: The 1992 Greenville Braves won a league-record 100 games, going 50-20 at home, 50-23 on the road.

Huntsville, Alabama

Team: Stars

Affiliates during the Southern League era: Oakland (1985-1997), Milwaukee (1998-current)

Stadiums: Joe Davis Stadium, opened in 1985 (340' LF, 410' CF, 330' RF)

Joe Davis Stadium was built just in time for the 1985 season and named for the city's mayor at the time. Davis struggled to get the five-person city council to approve the stadium construction and bring the team to town from the outset, then hit another snag once plans were in place. Some of the council members were against the sale of alcoholic beverages at the stadium. Davis managed to do some 11th-hour arm-twisting to make it happen.

Top graduates from the Southern League era:

Jose Canseco
Mark McGwire
Miguel Tejada
Terry Steinbach
Walt Weiss

Jason Giambi
Ryan Braun
Prince Fielder
Ben Sheets
Nelson Cruz

Notable: The Stars' nickname came from the city's strong affiliation with NASA and the space program, but their mascot is a skunk named Homer, a tribute to the varmints that would occasionally appear on the field during the franchise's early days.

Jackson, Tennessee

Team: Diamond Jaxx, Generals

Affiliates during the Southern League era: Chicago Cubs (1998-2006), Seattle (2007-current).

Stadiums: Generals Park, opened in 1998 (310' LF, 395' CF, 320' RF). There had been no pro baseball in Jackson since 1954, with the old Generals of the Kentucky-Illinois-Tennessee Class D league, until the Memphis franchise was moved 100 miles northeast up Interstate 40 as Memphis went to Triple-A. The stadium was originally known as Pringles Park, with the naming rights sold to the potato chip company that had a presence in Jackson. The Generals' nickname is in tribute to Gen. Andrew Jackson, a Tennessee native.

Top graduates from the Southern League era:
Carlos Zambrano
Kyle Farnsworth
Mark Prior
Ryan Theriot
Geovany Soto
Dustin Ackley
Jose Molina

Notable: One of the team's original owners was Wink Martindale, the quiz-show host and a Jackson native.

Jacksonville, Florida

Teams: Expos, Suns

Affiliates during the Southern League era: Cleveland (1970-1971), Kansas City (1972-1983), Montreal (1984-1990), Seattle

(1991-1994), Detroit (1995-2006), Los Angeles Dodgers (2001-2007), Florida/Miami (2008-current)

Stadiums: Wolfson Park (320' LF, 390' CF, 320' RF), Baseball Grounds of Jacksonville, opened in 2003 (321' LF, 420' CF, 317' RF). The Baseball Grounds sit near Jacksonville's Veterans Memorial Arena and far from EverBank Field, previously known as Gator Bowl, host to that annual game as well as the Jacksonville Jaguars of the NFL. In 2003, the Baseball Grounds replaced Wolfson Park, a classic old park adjacent to the Gator Bowl where, legend has it, a young Elvis Presley had to hide out in a bathroom and in a ticket booth trying to escape adoring female fans after a performance there.

Top graduates from the Southern League era:
Frank White
Dan Quisenberry
Willie Wilson
Bret Saberhagen
Andres Galarraga
Randy Johnson
Larry Walker
Alex Rodriguez
Matt Kemp
Clayton Kershaw
Giancarlo Stanton

Notable: The later Peter Bragan, Sr., the team's principal owner, rang an old CSX railroad bell next to his seat to mark every Suns' home run and victory.

Knoxville, Tennessee

Teams: Smokies, Blue Jays

Affiliates during the Southern League era: Detroit (1964), Cincinnati (1965-67), Chicago White Sox (1972-79), Toronto (1980-2002), St. Louis (2003-04), Arizona (2005-06), Chicago Cubs (2007-current)

Stadiums: Bill Meyer Stadium (330' LF, 400' CF, 330' RF), Smokies Park, opened in 2000 (330' LF, 400' CF, 330 RF'). The Smokies moved to Kodak in 2000, some 25 miles from downtown Knoxville and adjacent to touristy Sevierville. Bill Meyer Stadium had the longest walk in baseball for players who were removed or ejected from games. Because there was no tunnel between the dugouts and clubhouses, they'd have to walk through the stands, or around to the far end of grandstands and up a ramp into the concourse.

Top graduates from the Southern League era:
Harold Baines
Hal McRae
Cecil Fielder
Fred McGriff
Jimmy Key
David Wells
Jeff Kent
Carlos Delgado
Chris Carpenter
Roy Halladay
Jesse Barfield
Yadier Molina
Starlin Castro

Notable: Though Bill Meyer Stadium has been razed, an amateur park is in its place, named for Neal Ridley, the Smokies' former owner, and major leaguer Todd Helton, a Knoxville native and former player at the nearby University of Tennessee.

Lynchburg, Virginia

Team: White Sox

Affiliates during the Southern League era: Chicago White Sox (1964-65)

Stadium: City Stadium, opened in 1939 (325' LF, 390' CF, 325' RF). The stadium, now named for Calvin Falwell, brother of evangelist Jerry Falwell, the founder of nearby Liberty University, remains in use in Class A ball after a few extensive renovations.

Top graduates from the Southern League era:
Duane Josephson
Ike Brown
Rich Morales

Notable: Joe DiMaggio had the first two RBI in City Stadium history. The Yankees and Dodgers opened the park with an exhibition game as they traveled north from spring training.

Macon, Georgia

Team: Peaches

Affiliates during the Southern League era: Cincinnati (1964), Philadelphia (1966), Pittsburgh (1967)

Stadium: Luther Williams Field, opened in 1929 (338' LF, 402' CF, 338' RF). A black iron gate welcomes fans with the word, "Macon Base Ball Park," though the official name is in honor of the former Macon mayor. The stadium was built for the tidy sum of $60,000. When Macon hosted its first game, Judge Kennesaw Mountain Landis threw out the ceremonial first pitch.

Top graduates from the Southern League era:

Dock Ellis

Al Oliver

Bob Oliver

Bruce Del Canton

Lee May

Notable: Luther Williams Field has been used as the setting for movies "The Bingo Long Traveling All-Stars & Motor Kings," "42" and "Trouble With The Curve."

Memphis, Tennessee

Team: Chicks

Affiliates during the Southern League era: Montreal (1978-1983), Kansas City (1984-1994), San Diego (1995-96), Seattle (1997)

Stadiums: Tim McCarver Stadium, opened in 1963 (323' LF, 398' CF, 325' RF). The park was named in 1977 for the city's biggest major-league name, the former Cardinals and Phillies catcher more familiar to today's fans as a broadcaster. The stadium had a construction unique in contrast to other Southern League parks. Located near the city's Liberty Bowl, it was demolished in 2005 as the Triple-A franchise moved to a downtown stadium.

Top graduates from the Southern League era:

Bo Jackson

Tim Raines

Derrek Lee

Tim Wallach

Charlie Lea

David Cone

Notable: The infield had artificial turf and there was a grass out-field. The artificial turf was to have consistency with the Royals' organization, which built a speedy team and was one of the organizations that tried to as much as any to capitalize on the advantage of turf.

Mobile, Alabama

Teams: A's, White Sox, BayBears

Affiliates during the Southern League era: Oakland (1966), Chicago White Sox (1970), San Diego (1997-2006), Arizona (2007-current)

Stadiums: Hank Aaron Stadium, opened in 1998 (325' LF, 400' CF, 310' RF). The ballpark was named for the city's most famous major leaguer, and the house in which Aaron grew up was uprooted and transplanted on stadium grounds. (Its address is 755 Bolling Blvd., a tribute to Aaron's career homer total and to Frank and Milt Bolling.) It also pays homage to the city's remarkable baseball heritage with a plaza that honors greats like Billy Williams, Ozzie Smith, Willie McCovey and Satchel Paige, other Hall of Famers who are natives of the area.

Top graduates from the Southern League era:

Carlos Gonzalez

Paul Goldschmidt

Jake Peavy

Josh Barfield

Justin Upton

Ben Davis

Sal Bando

Blue Moon Odom

Rick Monday

Notable: The luxury boxes at Hank Aaron Stadium are located at field level rather than on an upper tier.

Montgomery, Alabama

Teams: Rebels, Biscuits

Affiliates during the Southern League era: Detroit (1965-1980), Tampa Bay (2004-current)

Stadiums: Paterson Field (330' LF, 380' CF, 330' RF), Riverwalk Stadium, opened in 2004 (314' LF, 400' CF, 333' RF). Riverwalk Stadium incorporates an old railroad station along the right-field side and a railroad track runs behind the left field fence, with trains often streaming past while games are in progress. A few monster home runs have actually struck passing trains. The ballpark was built when baseball returned to the city in 2004. Previous Montgomery teams played at nearby Paterson Field.

Top graduates from the Southern League era:
Lou Whitaker
Alan Trammell
Matt Moore
Evan Longoria
David Price
James Shields
Mark Fidrych
Jack Morris
Lance Parrish

Notable: The Rebels, a Detroit affiliate, won five titles in a span of six years at old Paterson Field.

Nashville, Tennessee

Teams: Sounds, Xpress

Affiliates during the Southern League era: Cincinnati (1978-79), New York Yankees (1980-84), Minnesota (1993-94)

Stadiums: Herschel Greer Stadium, opened in 1978 (327' LF, 400' CF, 327' RF). Greer Stadium was host to a pair of teams for two seasons, the Class AAA Sounds and the Southern League's Xpress. Nashville became a Triple-A city in 1985 after owner Larry Schmittou moved his Southern League team to Huntsville, but picked up the Xpress when Charlotte moved to Triple-A. The Xpress later moved to Wilmington, N.C. The stadium is named for a civic leader who was instrumental in professional baseball in the incarnation before the Sounds, when the old Nashville Vols played at storied Sulphur Dell.

Top graduates from the Southern League era:
Don Mattingly
Willie McGee
Buck Showalter
Steve Balboni

Notable: Greer Stadium has one of the most famous scoreboards in minor-league ball—a 116-foot long guitar that has the line score on the neck of the guitar. At its highest point, it towers 53 feet over left field.

Orlando, Florida

Teams: Twins, Sun Rays, Cubs

Affiliates during the Southern League era: Minnesota (1973-92), Chicago Cubs (1993-97), Seattle (1998), Tampa Bay (1999-2003)

Stadiums: Tinker Field (340' LF, 424' CF, 320' RF), Cracker Jack Stadium, opened in 2000 (335' LF, 400' CF, 335' RF). The antiseptic Cracker Jack Stadium, on the Walt Disney World campus, hosted Southern League ball for four years in a failed experiment to capitalize on the tourist trade. It replaced the storied Tinker Field, built in 1914, which sits in the shadow of the home-field stands of the Citrus Bowl. The prior park was named for Hall of Famer Joe Tinker, one of the principals in Franklin Pierce Adams's famed "Baseball's Sad Lexicon," noted for its "Tinker to Evers to Chance" double play chorus. It was a romantic ode for old baseball fans that belied the fact shortstop Tinker and second baseman Evers barely spoke to one another.

Top graduates from the Southern League era:
B.J. Upton
Carl Crawford
Josh Hamilton
Kerry Wood
Chuck Knoblauch
Gary Gaetti
Frank Viola
Lyman Bostock

Notable: Though the regular season was never a rousing success at Cracker Jack Stadium (which would later go through two name changes), the ballpark is now regularly packed as the spring-training home of the Atlanta Braves.

Pearl, Mississippi

Team: Braves

Affiliates during the Southern League era: Atlanta (2005-current)

Stadiums: Trustmark Park, opened in 2005 (335' LF, 402' CF, 332' RF). Just on the eastern fringe of Jackson, the state capital, sits the Braves' handsome park. When the franchise moved from Greenville, it was the second time Jackson had an affiliation with the Braves. When the Braves were in Boston, they had an affiliate in the city called the Senators, whose downtown stadium was destroyed by a tornado in 1954.

Top graduates from the Southern League era:
Brian McCann
Craig Kimbrel
Jason Heyward
Freddie Freeman
Andrelton Simmons
Mike Minor

Notable: Perhaps it's not surprising, in a state with such a bitter rivalry between Ole Miss and Mississippi State University, a game between those two schools at Trustmark Park in 2012 set the stadium attendance record.

Pensacola, Florida

Team: Blue Wahoos

Affiliates during the Southern League era: Cincinnati (2012-current)

Stadium: Pensacola Bayfront Stadium, opened in 2012 (320' LF, 400' CF, 335' RF). Built on the site of an old oil refinery, the stadium offers a beautiful view of Pensacola Bay; a homer to left field that travels more than 400 will splash into the water. The stadium welcomed the Reds' Southern League affiliate in 2012 after it moved from Zebulon, N.C.

Notable: The Blue Wahoos' name was chosen in a contest where fans submitted nominations. Other suggestions included the Aviators, Mullets and Salty Dogs. The "blue" attached to Wahoo is somewhat redundant, but Wahoos as a nickname is intellectual property of the University of Virginia so Pensacola had to add the color.

Savannah, Georgia

Team: Senators, Indians, Braves

Affiliates during the Southern League era: Washington (1968-69), Cleveland (1970), Atlanta (1971-1983)

Stadium: Grayson Stadium, opened in 1926 (322' LF, 400' CF, 310' RF). The original park was virtually destroyed by a hurricane in 1940, but General William Grayson led an effort to rebuild the park, at the cost of $150,000. The new park was named in his honor.

Top graduates from the Southern League era:
Dale Murphy
Glenn Hubbard
Steve Bedrosian
Bruce Benedict
Toby Harrah
Bob Watson
Fred Stanley

Notable: In 1953, the South Atlantic League color barrier was broken at Grayson Stadium as the Savannah club started African-Americans Izzy Israel and Junior Reedy.

Wilmington, North Carolina

Team: Port City Roosters

Affiliates during the Southern League era: Seattle (1995-96)

Stadium: Brooks Field, opened in 1989 (340' LF, 380' CF, 340' RF). This short-lived franchise, which had been the Nashville Xpress for two seasons, played at Brooks Field on the campus of the University of North Carolina-Wilmington. After drawing fewer than 200,000 fans in two years, the team moved to Mobile (though initial reports had the team bound for Springfield, Mo.)

Top graduates from the Southern League era:
Derek Lowe
Jason Varitek
Raul Ibanez

Notable: Wilmington is the hometown of the most internationally famous former Southern League player, the Birmingham Barons' outfielder named Michael Jordan.

Zebulon, North Carolina

Team: Mudcats

Affiliates during the Southern League era: Pittsburgh (1991-98), Colorado (1999-2002), Florida (2003-2008), Cincinnati (2009-2011)

Stadium: Five County Stadium, opened in 1991 (330' LF, 400'

CF, 309' RF). Zebulon inherited the team from Columbus, Ga., as well as the nickname perfect for the previous setting—the catfish-filled Chattahoochee River that flowed through Columbus—but a bit incongruous for the small town 30 minutes east of Raleigh. The five counties, for the record, resemble a law-firm title: Wake, Wilson, Franklin, Nash and Johnson. Zebulon lost the team to Pensacola in 2012, with an A-Advanced Carolina League team moving in that season as a replacement.

Top graduates from the Southern League era:

Tim Wakefield

Jason Kendall

Kris Benson

Matt Holliday

Miguel Cabrera

Josh Willingham

Josh Johnson

Juan Pierre

Aaron Cook

Notable: One reason for the distant location was to enable owner Steve Bryant to avoid infringing on other minor-league franchises in the Research Triangle area of North Carolina.

THE TOP 50 SOUTHERN LEAGUERS WHO DIDN'T MAKE IT

Memorable Southern League players who either didn't reach the majors or only had the proverbial "cup of coffee" (fewer than 100 MLB at-bats or 10 pitching appearances).

Rogelio Alvarez, 1B, Macon, Knoxville, Evansville. Batted .265 in 383 games in Double-A. Led Southern League with 19 homers split between Knoxville and Evansville in 1967

Don Anderson, 1B, Asheville. Batted .300 in 368 games in Southern League. Led league with .324 average, 18 homers and 100 RBI in 1969.

Blaine Beatty, P, Charlotte, Chattanooga, Carolina. Pitched in 140 games across seven years in Southern League, going 57-35.

Jim Bowie, OF, Jacksonville, Huntsville. Only player to lead the league in batting for two different teams. Had .301 average in six seasons in Double-A, also led league with 101 RBI in 1993.

Jim Brown, P, Knoxville, Montgomery. Pitched a pair of no-hitters in a span of three starts. Went 14-9 for Rebels in 1968.

Mike Coolbaugh, 3B, Huntsville. Led the league with 30 homers and 132 RBI in 1997. Batted .275 in 330 Southern League games. Tragically killed by a line drive while coaching first base for Tulsa in 2007.

Mark Corey, OF, Charlotte. Batted .307 in 307 Double-A games, with a 15-homer, 76-RBI, .310 season for Orioles in 1977.

Kevin Coughlin, OF-1B, Birmingham, Chattanooga. .385 average for Barons in 1995 set league record. Batted .305 in four years in Double-A.

Pete Dalena, 1B, Nashville. Led league with a .322 average in 1983. Batted .307 in 214 Southern League games.

Bobby Darula, OF, Huntsville, Chattanooga, Mississippi. Won 2002 Southern League batting title with .325 mark for Chattanooga. Hit .310 across six years in the SL.

Jamie Dismuke, OF, Chattanooga. Batted .294 in 300 games spanning four years in the league. Returned as hitting coach for Lookouts.

Tom Dodd, 3B-OF, Nashville, Knoxville, Charlotte. Won league MVP award in 1987, batting .289 with 37 homers and 127 RBI. Played in 471 games in SL.

Doc Estes, 1B-OF, Orlando, Savannah, Greenville. Composite .308 average in six years and batted .341 for Greenville in 1984.

Greg Field, P, Orlando. SL Pitcher of the Year in 1977 with 14-7 record and 2.78 ERA. Amassed 42 wins in five Double-A seasons.

Chris Floethe, P, Birmingham. Though only 12-23 in three seasons with the Barons, notched 225 strikeouts in 174 innings in 1971, with 11 games of 10 or more Ks.

Larry Foster, OF, Knoxville, Jacksonville. 1976 SL MVP (.311,

57 RBI). Hit .275 in 383 games in the Southern League from 1974-78.

Mike Fuentes, OF, Memphis. Led the league in HRs and RBI (37, 115) for Chicks in 1982. Had career SL marks of .277, 71 HRs, 236 RBI in 353 games with Memphis.

Mark Funderburk, 1B-OF, Orlando. Spent five seasons with Orlando, socking 117 homers, driving in 379 runs in 558 games. Was league's homer and RBI champ in 1985.

Eddie Gates, OF, Memphis, Montgomery, Birmingham. The league MVP in 1978 (.315, 25 HR, 67 RBI) for Memphis.

Joe Gates, INF, Jacksonville, Knoxville. Batted .295 in three seasons in the league, taking the batting title in 1978 at Knoxville with .332 mark.

John Gregory, P, Montgomery. Made 130 appearances, including 20 starts, across four years with the Rebels, with a 29-16 record and 2.83 ERA.

Terrel Hansen, 1B-OF, Jacksonville. Spent 13 years toiling in the minors, including four with the Suns, for whom he batted .273 with 80 homers in 392 games.

Ken Hottman, OF, Mobile, Asheville. Led league with 99 runs, 37 homers, 116 RBI alongside .302 average at Asheville in 1971.

Manley Johnston, P, Lynchburg. The league's only 20-game winner, in the SL's inaugural season. Former outfielder who batted .292 with seven homers in 1964.

Derek Lee, P, Huntsville. Twice an 11-game winner for the Stars, he made 136 appearances in five seasons for Huntsville as starter and reliever.

Richard Lewis, 2B, Greenville, West Tenn. Batted .329 as the league MVP in 2004 and had career mark of .270 in five Double-A seasons.

David "Spike" Lundberg, P, Jacksonville. Went 15-2 with a 2.27 ERA for the Suns in 2006, his only year in the league, and the best of 13 seasons in the minors.

James MacDonnell, P, Mobile, Asheville, Knoxville. 17-game winner for Asheville in 1971. 29-19 with 2.57 ERA in three Southern League years.

Bob Maneely, Orlando P. The Southern League Pitcher of the Year in 1975, going 14-8 with 2.78 ERA, the best of his three seasons with Orlando.

Gabriel "Gabby" Martinez, INF-OF, Montgomery, Chattanooga. Played in 523 games in the league, mashing 62 HRs and driving in 310 runs, with five of his 11 minor-league seasons in SL. One of the rare players to homer off a train at Montgomery's Riverwalk Stadium.

Tydus Meadows, OF, West Tenn, Jacksonville. Never hit below .261 in four seasons in the league. Batted .285 in seven years (out of 12 in the pros) at Double-A.

Cristobal "Minnie" Mendoza, INF, Charlotte. Eight of 20 minor-league seasons were in the Southern League. Two-time league batting champ (1967 and 1971).

Mark Naehring, INF, Knoxville, Charlotte. Hit for a .279 average over five seasons.

Mike Neill, OF, Huntsville. League-record 129 runs scored in 1997 with .340 average. Played in 226 games for the Stars, batting .310. Member of Team USA's gold medal team at the 2000 Olympics.

Jim Obradovich, 1B, Orlando. 70 homers over four years and 240 RBI and .260 average. Back-to-back home run champion.

Matt Peterson, RP, Jacksonville. League record 37 saves in 2009; recorded 18 more saves in 2010 with 1.47 ERA.

Mike Reinbach, OF, Asheville. 1972 league MVP and Triple Crown winner

Sal Rende, 1B, Chattanooga. 97 homers in six years and 1978 RBI champ. Managed at Chattanooga and Memphis.

Cohen "Laddie" Renfroe, RP, Charlotte. Appeared in a league record 78 games in 1989, going 19-7 with 15 saves and 3.14 ERA.

Kevin Rhomberg, 2B, Chattanooga. League-record 187 hits in 1981 for Lookouts, leading league with .366 average and 74 stolen bases.

Rondal Rollin, OF, Birmingham, Greenville. 30 homers and 108 RBI for Barons in 1985. Led the league with 39 homers in 1987. Had 97 homers in four SL seasons spanning 500 games.

William "Buck" Showalter, INF, Nashville. League-record 155 singles for Sounds in 1980. Played 453 games in Southern League and was a .291 hitter across six years in Double-A.

Charles "Chips" Swanson, P, Montgomery. Threw six shutouts for Montgomery in 1973 and had a perfect game in 1970. Career 30-21 in 99 Southern League appearances.

Fernando Tatis, INF, Columbus. Six of 10 minor-league seasons were spent in Columbus, with a .301 mark in 1977. Not to be confused with the more recent Fernando Tatis of dual grand slam fame.

Nic Ungs, P, Carolina, Huntsville, Jacksonville. Went 35-21 in 85 starts, mostly at Carolina (2003-05), with 3.40 ERA.

Federico "Freddie" Velazquez, C, Savannah. First year in the Southern League was 1964, the last in 1976. In seven Double-A years and 587 games, hit .267.

Jamie Werly, P, Nashville, Charlotte. Struck out 193 batters to lead the league in 1981, with a 13-11 record and 2.59 ERA. Had 365 Ks in 434 1/3 Southern League innings.

Stefan Wever, P, Nashville. Followed Werly as strikeout king, with 191 in 1982. Went 16-6 with a 2.78 ERA. In lone big-league appearance, gave up nine runs in 2 2/3 innings.

Jack Whillock, P, Montgomery. Pitched in five Double-A seasons. Excelled in 1971 at Montgomery with 5-2 record, 1.19 ERA and league-best 15 saves.

Stan Wojcik, OF, Birmingham, Mobile. Batted .261 in eight years in the SL, including .296 average in 1967.

THE TOP 50 BEST MAJOR LEAGUERS WHO GRADUATED FROM THE SOUTHERN LEAGUE

(1964-present, with their SL stats)

Harold Baines—13 HRs, 72 RBI, .275 in 137 games at Knoxville, 1978

Vida Blue—10-3, 3.20, 112 strikeouts in 104 innings at Birmingham, 1969

Miguel Cabrera—.365, 10 HRs, 59 RBI, 1.038 OPS in 69 games at Carolina, 2003

Jose Canseco—25 HRs, 80 RBI, .318, 1.146 OPS in 58 games; SL MVP at Huntsville, 1985

Bert Campaneris—.325, 69 runs, 18 doubles, 11 triples in 86 games at Birmingham, 1964

Dave Concepcion—.294, 47 runs, 11 doubles, 11 steals in 96 games at Asheville, 1969

David Cone—8-12, 4.28, 27 wild pitches in 29 starts at Memphis, 1984

Carlos Delgado—25 HRs, 102 RBI, .303, 102 walks in 140 games at Knoxville, 1993

Darrell Evans—.241, 3 HRs, 25 RBI in 56 games at Birmingham, 1968

Rollie Fingers—16-9, 2.61, in 36 games, 31 starts at Birmingham, totaling 1967-68

Andres Galarraga—.289, 27 HRs, 87 RBI in 143 games at Jacksonville, 1984

Tom Glavine—11-6, 3.41, 114 strikeouts in 22 starts at Greenville, 1986

Luis Gonzalez—.265, 24 HRs, 89 RBI in 138 games at Columbus, 1990

Roy Halladay—2-3, 5.40, 30 strikeouts in 7 starts at Knoxville in 1997

Josh Hamilton—.180, 5 doubles, 4 RBI in 23 games at Orlando, 2001

Trevor Hoffman—4-0, 1.65 ERA, 8 saves in 20 games at Chattanooga, totaling 1991-92

Tim Hudson—10-9, 4.54, 104 strikeouts in 22 starts at Huntsville, 1998

Reggie Jackson—.293, 17 triples, 17 HRs, 58 RBI in 114 games at Birmingham, 1967

Ferguson Jenkins—10-6, 3.11, 149 strikeouts in 21 games, 20 starts at Chattanooga, 1964

Randy Johnson—11-8, 3.73, 128 walks, 163 strikeouts in 140 innings at Jacksonville, 1987

Andruw Jones—.369, 10 doubles, 12 HRs, 37 RBI in 38 games at Greenville, 1996

Chipper Jones—.346, 11 triples, 9 HRs, 42 RBI in 67 games at Greenville, 1992

Jeff Kent—.256, 34 doubles, 12 HRs, 61 RBI, 25 steals in 139 games at Knoxville, 1991

Clayton Kershaw—3-5, 2.41, 88 strikeouts in 18 games at Jacksonville, totaling 2007-08

Mike Marshall—2-4, 3.12, 26 innings, 21 strikeouts in 8 appearances at Chattanooga, 1965

Dennis Martinez—4-1, 2.60, 45 innings, 18 strikeouts in 6 starts at Asheville, 1975

Edgar Martinez—.261, 44 2Bs, 9 HRs, 124 RBI at Chattanooga, totaling 1985-86

Don Mattingly—.316, 35 doubles, 7 HRs, 98 RBI in 141 games at Nashville, 1981

Fred McGriff—.249, 13 doubles, 9 HRs, 25 RBI in 56 games at Knoxville, 1984

Mark McGwire—.303, 15 doubles, 10 HRs, 53 RBI in 55 games at Huntsville, 1986

Jack Morris—2-3, 6.25, 36 walks, 18 strikeouts in 12 games, 9 starts at Montgomery, 1976

Dale Murphy—.267, 13 doubles, 12 HRs, 55 RBI in 104 games at Savannah, 1976

Eddie Murray—.298, 15 doubles, 12 HRs, 46 RBI in 88 games at Charlotte, 1976

Graig Nettles—.232, 18 doubles, 19 HRs, 86 RBI in 140 games at Charlotte, 1967

Al Oliver—.222, 1 double, 2 triples, 1 HR, 4 RBI in 38 games at Macon, 1967

Dan Quisenberry—7-5, 1.88, 22 saves, 70 strikeouts in 96 games at Jacksonville, 1975-78

Tim Raines—.290, 104 runs, 50 RBI, 59 steals, 90 walks in 145 games at Memphis, 1979

Cal Ripken, Jr.—.266, 28 doubles, 28 HRs, 86 RBI at Charlotte, totaling 1979-80

Alex Rodriguez—. 288, 4 doubles, 1 HR, 8 RBI, 10 walks in 17 games, Jacksonville, 1994

Joe Rudi—.288, 26 doubles, 13 HRs, 70 RBI in 121 games at Birmingham, 1967

Bret Saberhagen—6-2, 2.91, 48 strikeouts in 11 starts at Jacksonville, 1983

Curt Schilling—5-2, 3.18, 23 walks, 32 strikeouts in 7 starts at Charlotte, 1988

Frank Thomas—.323, 18 HRs, 71 RBI, 112 walks in 109 games at Birmingham, 1990

Alan Trammell—.278, 19 triples, 3 HRs, 50 RBI at Montgomery, totaling 1976-77

Robin Ventura—.278, 75 runs, 3 HRs, 67 RBI, 93 BBs in 129 games at Birmingham, 1989

Larry Walker—.287, 91 runs, 26 HRs, 83 RBI, 24 SBs in 128 games at Jacksonville, 1987

Tim Wallach—.327, 16 2Bs, 18 HRs, 51 RBI, 1.048 OPS in 75 games at Memphis, 1979

Lou Whitaker—.280, 81 runs, 3 HRs, 48 RBI, 38 steals in 107 games at Montgomery, 1977

Frank White—.252, 12 doubles, 2 HRs, 23 RBI, 13 SBs in 91 games at Jacksonville, 1972

Willie Wilson—.253, 54 runs, 35 RBI, 37 SBs in 107 games at Jacksonville, 1976

ACKNOWLEDGMENTS

It was well after bedtime, well after the game ended, but I was tromping around in thigh-high weeds behind the concrete right wall of Chattanooga's Engel Stadium, hoping to come across baseballs that had been launched there during batting practice or games. That my parents, Frank and Dot McCarter, were alongside me, having brought me to the game and now tolerating that scavenger adventure, speaks volumes. They tolerated so many adventures and misadventures, and I miss them every day.

My younger brother, Bryan, put up with incessant demands that he go play Wiffle ball or in the backyard with me. He got the ultimate revenge by being a much better player than I was and is an even better person. And while on family, I probably inherited my love of baseball from my maternal grandfather, Floyd Watkins. I was once interviewing Hank Aaron while standing in foul ground before a game only to look over Aaron's shoulder and see Granddaddy in the stands watching me interview Aaron. The pride in Granddaddy's eyes I can still feel, 35 years later.

Now, as for the people who helped make this book happen, thanks to Kevin Reichard at August Publications, who thought the idea worthy of print, and to Jesse Goldberg-Strassler, who has done his share of time in the Southern League and who made this book better than it was when it landed in his computer. And a special thanks to Cliff Pate, an old pal from his days at the Huntsville Stars, who suggested the book.

I was lucky to have unflagging Cubs fan Joe Distelheim, a baseball guy and a word guy, as editor and, more importantly, friend. His guidance and fingerprints are all over this book.

A number of my sportswriting friends pitched in eagerly with insight, quotes, clippings and encouragement, including Tommy

Hicks, Stacy Long, David Jenkins, Bill Vilona, John Pruett, Mark Bechtel, Stan Olson, and Mark Wiedmer. None were more important, though, than Wayne Martin, formerly of the *Birmingham News*. He offered invaluable advice in 1976 as I embarked on covering the Southern League and spent hours with me this past summer at Rickwood Field. He opened the door to the Rickwood roof that day – and to so much else through the years.

Both Roy Exum, my old boss at the *Chattanooga News-Free Press*, and Allan Morris, the inimitable sports editor, gave me a chance to learn and grow when I got thrown onto the minor-league baseball beat as a 21-year-old kid. Larry Fleming of the *Chattanooga Times* became both a competitor and friend. My current employer, Alabama Media Group and the *Huntsville Times*, was understanding during the writing of this book, in particular Anthony Cook and Shelly Haskins.

Lori Webb and P.J. Webb of the Southern League office and Tom Kayser of the Texas League opened their files to me. Thanks to players, managers, journalists, wives, officials and others who shared time and assistance, including Bryan Dingo, Don Rizzardi, Bruce Baldwin, Doug Scopel, Jill Cacic, Nick Dobreff, Greg Tubbs, Eric Jokisch, Jim Bouton, Bruce Robinson, Brian Kingman, Ron Beaurivage, Steve Kornya, Mark Hauser, Curt Bloom, David Paschall, Adam Johnson, Jake Marisnick, John Arnold, Dave Fendrick, Billy Gardner, Sr., Billy Gardner, Jr., Darnell Coles, Buck Showalter, Larry Ward, Dominic Latkovski, Farrell Owens, Jim Baker, Jake Peavy, Jonathan Bailey, Alex Ransom, Garrett Patterson, John Varner, Van Snider, Chris Hook, Pat Darcy, Mike Hostetler, Manley Johnston, Art Clarkson, Craig Kimbrel, Tommy Runnells, Rene Lachemann, Fran Kalafatis, Bob Kesling, Don Money, Greg Tubbs, Carolyn Aaron, Dan Evans, Brad Rippelmeyer, Bryan Lambe, David Sharp, Phillip Wellman, Buck Rogers, Peter Bragan, Jr., Sarah Bragan, Art Clarkson, Eric Jokisch, Larry Schmittou, Ryan Christensen, Jimmy Jones, Ed Romero, Charles Farmer, Jonathan Nelson, David Thomas, Roger Hoover, Pat Mincher, Bob Mayes, Rudy Jones, Steve Connelly, Brian Cox, John Mueller, Al Harazin, Jane Des Ormeaux, Harold Justice, Chips Swanson, Earl Altshuler, and Grady Little.

A nod as well to Dr. Kevin Dupre and Dr. Bob Glenn at Athens State University.

Now, we circle back to home: There are my stepsons, Miles and Jackson Stumb, who have brought more into my world in these past nine years than I could ever bring to theirs. There are "The Ice-breakers," who've added a special dimension to my life. And thanks to friends who didn't walk away from all those conversations that included the phrase "busy writing my book..."

There is my daughter, Jordan. Poor kid never stood a chance. She was going to Chattanooga Lookouts games in the womb. Thanks to her mom Susan for that, and so much else. On my desk is a photo of Jordan, wearing a Red Sox jersey, the very instant her beloved Sox clinched the 2004 World Series. The Daddy-Daughter Baseball Trip—Atlanta-Boston-Milwaukee-Wrigley-Comiskey-Cleveland-Pittsburgh-Cooperstown, whew!—remains a highlight of my life.

The first book I wrote, more than a decade ago, I thanked my then-girlfriend Patricia in print for her "editing and patience." That's become an oft-repeated punch line around our house. Once again, I'm thankful for Patricia's editing and patience—and even more thankful she's now my wife.

BIBLIOGRAPHY
AND CREDITS

Books

Aaron, r.f. Hank Aaron and Furman Bisher. World Publishing, 1966.

Ball Four. Jim Bouton. Collier Books, 1970.

Baseball's Great Experiment: Jackie Robinson and His Legacy. Jules Tygiel. Oxford University Press, 2008.

Baseball in Chattanooga. David Jenkins, Arcadia Press, 2005.

Baseball in Mobile. Joe Cuhaj and Tamra Carraway-Hinckle. Arcadia Press, 2003.

Francona: The Red Sox Years. Terry Francona and Dan Shaughnessy. Houghton Mifflin Harcourt, 2013.

If I Ever Get Back To Georgia I'm Gonna Nail My Feet To The Ground. Lewis Grizzard. Villard Books, 1990.

The Chattanooga Lookouts & 100 Seasons of Scenic City Baseball. Stephen Martini. Dry Ice Publishing, 2005.

The Girl Who Struck Out Babe Ruth. Jean L.S. Patrick. Carolrhoda Books, 2000.

The Southern League. Bill O'Neal, Eakin Press, 1994.

Your Lookouts Since 1885. Wirt Gammon Sr. *Chattanooga Times.*

Newspapers, Websites and Periodicals

The Huntsville Times

The Birmingham News

The Mobile Press-Register

The Chattanooga Times-Free Press

The Atlanta Journal-Constitution

The Montgomery Advertiser

The Columbus (Ga.) Ledger-Enquirer

The (Memphis) Commercial Appeal

The Jackson (Tenn.) Sun
The Jackson (Miss.) Clarion-Ledger
The Knoxville News-Sentinel
The (Jacksonville) Florida Times-Union
The Orlando Sentinel
The Los Angeles Times
The New York Times
The Washington Post
The Winston-Salem Journal
The St. Petersburg Times
The Baltimore Sun
Ballparkdigest.com
Vanderbilt.com
Southernleague.com
Minorleaguebaseball.com
Majorleaguebaseball.com
Baseball-Reference.com
Sports Illustrated
The Sporting News
Baseball America

ABOUT THE AUTHOR

Mark McCarter is a columnist and sports reporter for the *Huntsville (Ala.) Times* and Alabama Media Group. A four-time Alabama Sportswriter of the Year and four times the Southern League Writer of the Year, he began covering the Southern League in 1976 for the *Chattanooga News-Free Press*. He is also the author of *The Racetracks Book*, published by *The Sporting News*. Mark lives in Huntsville with his wife, Patricia. In 2012, he was inducted into the Greater Chattanooga Sports Hall of Fame, a bittersweet honor when he learned it was for his writing—not for having led the Brainerd Dixie Youth League in home runs in 1966.